# Essays on
# Spirituality and Charism:

## A Message of Hope and Reconciliation

LA SALETTE LAITY

September 19th, 1846

LAICOS DE LA SALETTE

**Editor: Fr. James A. Henault, M.S.**

Missionaries of La Salette Corporation
915 Maple Avenue
Hartford, CT 06114-2330, USA
Website: www.lasalette.org

**Imprimi Potest:**

Very Rev. Fr. Rene Butler, M.S., Provincial Superior, Missionaries of Our Lady of La Salette, Province of Mary, Mother of the Americas, 915 Maple Avenue, Hartford, CT 06114-2330 USA

Printed in the United States of America

**Editor:** Fr. James A. Henault, M.S.; content from past and present members of the La Salette Missionaries and La Salette Laity.

**Booklet Design and Digital Formatting:** Jack Battersby and Fr. Ron Gagne, M.S.

This and other La Salette titles available in paper and E-book formats at www.amazon.com and www.lasalette.org

**IBSN:** 978-1-946956-39-2

All our authors – Laity, La Salette Laity and Religious - are closely connected with our La Salette Misionaries around the world. We are very grateful to them for their contribution to this book.

Chris Austgen: Chapter 19

Fr. Joseph Bachand, M.S.: Chapter 16

Fr. Ron Beauchemin, M.S.: Chapter 11

Fr. Paul Belhumeur, M.S.: Chapter 20

Fr. Ted Brown, M.S.: Chapter 24

Very Rev. René J. Butler, M.S.: Chapter 1

Fr. Raymond Cadran, M.S.: Chapter 3

Fr. Roger Castel, M.S.: Chapter 6

Fr. Ron Foshage, M.S.: Chapter 21

Fr. Ron Gagné, M.S.: Chapter 18

Fr. Flavio Gillio, M.S.: Chapters 4 & 7

Fr. Jim Henault, M.S.: Chapters 5 & 9

Very Rev. Silvano Marisa, M.S.: Chapter 13

Fr. Cyriac Mattathilanickal, M.S.: Chapter 10

Fr. Phil "Skip" Negley, M.S.: Chapter 8

Fr. Terry Niziolek, M.S.: Chapter 23

Fr. Jack Nuelle, M.S.: Chapters 14 & 15

Fr. Isidro Perin, M.S.: Chapter 12

Fr. Paul Rainville, M.S.: Chapter 2

Elizabeth Vasquez: Chapter 22

Fr. Thomas Vellappallil, M.S.: Chapter 17

# Contents

V

# Prologue: Peeling an Onion
## By Fr. Jim Henault, M.S.

The word, *hermeneutics,* is often applied to the study of Scripture with a view to understanding the genre, the context, the meanings and interpretations, and the applications of a passage or chapter or book of the Bible through various applied "criticisms" or perspectives. It has a broader meaning though and allows any of us to explore events, messages, realities in their proper context for their time and for today. When I want to apply this to La Salette and the breath of the event I use a simpler term: peeling an onion.

Onions are such an interesting vegetable. They have an outside skin that protects what is inside – multiple layers of tasty food that can be sliced, quartered, diced, or pureed. In this context I would see the outer skin as the Story of the Apparition itself: all that happened on that wonder few minutes when Mary appeared to Maximin and Melanie on September 19, 1846. In this case the skin is most valuable, but it is just the start of the reality. We cannot stop there or even worse pick and choose snippets of the message.

We need to realize that the apparition has an historical context of France in the 1840's. In the south of France rural society was very much agricultural; many other parts of the country and the world were being impacted by the industrial revolution. The faith of the average person was not well developed or practiced. The concepts of individual and freedom were abounding in society and political turmoil was rampant. Spirituality was focused often upon a God who punishes and tries the lives of people with famines and shortages and instability. The two cowherders were poor children, had little education in school and in their faith. Their families were suffering, and they had to struggle to assist themselves and those they loved.

Another layer of the onion is *the genre of apparitions*. Mary speaks of the sins of the people, primarily those core to their relationship with God and the Church. She has a lot of prophetic statements that always have "ifs" involved. Mary in her appearances over the centuries has called people to relationship. Prayer, fasting, sacrificing, authenticity are all called for by her. Many of those who are visionaries are young in their age or in their faith life and all are open to hearing a message and acting upon it. There is often a pushback, a resistance from some officials of state or church or local townsfolk and sceptics throughout the world who will question, bribe, threaten, and just reduce the credulity of the message. But one constant is there: the receivers of the message are fearless in their actions and are clearly changed by the event and the future realities of their ministry as messengers.

A further layer of the onion is *the investigations* by church, press, saints and sinners, and the local powers. The changes in the population in their lives is central to this investigation. The details of the children's lives and prior religious practices were closely examined. While it took five years for the official approbation to be issued by Bishop Philibert de Bruillard of Grenoble, the common folk made judgements rather quickly. Pilgrimages up the mountain by individuals and by organized groups began almost immediately and continued through the years before the final approval. The use of God's name in vain was frowned upon and unacceptable in the local society. Church attendance grew on Sundays and religious groups of men and women were focused on prayer and conversion through penitence. People prayed for miracles and drank of the miraculous waters that led to restoration of health of body and soul.

The next layer is the *comparison of the apparition message* to the Scriptures, to Church teaching, to the dogmatic and doctrinal proclamations of the Church, to the practical teachings of homilies and witness testimony. Are they consistent? This is the start, but further knowledge comes as we relate one to the other. If we look to see how the apparition message and charism speak to the Scriptures and to how the Scriptures compare to the Apparition enlighten my understanding and appreciation of the La Salette event can be furthered. Let me give an example by comparing the La Salette message and the Parable of the Prodigal Son. As we study the two we are able to understand better who God is, who am I as a sinner, how am I like the good brother who react to the brother or sister who have been away and come back to the family.

Another onion layer, possibly *the "nugget" or core*, is to center on a theme or part of the charism and explore its many dimensions. You could focus on Reconciliation or Conversion, on Hospitality and Welcome. You can also take modern issues and see what La Salette has to say about them in the world today. Essays here focus on Youth, Mission, Social Justice and Action, and Ecology. In a presentation at the Second International Laity Gathering I used the concept of Famine. I will repeat that here for you as an example of what you can do.

## Famine: Peeling an Onion

### Famine: A lack of food

- Natural condition of drought, pestilence, lack of sunshine, flood
- Condition of man's action: overplanting, poor seeds, no seeds
- Wasting resources: Distribution of food poorly, lack of agricultural knowledge

### Famine: A natural disaster

- Famine, hurricanes, typhoons, tsunamis, cyclones, tornadoes, blizzards, avalanches, droughts, and floods are all realities of nature.
- Insurance companies see them as acts of God.
- Pray for relief as we are not usually personally responsible.
- Global warming and climate change are our participation in these problems.
- Know that some of these can be relieved by our actions but most are an inevitable part of our world.

### Spiritual Famine

- Leaving God out of our lives. Going it alone.
- Prayer without sacraments: personal relationship with God that excludes Church and community.

- Occasional Eucharist and devotions
- God is compartmentalized: reserved for Sundays or major crises.
- Lack of spiritual direction
- Poor image of God
- Social Famine Xenophobia and agoraphobia
- Lack of friends and companions
- Cutting off family ties
- Fear of crime, violence, terrorism, injury
- Afraid to be myself (John Powell "Why am I afraid to tell you who I am?" Because you might not like me)
- Coming out of the "closets" of life
- Insisting on my independence, my own way

## Famine of Social Justice

- Famine is unnecessarily causing death.
- Approximately 25,000 children a day die of malnutrition
- We have enough food today to feed everyone well. Food mountains for price support
- Soup kitchens feed thousands upon thousands in countries around the world when food is bought.
- Food is wasted wholesale
- $54,000,000,000. ($54 billion US) annually would wipe out global poverty. Less than 8% of USA defense budget.

## Economic Famine

- Unemployment or underemployment
- Lack of proper housing
- Water and sanitation problems
- Lack of education opportunities or in fact
- Personal freedom and societal slavery – Human Trafficking
- Lack of financial resources

• Lack of civil and religious rights

• Lack of opportunities to ...

**Reflection Questions:**

• What is the best way for me to conquer famine?

• What famines am I currently facing in my life? Or have I faced?

• How do I grow from the challenges that my famines present?

• What "onion layer" of the La Salette message can I peel?

• What was the most important thing I learned today?

# Section 1 –
# The Message Background

# Chapter 1 —
# La Salette: A Mystery of Presence

By Very Rev. René J. Butler, M.S.,
Provincial Superior of the Province of
Mary, Mother of the Americas

In September 1982, I was present at a month-long renewal program for Missionaries of Our Lady of La Salette. It was taking place at the original La Salette Shrine, in the French Alps. One of the speakers was a French priest, Fr. Roger Castel, M.S. He began by defining what an apparition is.

Here is his definition. *An apparition is the extraordinary manifestation of God's ordinary presence.* It struck me like lightening, and I have never forgotten it.

This definition applies wonderfully well to La Salette, as I hope to show in the following paragraphs.

Presence:

First, however, let us look at the various possible meanings of presence. We can just happen to be in a certain place when something occurs near us or around us (e.g., a rainbow); or we can be casually observing something (a parade passing by); or we can be participants without much caring about what is happening (a boring meeting); or we can be active participants, invested in the activity or event.

Our Lady of La Salette shows us, by her own manner of being present, that God's ordinary presence is not a matter of just being there, or mere observing. Rather, like the prophets, she highlights his active participation in the life of his people, his caring deeply about them.

And at the very heart of this kind of presence is connectedness, in the form of an encounter.

## My Children, my People, my Son:

On that September 19, 1846, Mélanie Calvat and Maximin Giraud were terrified at what was happening near them, right before their eyes. They were prepared to defend themselves if necessary. Then a gentle voice called, *"Come closer, my children; don't be afraid."*

I like to compare Mary's words, "Don't be afraid," to a musical phenomenon called ostinato. Meaning "obstinate," it is a melodic or rhythmic element that is insistently repeated throughout a composition. In this sense, the Beautiful Lady's first words set the tone for everything that is to follow, quietly echoing as it were, like an *ostinato*, through her whole discourse: *"A great famine is coming* (but don't be afraid)... *If they are converted, the rocks and stones will turn into heaps of wheat* (so don't be afraid)... *You will make this known to all my people* (and don't be afraid)."

She called them *"my children."* Notice in particular the use of "my." Mary is letting the children know that she already has a relationship with them, as Mother. I am reminded, here, of the words of one of the documents of Vatican II, which reflects on the "maternity of Mary in the order of grace." We read: "Taken up to heaven she did not lay aside this salvific duty, but by her constant intercession continued to bring us the gifts of eternal salvation. By her maternal charity, she cares for the brethren of her Son, who still journey on earth surrounded by dangers and difficulties, until they are led into the happiness of their true home." (*Lumen Gentium*, 62)

**A little quiz:** How many times does Our Lady of La Salette say, *"my children"*? How many did you remember? At least two, for sure, at the beginning and the end. And she says it twice at the end, in fact; so that makes three. But where else? Here is the complete list:

*Come closer,* **my children;** *don't be afraid.*

*Don't you understand,* **my children?** *Let me find another way to say it.*

*Do you say your prayers well,* **my children?**

*Ah,* **my children,** *you should say them well.*

*Have you never seen wheat gone bad,* **my children?**

*Well,* **my children,** *you will make this known to all my people.*

*Very well,* **my children,** *make this known to all my people.*

Seven times. Who could doubt the importance of this connectedness?

The Beautiful Lady also cleverly engages the children's curiosity, "*I am here to tell you great news.*" They run down the slope to join her, standing so close, Maximin said, that "no one could have passed between her and us."

Her very next words are, "*If my people...*" There's that "my" again. The phrase "*my people*" turns up twice more, at the very end of the message. He we see a broader connectedness.

"*If my people,*" she says, "*refuse to submit, I will be forced to let go the arm of my Son.*" This is the Son whose crucified image she wears over her heart. He is the one St. Paul describes as "making peace by the blood of his cross." (Colossians 1: 20)

With the phrase "*My Son,*" which occurs six times, the circle is complete. *My children... my people... my Son...* Mary is deeply connected to each, and has come in the hope of restoring the relationship among them.

## The Language of Her People (Part One):

She goes on to demonstrate that she is intimately aware of what is going on in the life of her people, in two areas especially: religion, and economics. But she is no passive observer. As she describes her people's lack of respect for her Son's name and their neglect of Sunday worship and Sabbath rest, she weeps. As she lists the sufferings of her people — blighted crops, famine looming on the horizon, children dying — she weeps. What matters to her people, matters to her. Or, as Fr. Marcel Schlewer, M.S., puts it, she speaks the language of her people. This is part of the prophetic character of the message of La Salette.

Even when she offers a more hopeful prospect for the future, her tears continue to flow. After all, her people had failed to notice past warnings. Even if they responded now, they would never, as she herself declares, be able to pay her back for the pains she has taken for them. More than a complaint, this constitutes a challenge. (For many decades, the appropriate response was seen as "reparation.")

Maximin Giraud and Melanie Calvat, the two
witnesses to the La Salette Apparition

At a certain point, Mary made her encounter with Maximin and Mélanie deeper still. Observing that they were not understanding her very well, she made a simple adjustment, switching from French to the local dialect, or patois, used by less educated persons, and the only language either of the children had ever spoken. Now she was literally "speaking their language," entering into their world more intimately, and thereby drawing them into hers.

A couple of early accounts of the apparition mistakenly state that Mary noticed at the very beginning that children did not understand French, and that she pronounced her entire discourse in the patois. But all the best accounts, written during or immediately after interviews with the children, place the change at the point where, speaking of the potatoes, she says, "*... and by Christmas this year there will be none left.*" Then she went back and repeated, this time in dialect, part of what she had already said, beginning with, "*If the harvest is ruined ...,*" and continued in the dialect until just before the final commission, "*Well, my children, you will make this known to all my people.*"

Sometimes people wonder how it could be that Our Lady was unaware that Mélanie and Maximin did not know French. It is an intriguing question. To answer it, we must first recognize that nothing about the apparition happened by chance. The Beautiful Lady chose two poor, uneducated children as her witnesses. She chose the place. She chose the date, Saturday, September 19, the Vigil of the Feast of Our Lady of Sorrows, celebrated in those days on the Sunday after September 14, the Feast of the Holy Cross.

She knew what she was going to say; surely she knew how she was going to say it! Why two languages? She offered no explanation, but the most reasonable interpretation is that she wished to include both "her people" (ignorant of the dialect) and "her children" (Maximin and Mélanie). Plus, the history of the approval of the apparition shows that the children's ability to repeat the lengthy first part of the discourse in a language they did not know was one of the factors in favor of the authenticity of the event.

## The Language of Her People (Part Two):

In the message of La Salette, there is a yet another relationship that opens up to us. It does not concern any person or group of persons as such. Rather, in a somewhat subtle way, it connects us with the Scriptures, the Word of God.

Various lists have been drawn up, of phrases in the discourse of Our Lady of La Salette or aspects of the apparition itself, that echo or parallel passages in the Bible. They are interesting and helpful, but the perspective I wish to present is different.

The most important context for understanding La Salette is the Bible. Every part of the Message reflects that world. Without the Scriptures, La Salette is subject to every sort of interpretation.

This applies most especially to the Prophets. Mary at La Salette can be seen not only as Our Lady of Sorrows, as implied above, but also — as she is called in the Litany of the Blessed Virgin Mary — Queen of Prophets. This helps us to understand certain expressions that can trouble theologians and the ordinary faithful alike.

Earlier I quoted Fr. Marcel Schlewer, M.S., who pointed out that, in mentioning the concrete things that concerned her people, she was speaking their language. When he turns his attention to the style of the message, he says again that she is speaking the language of her people, but in this case he means, literally, her people, the people among whom she lived during her years on earth, speaking the kind of language they spoke. Hers was a Hebrew heritage, and this is reflected in many ways in the message of La Salette.

In particular the prophetic style of the message echoes that of the Prophets themselves. Like them, she criticizes her people's sinful ways, but offers a vision of hope as well. Like them, she sometimes has harsh words. *"In Lent they go to the butcher shops like dogs,"* she says. But, compared to certain passages in Ezekiel, which I guarantee you will never hear in church, this is really quite gentle.

Similarly, one might wonder why Mary says, *"I gave you six days to work; I kept the seventh for myself, and no one will give it to me."* The Sabbath rest was not given by her, but by God, institutionalized in the commandments. The Prophets, however, often spoke God's word in the first person, usually, but not always, adding, "says the Lord," or words to that effect. Even when they do not, there is never any doubt on whose behalf they are speaking. In Mary's case, the next sentence makes it perfectly clear whose thought she was expressing: *"This is what makes the arm of my Son so heavy."*

Besides the prophetic content and style, there are other indications of biblical thought patterns in the message. So as not to belabor the point, I will give just one example.

But first, another quiz question for you. At what times does the Beautiful Lady say we ought to pray?

Most of my readers will say, "Morning and evening." That is, however, incorrect. When the children answered the Lady's question, and said they hardly prayed, she insisted: *"Ah, my children, you should say them well, at night and in the morning."* The meaning is of course the same as morning and evening, but the turn of phrase she used has strong biblical overtones. In the first chapter of Genesis we read six times: "Evening came, and morning came — the first, [second, third, etc.] day." In Jewish practice, the day begins at sunset.

As I say, this is subtle. Nonetheless, in drawing us thus into her world, Mary helps us to encounter God in his word, in a more intimate and personal way.

## Beyond Language:

So far, I have focused mostly on the words of the message of La Salette to show how they demonstrate different aspects of God's presence, as expressed by Mary's apparition. But I would not wish to forget another element, visual in nature.

Recently I attended two different dramatizations of the La Salette story. They were well done, but I was disappointed to see that Mary's costume was that of a classic Madonna, with little resemblance to that described by the children. I am not thinking particularly of the unique features: the crucifix with the hammer and pincers, or the roses, or the chains, or the crown of light. Rather, I am more interested in the ordinary clothes she wore.

Look at the statue of Mary talking to the children. Take away all the special items listed above. What is left? A long dress, an apron, a shawl and a bonnet.

Now notice what Mélanie is wearing: a long dress, an apron, a shawl and a bonnet. She, and any girl or woman of the locality, seeing the Beautiful Lady, could have said, "She is one of us." And that is my point. Even in her garb, before speaking a word, Mary chose to be as close to her people as possible.

## The Corner Field (Le Coin):

I have saved the best for last, however. At the end of her discourse, Our Lady of La Salette told a story, illustrating, better than anything else, the mystery of God's presence.

She asked the children if they had ever seen blighted wheat. When they said no, she spoke to Maximin, to remind him of a time he and his father had gone a field known as "The Corner" (*Le Coin*, in French), where the farmer showed them how his wheat was going bad. Walking back home, Mr. Giraud gave his son a piece of bread, wondering out loud how much longer there would be any bread to eat.

**Window in La Salette Basilica on the Holy Mountain – the event at the corner field**

When the people of Corps, where Maximin's home was, heard of the apparition, some laughed at his father, not a religious man, while others kept coming to the door to find out more from Maximin. It wasn't long before Mr. Giraud had had enough! He forbade his son to talk about these things to anyone. During one of these tirades, the boy answered, "But, Daddy, she spoke about you!" That got his attention, and Maximin was able to tell him the story about their visit to The Corner and the piece of bread, as the Beautiful Lady had told it.

Mr. Giraud knew that he and Maximin were alone on the road that day. He also knew that his son, a scatterbrained child if there ever was one, could not possibly have remembered this episode on his own. Only one conclusion was possible: God was there, too.

He was, as the saying goes, blown away. Still, he needed confirmation, a sign. He went up the mountain with his son, he drank from the stream near where Mary had stood, asking to be cured of his asthma. His prayer was heard. He returned to the sacraments, and attended Mass every day until his final illness less than three years later.

Maximin's father had experienced the extraordinary manifestation of the ordinary presence of God. His story is our story. God is truly Emmanuel, God-with-us.

# Conclusion:

The title of this chapter speaks of presence as mystery. In a spiritual context, mystery has a special significance. It is not a riddle to be deciphered, nor a secret to be discovered, and much less a puzzle or problem to be solved. Rather, it is so vast and deep that we will never fully grasp it. Each time we reflect on it or simply experience it, there is something more, something new. The most obvious example in most people's lives is love.

So it is with God's presence. The Beautiful Lady opens our eyes, and especially our hearts, to that reality, which continues to amaze us and — to use the image of light — dazzle us every time we realize that God is indeed with us, that he loves us, that what matters to us matters to him, that he wants us to be present to him.

## Reflection Questions:

• How do you identify with the personal relationship with Mary on which the article focuses? Are you "my children"? Are you a part of "my people"? Is Mary your Mother? Her Son your Brother? How do you see this closeness in your spirituality?

• How would you describe your reaction to the apparition? Reconciliation? Reparation? Welcome? Don't be Afraid? Come closer? Tears?

• What really struck you as new or central or most important in the article? How does your relationship with God, Mary and the People of God need to change?

# Chapter 2 —
# La Salette Spirituality in Everyday Life
## By Fr. Paul Rainville, M.S.

### Introduction:

On September 19, 1846, Our Blessed Mother appeared and spoke to two Children, Melanie Mathieu and Maximin Giraud. At one point she asked them: *"Do you say your prayers well, my children?"* The two of them answered with a "no." The reality is that neither of them was very religious. Both were baptized in the Catholic Church. They both knew where the local church was located in Corps, their native village. That was probably the full extent of their religious knowledge. And like most of the people around them, Faith in God and in Jesus was not a high priority, if even it ever came to mind.

Melanie, the oldest of many children in the poorest of families, had been "farmed out" as a servant since the age of five or six. She was at home in the wintertime when there was not much work or much food. Maximin's mother had died in childbirth and his father had quickly remarried. With other children coming into the family, Maximin was pretty much on his own in the village of Corps. Each of the children adopted a sort of "survival mode" in their everyday life. And God did not appear to be a part of it.

The question the Beautiful Lady asked was a very simple one, filled not with condemnation, but with interest. In some ways it was a loaded question. It opened new, unexpected perspectives. It was the religious dimension, the connection with God. And this is where spirituality comes in.

# Spirituality:

For most people, even many very religious persons, the word spirituality evokes something very foreign to their life. They may have heard of the word and associate it with great saints and heroes of the Faith. And they then conclude that it is something far beyond their reach.

Church teaching is very different. Saint John Paul II made it a point of his papacy to recall that by our baptism we are all called to holiness, each one of us without exception. In this, he was echoing the sentiments and the documents of the Second Vatican Council. The pope did not say that we are all called to be canonized saints. The canonized saints are the exceptional ones that encourage us on our way.

The Holy Father's understanding of holiness led him to reform the whole process of canonization, to simplify it. He canonized more people than all of his predecessors put together. And we see these saints, warts and all because spiritual perfection is a limited perfection. And the saints are real people, just as we are. In their life here on earth they were in fact sinners who kept on trying.

When our Blessed Mother appeared at La Salette that Saturday afternoon, there was a coming together of the ordinary and the extraordinary, the secular and the spiritual. It is the same in our own lives.

When Our Lady came at La Salette, she did not appear to Church leaders. No, she appeared to two children, and she came as one of them, a peasant woman from the area and wearing peasant clothing. Melanie and Maximin saw her as a local person, one whose life is similar to theirs. Because of the similarities the children identified with her and a relationship could and in fact was established. A relationship with Mary always leads to a relationship with her son, Jesus, a relationship to God the Father, a relationship to the Holy Spirit.

Three elements of that reality need to be elaborated: they need unpacking. The first is that it always begins with God: He initiates. A second point is taking a look at what spirituality is all about from our perspective. And finally, what did the Beautiful Lady have to say about that, and how that reflects what is in the Holy Bible and in our own Catholic traditions.

## God Initiates:

Our Catholic Faith is rooted in the call of Abraham, our spiritual ancestor. God initiated the call and Abraham followed; from Ur of the Chaldeans he and his family became wanderers in the land of Canaan and the land of Egypt.

God also called Moses. He captured his attention with the burning bush and invited him to remove his sandals and draw closer. God told Moses that he had heard the cries of his people in Egypt. And He sent Moses to deliver them. God took care of his people through thick and thin, even when they grumbled against God.

Samuel was but a child when God called him in the middle of the night. Years later God let Samuel know that it was David that he had chosen, the youngest son of Jesse, and he was the one to be anointed, not any of his older brothers.

When we look at other prophets of the Old Testament we see the same thing. The prophet Jeremiah was chosen to speak in God's name before he was born. Amos was a "dresser of sycamore trees" when God called and sent him.

Jesus began the conversation with the woman at the well in Samaria. He asked her for water and announced that he had greater water, water that did not leave one thirsting. This was a great surprise to her and to the disciples. In speaking with her Jesus broke away from many customs and accepted behaviors of the time.

Mary, our Blessed Mother and the Mother of Jesus, follows the lead of her Son and her God: At the foot of the cross Jesus gave John to his mother as her son and gave his mother to John as his mother. At that moment John represented each and every one of us. Mary became your mother and mine at that moment.

Mary takes her role as our mother very seriously. She sees our infidelities as the root cause of our drifting away from God. So, she takes the initiative.

As she appeared to the children, her pain and tears were obvious. The

**Mary speaks to
Maximin and Melanie**

tears kept flowing throughout the apparition, and through her words also. The first of those words: "*Come closer, my children; don't be afraid*" were so soothing and comforting that both children instantly lost their fear and approached her. They were so close to her, they said, that no one could have come between them. She began it all: she appeared in the bright light, she invited them to come closer, she spoke lovingly through her tears.

The Beautiful Lady told them of her suffering: "*How long a time I have suffered for you!*" We can easily think of her Seven Sorrows as depicted in Scripture and in the rosary meditations that speak of those sufferings. But she spoke of her ongoing suffering, not of things in past history. The arm of her Son was heavy with the burden of our sins, with our lack of respect and with our neglect of the One who did so much for us.

## Respecting the name of her Son:

She spoke about cart drivers who swore and abused the name of her Son. Things have not changed much. In present day society it is offensive to use vulgarity, because it disturbs sensitivities. But using the name of Our Lord even in the most offensive ways is almost as "normal" as breathing. We might ask ourselves this question: can we respect ourselves and others if we don't respect our God? Love needs respect as its foundation.

## Respecting the Lord's Day:

The Beautiful Lady mentioned how few people went to Church on Sunday. In the wintertime, as a pastime many went to church only to mock at religion. When the children told her that they did not pray, she invited them to say at least an *Our Father* and a *Hail Mary* in the evening and in the morning; and when the opportunity would arise, she invited them to say more.

After speaking privately to each of the children, she asked them if they had ever seen spoiled wheat. After a negative answer from each of them, she turned to the young boy, Maximin, and reminded him of an event that only he and his father had experienced: *"la terre du coin"* and the piece of bread given to him by his father out of concern for what was to come in the next few months. All of this is very personal. She showed them how much she cared and how much she was concerned.

## What does this mean?

God created us out of love. His desire is for a mutual relationship. Our first parents with their sin distorted that relationship. God promised to reinstate it. God the Father has done just that by sending us his Son. Through his suffering, his death and his resurrection Jesus has even enabled us to become part of the divine family: Saint Paul tells us that by our baptism we are adopted into God's family. And Saint Paul calls each baptized person a saint.

We recognize that each and every one of us, though similar, is a unique individual. It follows that our relationship with God will be similar to the spirituality of others and yet at the same time be very unique. Saint Francis de Sales, a doctor of the Church, described this at length some four hundred years ago. Spirituality needs to be adapted to the life of an individual. It is not a one size fits all kind of reality. He used contrasting imagery to make his point. Bringing his imagery up to date we might say that an astronaut cannot have the same spirituality as a stay at home mom with a couple of little ones in diapers, a high-powered executive will not be praying in the same way as a contemplative monk, a construction worker and a priest will have different approaches, a school teacher and an interstate truck driver will have very different lives.

# Finding our way:

It is obvious that the Beautiful Lady who came to speak to Maximin and to Melanie was concerned that peoples' lives were aimlessly moving about, we could say like a boat without oars, or sail, a boat at the mercy of everything around it. She came to remedy the situation: to help re-establish our relationship with God, maintain it, and enable it to grow.

After removing the fear factor with her first words "Come closer, my children," and making them aware of the situation, she presented the children with a small spiritual toolkit that every person can use, and in fact that every person already possesses. These simple tools are: prayer, mass (and by extension the other sacraments), discipline, and finally respect for Jesus' name. These need to be examined more closely, remembering at the same time that each one of us is a unique person, created in the image of God.

## Prayer:

*The Annunciation*
by El Greco (1541–1614)

We often tend to complicate things. Thousands of volumes have been written about prayer. Many more thousands will be written. They all have their place. What is most important though is a good foundation. The Beautiful Lady kept it simple. Our Lady asked the children if they prayed well and they gave an honest answer: no. She responded in turn by asking them to say an "Our Father" and a "Hail Mary" at night and in the morning, and when the opportunity arose to say more.

Relationships evolve. They begin slowly and then they grow. For us human beings it takes time to get to know another person. It takes time to learn to appreciate the gifts and strengths of another, as well as that person's weaknesses and limitations. Our Lady asked the children to pray at night and in the morning. The rising and the setting of the sun are natural moments in life, as the day begins and ends. For most of us it is a good time to be in touch with God.

We might say that the *Our Father* and the *Hail Mary* are the rock foundation on which all else is built. Both prayers are biblical in origin. For those of us who are born catholic, we have learned them early in life, in the presence of loving parents and family. For many others who come from other Christian communities, the "Lord's Prayer" is the most sacred of prayers. The "Hail Mary" is also very biblical, though not as immediately obvious to many people. It contains the greeting of the archangel Gabriel when he came to speak with her: "Rejoice, you who enjoy God's favor! The Lord is with you" (Luke 1:28). It is followed with the greeting of her cousin Elizabeth: "Blessed is the fruit of your womb" (Luke 1"42b). Eventually the name of Jesus was added, since he is the fruit of her womb. Later still a petition for prayer was also added: "Holy Mary, Mother of God..."

All of this is most appropriate since, as was mentioned earlier, at the foot of the cross Jesus gave the apostle John to her as her own son. Mary is indeed our Mother. Just as Jesus called the Father, "Abba" that is to say daddy, denoting a very close and deeply personal relationship with the Father, Mary can be addressed as our mother, with terms of intimacy.

In our own prayer life, we begin with simple basics: two simple prayers. We need to grow into catholic Christians with more mature spiritual lives. But we need to begin slowly. Saint Paul himself spoke of his human and spiritual growth when he mentioned when he was a child he spoke and he ate like a child, but as he grew things changed. We also know from our own life experiences that too much of a good thing is not healthy. We can easily note this when we are overeating or over exercising; we can easily injure ourselves or make ourselves sick. A good exercise program begins slowly and once it is solid and well established, it is easier to build on it. Similarly, if we can begin slowly and be consistent in maintaining our prayer life, brief as they might be, our yearnings will enable us to recognize when it is time for more. The Holy Spirit will not fail us.

## Mass and Respect for the Lord's Day:

The Beautiful Lady complained that only a few elderly women went to mass during the summer time and that during wintertime, many went just to mock at religion. Church participation, more specifically Sunday mass attendance, is a problematic issue to this day. While it is true that many of our church buildings may be full, generally less than half of the people who identify themselves as catholic actually go to mass weekly. As Catholic Christians, the Eucharist is at the heart of our Faith. Yet most of us highly under appreciate it. The Church tells us that Mass is the primary way to celebrate and observe the Lord's Day.

At the Last Supper Jesus said: "Take it and eat, 'this is my body'... drink from this... for this is my blood" (Matthew 26:26). And as he did so, he forever linked that incident with his death coming the following day. Jesus mandated his disciples to "do this in remembrance of me" (Luke 22:19b). Because Jesus said it and did it, the Cross and the Last Supper are forever one and the same. When we participate at mass we participate in the very act of Redemption. We are nourished by his Body and Blood. We also deepen the understanding of our Faith as we listen to the living Word in the readings that are from Sacred Scripture.

The words of Our Lady at La Salette were themselves prophetic as she spoke in the name of her Son. Her words are an invitation to look at Sunday mass not so much as an obligation, but as an incredible gift. Jesus gives himself to us, the fullness of life and love, adopts us into the divine family and gives us his Kingdom as our heritage. We are given all of that and we hardly ever take notice.

## "Abusing the Name of My Son:"

In the Ten Commandments we are told to "not take the name of the Lord in vain". There are many ways we can disrespect the Lord's name. As Christians we have come to know that Jesus is the Son of God. As God, his name too requires respect. Twice the Beautiful

Lady speaks of abusing "the name of her Son": first in speaking about the cart drivers, who seem unable to speak without throwing in the Lord's name, and again as people react to the discovery of spoiled crops.

In our own day we see pretty much the same reality. It is now an endemic situation in many if not most western cultures and societies. Some societies such as our own American society, claim to be religious with a majority claiming Christianity as their root belief system. Yet at the slightest surprise, challenge or difficulty, the Lord's name comes out as the easiest of exclamations. And far too frequently it comes out as an expletive.

Vulgarity is offensive in its own way. It indicates a lack of respect as well as a lack of sensitivity. This is dehumanizing and therefore wrong and against God's plan. It is far less of an offense than using the Lord's name in vain. For many people, though, it is personally more offensive and using the Lord's name in vain is more acceptable. Our value system is distorted.

## Church Discipline:

The Beautiful Lady also spoke some words that appear to be quite harsh: "*In Lent they go to the butcher shop like dogs.*" Comparing people to dogs or calling them dogs is not a compliment. All of us can think of words, legitimately used to describe dogs, which become very demeaning when used about people. Was Our Blessed Mother demeaning us? Absolutely not and quite to the contrary she was showing us how easily we demean ourselves. Every time we sin, we are less than we could be.

The words of Our Lady had to do with peoples' attitude about Church discipline. Ignoring their own good and their spiritual welfare, the Church's discipline became meaningless. But that discipline did not just drop out of the blue. It is part of a very long tradition. It goes back to our Judeo-Christian roots. It is a part of our spiritual DNA.

The Old Testament of the Bible often speaks about folks fasting in times of strife and even more so as repentance for sins. That along with prayer and almsgiving, what we now perceive as charitable giving, were traditional ways of approaching the Lord and to be renewed spiritually.

The Church has accepted this reality as beneficial both to individuals and to the Church as a whole. The Church has both regulated and suggested various forms of these disciplines to this day.

The Beautiful Lady spoke specifically about the discipline of abstinence. Abstinence, the avoidance of meat in the diet, which for our understanding, we might describe as a kind of subset or added form of fasting. It also has varied with time and place. Current discipline of abstinence in the Church is simpler: Ash Wednesday, the six Fridays of Lent and Good Friday. Other Fridays through the year are highly recommended, but not mandatory.

The purpose of abstinence is simple: a discipline to help us recognize our sinfulness and brokenness, to make amends for our sins as well as to help us be stronger on our spiritual journey. At its most basic, discipline is an act of the will, a spiritual muscle if you will. Acts of the will are our decision makers. Through exercises

*The Deposition*
by Michelangelo (1475-1564)

of spiritual discipline, we enhance our ability to choose to do what is correct or incorrect, to do what is wright or what is wrong.

## Guideposts:

Abstinence and fasting, almsgiving, observing the Lord's Day as well as respect for the name of Jesus her Son can be seen as guideposts and tools on our faith journey. That is the hope and expectation of the words of our Blessed Mother as she spoke to the two children on that September Saturday afternoon. They are basic tools needed for our spiritual growth. Adapted to our own lives, they are part of the foundation of a rich spiritual life.

**Reflection Questions:**

• Mary mentions three important actions that are part of the Catholic identity: participating in Sunday Eucharist, Respecting God's Name, and fasting and abstaining on appointed days. Do you see these as more than obligatory things to do? How are they foundational to Christians?

• How does the *Our Father* and *Hail Mary* create this relationship with God, Mary and the Church in your life?

• Do you live out the call – response nature of our Faith? God initiates by calling us with his grace and love and we respond to Him; do you let God's love and goodness have that power over your life?

# Chapter 3 —
# Come Closer, My Children
### By Fr. Raymond Cadran, M.S.

*Let the Little Children Come unto Me* **by Carl Bloch (1834-1890)**

As often as I read this opening message from the Apparition of Mary at La Salette, I am reminded of the beautiful, but challenging, invitation Jesus gives in the Gospel: "Let the little children alone, and do not stop them from coming to me; for it is to, such as these, that the kingdom of Heaven belongs." (Matthew 19:14). The life of children is especially precious to the Lord. He sees them and their world of joy and wonder, of creativity and questioning, of exploration and their hunger for love and affirmation; and he recognizes these as signs of the inbreaking of the Kingdom of God in our midst.

At another time, when the disciples were questioning who was greatest in the Kingdom of Heaven: "So he called a little child to him whom he set among them. Then he said, 'In truth I tell you, unless you change and become like little children you will never enter the kingdom of Heaven'" (Matthew 18:2-5). Jesus noted in children their willingness to trust and their complete dependence on their parents for life and guidance and held these up as a model to his followers for their relationship with God and for being his disciples.

I can only imagine that Jesus learned these insights about being beloved Children of God from his own home life, especially from the way he was raised by his mother Mary and his foster father, Joseph. For Jesus, the spiritual power that children hold and can offer to the world, was and is precious and needs to be nurtured and protected.

This is where I come to view Mary's visitation at La Salette as a reminder to the beautiful and precious relationship she has had with the younger brothers and sisters of her son, given to her to care for at the foot of the cross. For Mary, the spiritual life of children has a wonderful potential to transform the world, if we as adults can learn to listen to them more carefully.

I have often wondered why Mary chose young people to be bearers of the profound messages of such apparitions as La Salette, Lourdes and Fatima. What did she see in them that gave her such confidence that they could 'make this message known to all my people'?

Perhaps it was because when she herself was, as tradition holds, in her middle teens, that God invited her into the awesome drama of incarnating His Word, in and though her life.

How God had entrusted to her his Son, the living message of saving, reconciling love; and called on her to bring him to birth, nurture his life and educate him for his mission. Perhaps she experienced in that invitation God's affirming love of her at such a young age, trusting her to be open to his power at work in her, believing in her, and gracing her with the gifts that would help her to be a budding evangelist. Perhaps this was in Mary's heart and mind when she visited the children of La Salette, Lourdes and Fatima.

When Mary appeared at La Salette to Maximin, aged 11 and Melanie, aged 14, the encounter brought out in these young children some of the most beautiful aspects of what I see in the spiritual life of children:

- •wide eyed openness to the new
- •wonder and awe
- •an innocence leading to trust
- •creative and inquisitive minds
- •beautifully, simplistic hearts
- •a personal openness to experiences
- •a willingness to learn
- •a sense of adventure
- •a wish to be loved and valued

28

- an instinctive wish to help someone in need
- a responsiveness to being cared for
- the joy in being entrusted with a responsibility

So many of these gifts of and for life I have seen in parish life, in pre-school children and formation ministry to young children and teens.

The Apparition of Mary at La Salette celebrates and highlights God's care for all God's beloved sons and daughters and the expression of that care in the unique visitation of Mary, as mother care, a responsibility and gift she was given in the last moments of her Son's earthly life, at the foot of his cross. It also highlights how her new children respond to the nurturing and confident love she has for them as she missions them into the world.

The core message of what Mary said and did, with and through the children, at La Salette is as relevant and needed today as it was in 1846. How so?

First and foremost, Mary came to La Salette to visit two young children, Maximin Giraud, aged 11 and Melanie Mathieu, age 14. I underscore this spiritual reality because it is a vital one. Mary appeared with a special, divinely inspired, gospel-centered message to two young children. She did not appear to a Pope, Bishop or clergy, scholar or powerful leader of towns, cities or nations. No, she came and spoke her life transforming message to these two rustic children and entrusted them with beginning the Spirit inspired movement that would help reshape the world spanning time and geography. These young people heard, and took to heart, and were graced with the courage to: *"Very well, make this message known to all my people."* At its core, we might say that the La Salette event is profoundly a children's apparition.

From the heart of God's Kingdom, Mary came with a message of divine love for the children of God in need of mercy and direction and of tender care for the victims of the consequences of the selfish, sinful acts of those who were turning away from a life lived in the light of her Son. She came with a message that shared all the life-promoting effects that would follow a converted heart and a renewal of our relationship with God; a renewal fostered through prayer, acts of penance and a concern for the well-being of God's most vulnerable sons and daughters.

This is the powerful message Mary entrusted to the two young children. We might wonder, with a message of such importance, why to them, for they were seen as illiterate, not well schooled, not very religious, not very prayerful, or outgoing, or confident, why them?

I venture the possibility that it was because Mary saw in these two youngsters, something that we as adults need to be more attuned to in the spirituality of children, especially our own children today.

These first witnesses approached Mary with wonder and awe and a gradual growing respect for the one who they called 'the Beautiful Lady'. They sought to know her better. With a sympathy that we can learn lessons form, they saw her weeping and wanted to know why, to help dry her tears and to understand why she hurt.

They listened attentively to her story of sorrow and let her know when they could not understand her words, so she could adjust her language to help them know what she needed them to do.

They were highly observant to the symbolic, non-verbal, language she spoke and wore; the globe of light that enveloped her, the roses that draped her shoulders, head and feet, the tears flowing down her face, the chains that hung from her shoulders, the cross which bore the image of her Son and the hammer and pincers. All these spoke to them of her beauty, her sorrow, and the import of her message.

The children shared their lives with the 'Beautiful Lady', honestly answering her questions such as *"Do you say your prayers well, my children?"* and with no sense of denial or excuse, responded: "No madame, we don't."

The children had a great willingness to stay in the experience, not to run away in fear or be distracted by other cares and worries. They were eager to accept the mission, the work entrusted to them by the 'Beautiful Lady': "*Very well, my children, you will make this known to all my people.*" They carried out that mission over time with growing confidence, courage, and care, believing that they were her messengers of what was a life-changing story.

The children of La Salette bore to the adult church and world a reconciling, healing, and conversion inspiring message. The La Salette Missionaries have come into existence because of their young, prophetic voices. Their encounter with the one they called 'the Beautiful Lady'; whom the Church discerned to be Mary, the Mother of our Savior, and whom we know now as Our Lady of La Salette; set in motion the journey of many back to a stronger, deeper and more committed relationship with the merciful God. Perhaps this loving God had these children in mind and heart when he missioned Mary to visit the mountain of La Salette out of continuing, saving love for us.

As an integral part of the La Salette family now, we too are enfolded into that same reconciling mission the children received. We are invited to carry that message to the world using our own human gifts and abilities as we also accept the invitation of St. Paul to be 'ambassadors of reconciliation' (2 Corinthians 5:11-21).

If the simple, but vitally important children of La Salette can inspire such a healing, life-producing mission and ministry of reconciliation in and for God's people, how much more today can our children, the youth of our families, parishes, shrines and ministries, be an inspiration to us. We must nurture their souls, their spiritual hearts. We must protect and care for their precious lives, so capable of receiving such revelation from the heart of God's Kingdom.

For the love of God, our children and youth should inspire us to:

- create safe havens for them to grow up in peace and security,

- to care for and nurture their spiritual lives and journeys,

- to help them discern their special roles in following Christ as his youngest, but very precious disciples,

- to teach them, by our own growing example, to pray well, love the Eucharist, spend time with God and respect the name of Jesus,

by which we are saved,

• to learn with them the lessons of God's forgiving love and to live these in our daily and family lives,

• to respond carefully and faithfully to their many questions about God, Jesus, Mary, the Church and how to live peacefully and justly with all God's people,

• to help them grow in their sensitivity towards and knowledge of how to help the hurting and less fortunate,

• to spark their creativity, wonder and awe in God's creation and to live respectfully with all God's people in the world,

• to help them become attentive listeners for God's voice in their lives as caring parents, teachers, and mentors,

• to hear their stories of joy and sorrow, to seek to dry their tears with understanding and patience and to rejoice in their seemingly small, but very significant achievements and accomplishments,

• to do all we can to keep them safe and healthy so that they can grow up to confidently make known in their world of family, school and friendships, God's message of Divine love, mercy, and conversion of heart.

Mary cared deeply as a loving mother for Maximin and Melanie. She made known to them that she needed them to be her and her Son's prophets of hope. She wanted them to be close to her Son and know of his love for them.

Here at St. Ann's Catholic Church, in Marietta Georgia, we have a wonderful children's ministry called LAUNCH. Through it we hope to ignite the faith of our parish children, enflame them with the fire of God's Spirit at work in their lives and send them forth with confidence and joy on a 'Journey to the Son' — to a closer relationship with Jesus Christ, a truly La Salette mission.

I asked our director of the program, Jenny Kiehl, for some thoughts on what she saw as important areas of a children's spiritual life that need nurturing. This is what she said:

"I think the single most important area of a child's spiritual life that needs nurturing is a foundational and modeled relationship with Jesus, God the Father and the Holy Spirit. Everything else falls into place after that. The very first lesson we teach at LAUNCH is this: when you love someone or care about them or they are important in your life, you spend time building a relationship with that person.

"You get to know everything about them and what they like and do not like. You spend time playing with them or talking to them or just being with them. You do special things for them that will bring them joy. You even get them special gifts.

"Well, God is the most important person in your whole life, so your job is to talk to him, spend time with him, learn about him, do special acts for him, and even give him gifts, prayer, Biblical history, catechism, Sacraments, worship, acts of service, ministry, tithing, and so on."

I think Jenny has a wonderful feel for and understanding of the richness of the spiritual life of children. She sees them through a La Salette lens, the same one Mary saw Maximin and Melanie through. Like Mary, she appreciates their unique spiritual potential and seeks to ready them for the mission as Christ's youngest, but most precious disciples.

Jenny also says that: "...if the lessons that are taught in the classroom aren't reinforced at home in some way, children then see those lessons as less important because they aren't important to their parents, and if the parents don't think it is important, then many times, the lessons don't last. In order for children's religious education to take deep root, it should be modeled, reinforced, practiced or discussed in the homes." This is a profoundly important insight and stands as an urgent challenge for us all, especially parents and all ministers of catechesis. Jesus' spiritual life and lessons were surely reinforced and modeled at home.

As I close this reflection, I do so with thanksgiving for the many examples I have seen and experienced of our Adult Faith Communities using their time and talents to bring God's children and youth closer to Christ, to help them know that the Lord is deeply concerned for and cares about their lives and for all that takes place in them, that Jesus wishes to say to them through us: 'I want to be a special part of your lives, I want you to know that everything that happens to you is of interest and concern to me, your joys and sorrows, your hopes and dreams, your struggles and successes.' And to us as adults, Jesus continues to say, as Mary echoed at La Salette: "'Let the little children come to me, and do not stop them; for it is to such as these that the kingdom of God belongs" (Luke 18:16).

If you would like some further information on the spiritual life of children, please refer to the following:

- Christiane Brusselmans, *We Celebrate the Eucharist*, New York, Silver Burdette, 1972.

- _____. *We Celebrate Reconciliation*, New York, Silver Burdette, 1976.

- _____. *Religion for Little Children*, Huntington Press, 1970.

- Elizabeth Caldwell, *Making a Home for Faith*, Pilgrim Press, 2007.

- Robert Coles, *The Spiritual Life of Children*, Boston: Houghton Mifflin Co. 1991.

- Fr. Emile A. Ladouceur: *Vision of La Salette: The Children Speak*, Hartford: Missionaries of La Salette, first edition, 1956, Revised edition, 2016.

- Bonnie J. Miller-Mclemore, *Let the Children Come, Reimagining Childhood from a Christian Perspective*, Fortress Press, 2019.

- Traci Smith, *Faithful Families: Creating Sacred Moments at Home*, Chalice Press, 2017.

**Reflection Questions:**

• How do you understand the reasons for Mary choosing to appear to the two children: Melanie and Maximin?

• How can we be childlike all the days of our lives no matter the number of years we have been on the earth? What stands in our way?

• How do we personally encourage, educate, and raise our youth of today by word and example to know our loving God?

# Chapter 4 —
# The Gift of Mary's Tears
## By Fr. Flavio Gillio, M.S.

*I have never personally met Fr. Normand Theroux, M.S. and yet we have
become good friends. Whenever I have a chance to visit his gravesite in the
small cemetery at the Shrine of Our Lady of La Salette in Enfield, New
Hampshire, we spend a little time together and we peacefully converse.
Yes, I guess we have become good friends. After all, we both share the same
passion for the Scripture, we both studied in Rome at the Pontifical Biblical
Institute and more importantly, both of us have been captivated by the same
"Beautiful Lady"!*

## We are on a Journey:

Bible stories constantly remind us that the idea of "journey" or "pilgrimage" bears a deeply interconnected anthropological and theological value. On the one hand, we are and belong to a pilgrim people, to
a pilgrim community. On the other hand, we do not walk alone. Like
the pilgrim community of Israel in the desert, we are found by the
One for whom we are searching: the God of Abraham, Isaac, Jacob,
and the Father of Jesus, the Messiah.

God introduces himself as a pilgrim God, looking for his wandering
people. It is not a coincidence that one the greatest modern Jewish
thinkers, philosophers and theologians, Abraham Joshua Heschel,
entitled one of his most known books, *God in Search of Man: A Philos-
ophy of Judaism*. And for us Christians, God's pilgrimage reaches its
highest point in Jesus of Nazareth, as Saint John Paul II reminds us in

his 1999 letter, *On Pilgrimage.*

The Biblical History of Salvation, from Genesis to Revelation, is conceived as a progressing and unfolding journey from the Paradise lost to the Paradise found. In between, we find a great number of characters who embarked on challenging journeys, both physical and spiritual: Abraham, a "wandering Aramean" (Deuteronomy 26:5) took the risk of journeying towards an unknown land (Genesis 12:1; 15:17; 17:1); Moses, the greatest prophet, led Israel into a collective pilgrimage (Book of Exodus); Hosea, who prophesied to the Northern Kingdom just before the destruction of Israel in 722 B.C., and himself embarked on a painful journey through the ebb and flow of love.

And in the New Testament, a young woman from Nazareth, named Mary, journeyed through the sometimes-dark pilgrimage of raw and heroic faith; Paul and the Apostles, those "pilgrims" for Christ, journeyed from the Torah to the Cross and the resurrected Jesus. They were all men and women "on the way." following and witnessing the One who is the "Way."

This collection of homilies invites us, its readers, to embark on a literary and spiritual journey between two mountains, Mount Sion and the Holy Mountain of La Salette, where the "Beautiful Lady" appeared on September 19, 1846 to two children, Maximin Giraud and Melanie Calvat.

Our guide for this journey is Father Theroux's gentle voice and sharp insight. He allows us to appreciate the height and depth, the width and the length of the many biblical and La Salette landscapes and panoramas that his love for Scripture and for the Beautiful Lady are able to decipher and unfold. These reflections highlight the deep connection between the Bible – and more specifically the Gospels – and the message delivered by Our Lady at La Salette. And, finally, these perceptive meditations can help us understand better and more deeply the Apparition of Our Lady of La Salette as the most biblical of the major Marian Apparitions.

## Mary is a Handmaid:

Throughout Fr. Theroux's homilies, Mary is discretely present, a handmaid. She never overshadows her Son, but rather she leads us to him – as in the Gospels and in her words and actions at La Salette. Even if, as Fr. Theroux writes in one of his homilies, Mary remains "in obscurity throughout almost the entire New Testament", she keeps on being a discreet but significant presence. Like in the Gospels, so on the Holy Mountain of La Salette, Mary's presence is simply and entirely Christ-centered:

> "The crucifix on the Lady's breast at La Salette is more than a symbol. (Jesus) is the 'Son' she mentions three times in her discourse. He is the center of her life. He is her life. She had given him his body, his humanity. She had given him the blood he had shed on Calvary. The Lady who had stood on Calvary now stands at La Salette. She was called 'mother' on Calvary and this was to prove more than a title. She weeps still up to this very day for all her people and for each one of them."

Regarding Mary's discrete but significant presence in her Son's life, the *Dogmatic Constitution on the Church*, *Lumen gentium*, one of the principal documents of the Second Vatican Council, points out:

> "In the public life of Jesus, Mary makes significant appearances. This is so even at the very beginning, when at the marriage feast of Cana, moved with pity, she brought about by her intercession the beginning of miracles of Jesus the Messiah. In the course of her Son's preaching she received the words whereby in extolling a kingdom beyond the calculations and bonds of flesh and blood, he declared blessed those who heard and kept the word of God, as she was faithfully doing.

> "After this manner the Blessed Virgin advanced in her pilgrimage of faith, and faithfully persevered in her union with her Son unto the cross, where she stood, in keeping with the divine plan, grieving exceedingly with her only begotten Son, uniting herself with a maternal heart with his sacrifice, and lovingly consenting to the immolation of this Victim which she herself had brought forth. Finally, she was given by the same Christ Jesus dying on the cross as a mother to his disciple with these words: 'Woman, behold your son'" (*Lumen gentium*, Chapter 8, #58).

# Mary as Prophet and Teacher:

While guiding his readers to climb the two mountains, Fr. Normand Theroux paints Mary as prophet, teacher, and tender companion and mother. With the biblical prophets, Mary at La Salette shares the "…grace and terrifying vocation…" of giving voice to someone else's words, demanding to be heard:

> "At La Salette, Our Lady spoke in the name of her Son. She clearly did not say what she said on her own authority. She reminds people of the Mass, the day, Sunday, reserved for the Lord, penance, prayer and respect and honor for the Name of her Son. These are all God-centered commandments and the Lady speaks them on the authority of her Son. She mentions this 'Son' repeatedly throughout the apparition, so that there is no doubt about the origin of her message."

As such, Mary's words at La Salette, are words that are "…riven with truth and the truth in them will not expire," as Fr. Theroux writes commenting on the Gospel. He adds, "At La Salette, (she) is Mary, the Queen of Prophets".

In this first volume, *Food for the Journey: the Biblical Roots of the La Salette Message*, Mary also appears as a teacher and catechist. She teaches us, through Fr. Theroux's meditations, how to cope "well with life and its tough problems", and the path to follow in order to grow in intimacy with the Lord.

Finally, the Beautiful Lady of La Salette also accompanies us on our journey, as a tender and vulnerable companion and mother – a compassionate mother who weeps for all those whom she loves. Hopefully all of us have learned from our own life experiences. I believe that Fr. Theroux is correct when he writes that "caring for people brings its share of pain – joys too, of course, but pain in abundance" – a pain born of love. And likewise, the "Beautiful Lady," out of love for her people, experiences a "…flow of tears that flood the heart and cannot be held back."

# Shedding Tears:

At La Salette, Mary's tears are not only among those traits that make the Apparition of La Salette the most biblical one among the major Marian apparitions, but they are also a key to understanding the message she delivered to Maximin and Melanie. Like in the Gospels, where Jesus' deeds bring to light his words and vice versa, at La Salette too, Mary's actions and attitudes are deeply connected to her words, and they mutually enlighten each other. In fact, the authors of the bible are not at all hesitant to show even the most well-known persons in our Salvation History coming to tears. And as ironic as it may appear, men in the bible are seen weeping more than women!

Our Lady of La Salette, our Weeping Mother

## Tears in the Bible:

For example, Abraham weeps over the dead body of his beloved wife, Sarah (Genesis 23:2).

Esau weeps at the feet of his father, Isaac, when he realizes that his brother, Jacob, has stolen the blessing from his father (Genesis 27:38).

Joseph the dreamer, the great Prince of Egypt, weeps six times. The first time happens in Genesis, chapter 42, verse 24. A second snapshot of Joseph weeping is also described (Genesis 43:30).

Later the narrator portrays Joseph to be even bolder in his expression of emotions: "...he wept so loudly that the Egyptians heard him" (Genesis 45:2). And once the family ties are almost reconciled, Joseph weeps once again (Genesis 45:14).

A similar reaction is found when Joseph is reunited with his father (Genesis 46:27). The last time Joseph weeps is at his father's death (Genesis 50:1). From these instances, we can infer that Joseph was not only a great charismatic and confident leader, but he also had a tender heart and did not hesitate to express his powerful emotion in tears.

Similar to the outstanding prince of Egypt is the greatest King of Israel, David. He wept often, and quietly. But one of his most emotional responses occurred when he saw the dead body of his dearest friend, Jonathan, and the body of Jonathan's father, Saul (2 Samuel 1:12).

Even though our male biblical heroes seem to weep quiet frequently, women are not forgotten. For example, Hannah is not ashamed to express her sadness of heart to her beloved husband, Elkanah, through her frequent tears: "Elkanah, her husband, would say to her: 'Hannah, why are you weeping? Why are you not eating? Why are you so miserable? Am I not better for you than ten sons?'" (1 Samuel 1:8).

As we shift our attention from the Old Testament to the New Testament, both Jesus and Peter, continue the biblical habit of expressing their feelings through tears! Twice, once in Luke and once in John, Jesus is said to weep. He wept while approaching Jerusalem, probably at the Mount of Olives: "As he drew near, (Jesus) saw the city and wept over it" (Luke 19:41). Then he also wept in seeing the dead body of his very dear friend, Lazarus: "When Jesus saw (Mary of Bethany) weeping and the Jews who had come with her weeping, he became perturbed and deeply troubled, and said, 'Where have you laid him?' They said to him, 'Sir, come and see.' And Jesus wept" (John 11:33-35).

## Tears – a Sign of Vulnerability:

From a biblical perspective, weeping is not necessarily a sign of weakness but rather can be a sign of tender vulnerability and surrender. Weeping unveils the height, width and depth of our own humanity and heart. Yet, as a culture, many of us are not comfortable disclosing times in our lives when tears came to our eyes. Many among us may even feel embarrassed and ashamed at being seen weeping in public.

Just a small example: oftentimes in confession, if a person confessing begins crying, he or she will often say, "Excuse me, Father...", as if this is a shameful or embarrassing response for them. Such a way of thinking may be rooted in the fact that we have been growing up with the tenet, "never let them see you cry". Or, we might feel that, as a modern, sophisticated person, we believe that crying doesn't accomplish anything and could even expose us even to being more deeply hurt. Perhaps we were taught to control our emotions in order to be seen as strong and competent, especially if we have a leadership role in our community, family or elsewhere.

## Tears as a Tender Expression of Love:

But this way of looking at tears is certainly not what we see in the Apparition of Our Lady at La Salette. At La Salette, the "Beautiful Lady" becomes alive and real through her tears. For example, when Maximin and Melanie saw her crying, they simply thought it was a peasant woman from the village down in the valley who was running away from her family. Mary at La Salette is not embarrassed to appear vulnerable and expose to us her deepest emotions, through her weeping.

And so, what do her tears mean? The liturgical readings for the Feast of Our Lady of La Salette disclose to us their meaning. In our first reading from the book of Genesis, we hear about the rainbow in the clouds as a welcome reminder of God's covenant with us (Genesis 9:13).

At La Salette, Mary's tears also remind us about the good news of God's love and mercy for his people. They speak to us about her and her son's communion with our broken and wounded world – expressing sorrow mingled with hope for our redemption (*"If they are converted ..."*). Her tears make her presence real, showing us her deep communion with the needy people in our world. Fr. Theroux highlights this attitude when he writes:

> "Mary at La Salette came to imitate her Son in what he had done and to share his mission. She showed the world the suffering of an abandoned Lord. She revealed, if it had to be revealed, that in some mysterious way, God grieves and weeps for people. It is nothing less than stirring to see that at La Salette, the Lord wanted to let us know that God, is indeed, caring for his people to the point of tears."

# Our Crucified Savior Suffers With Us and For Us:

In our brief gospel for the feast, Jesus is seen nailed to the cross, with Mary and one of his disciples faithfully present. Concerning this tragic scene, Fr. Richard Rohr describes the crucified God as one "who walks with crucified people, and thus reveals and redeems their plight as his own. Jesus is not observing human suffering from a distance, but is somehow in human suffering with us and for us."

Similarly, at La Salette, Mary bears, on her breast "the crucified Christ... in bright and shimmering evidence. This is a suffering Christ, who in some way, still bears the burden of the cross. The mother herself says clearly, *"How long a time have I suffered for you!"* Like the Son, the "Beautiful Lady of La Salette" is not observing the broken world from afar, from a distance. Instead she is *with* us and *for* us. This shows her desire to suffer with us – *"cum passio,"* "to suffer with" – and her tears indicate both her compassion and mercy. Both the Son and his Mother are burdened with suffering, out of love and for those they love.

Window of St. Paul the Apostle, St. Joseph's Church, Bristol, CT

Mary's tears at La Salette should awaken in us a sense of gratitude and thanksgiving, leading us to pray with the Psalmist: "O bless the Lord, my soul" (Psalm 103:2). This is because Mary's tears are neither a sign of dismiss nor of judgment.

On the contrary, her tears welcome us; they do not judge us or reproach us; they invite us to come closer to her and allow ourselves to be welcomed by her in the same way that the "Beautiful Lady of La Salette" invited and received the two little peasant children. And the opening words of her message emphasize even more her attitude and posture:

*"Come closer, my children... do not be afraid...I have great news to tell you."*

This is a picture of what it means to be unconditionally loved. We all hunger and thirst for such an experience. As Richard Rohr describes so well:

> "This is the kind of experience that we all want, that we all wait for, that we all need. Although we want it from one another and we get it occasionally, there is only One who can be relied upon to always receive us and mirror us perfectly as we are."

It is really a grace to be able, at least once in our own life, to experience being truly loved – not for what we are able to accomplish; not because of our good reputation; but rather to be loved simply for who we are. It is a transforming grace to experience such a moment of unconditional love. We should appreciate that it can be a transforming grace to be touched and moved by the tears of Our Lady of La Salette.

As Paul reminds us in the second reading from the La Salette Feast Day Mass, Mary's tears, when we allow them to touch our hearts, are able to recreate us – "a new creation" – to reconcile us, and thereby make us ambassadors of Christ's reconciliation.

## She Weeps for Those Who Do Not Deserve Her Tears:

Because of that, the tears that Mary shed at La Salette are a challenging call to direct our compassion, mercy and tenderness to those who live at the margins or peripheries of the Church and our world.

As in 1846, it's very easy to recognize that our contemporary world is still filled with people who weep. They may be responding to natural calamities happening around the world; or perhaps weeping over discrimination because of people's different beliefs, religious values, or sexual orientation; or perhaps they come to tears seeing mistreatment and injustice, within and outside the Church.

Mary's tears at La Salette are tears for all her people – without exclusion or discrimination. And if we delve more deeply into the message, Mary weeps for people who do not deserve her tears! In her own words, she weeps for people who "cannot drive the carts without bringing in my Son's name"; for people who do not go to Mass or, if they go, they do so "only to mock religion"; also for people who, during Lent, "go to the meat market like dogs." In short, she weeps for people who do not deserve her tears!

Once again, the Mother imitates the Son, as Fr. Theroux very well explains:

> "At La Salette, Mary said, 'Well, my children, you will make it known to all my people.' By the ministry of Maximin and Melanie, her words would stir the Church but go beyond it to the whole world. The entire world is thus called to faith and life. The gospel of John is predicated on faith, on the belief that the love of God for all people is not something one can understand. Only faith can grasp it. The Lady weeps at La Salette for all the people who do not know the beauty of faith which is an aspect of God's love for people."

Like her Son, Mary at La Salette wishes to reach out to her own people – where they are and whom they are. What a great lesson, modeling for us what compassion, mercy and tenderness are all about! What a wonderful lesson about how to extend our compassion, mercy and tenderness to the margins and peripheries of our Church and world! The Beautiful Lady of La Salette, appearing in this very remote and marginal place, reaches the neediest people where they are found. She is with them and for them!

## An Invitation:

This collection of homilies, volume one of *Food for the Journey: the Biblical Roots of the La Salette Message*, is meant to be, like the Eucharistic Bread and Wine, food to nourish a special friendship, and a special relationship, while encouraging us, its readers to take "... advantage of those habits of faith..." which Our Lady of La Salette lists in her message: prayer, Eucharist, Lenten observances, and respect for the name and person of her Son.

We can all be truly grateful for Fr. Normand Theroux's love for Scripture and Our Lady of La Salette; ultimately, they give us the opportunity to walk in the footsteps of the One who is the face of the mercy of the Father and in so doing reaffirm our own discipleship. They give us the opportunity to listen anew to Mary's reconciling message and to be transformed into reconciled reconcilers.

They give us the opportunity to open our hearts to the Father's tenderness, mercy and compassion as reflected by the Son through his Mother so that we can become what she preached. After all, in a single half-hour, Maximin and Melanie had learned to love "the Beautiful Lady of La Salette"! And we certainly have more time than that!

May this first volume of Fr. Normand Theroux's homilies be, as he himself expresses with great hope, a "good way to learn who Mary is, what she does and how she practices the gospel command of love". May we pledge to seek out and be ambassadors of reconciliation with and for those of her people who live on the margins of our Church and world.

May all her people, in addition to Maximin and Melanie, hear the great news: "*Come closer*, my children, don't be afraid." After all, the message of Our Lady of La Salette is a universal call. In Fr. Normand Theroux's own words: "La Salette gives us the sharp message that someone cares enough to call and call again. To speak. To upbraid. To weep" – all without judgment, dismissal, or discrimination. Enjoy this reflective journey and welcome its call to conversion of heart.

## Reflection Questions:

• When have you come to tears over an event or a person? How did others react that saw the situation?

• Who is a person of faith for you and why? Describe some aspects of that person that you admire.

• How have you been touched by the tears of others? What were your reactions when you saw people cry?

# Chapter 5 —
# "If They Are Converted..."
## By Fr. Jim Henault, M.S.

*"If they are converted"* is the key to understanding the entire La Salette message and the central action that needs to be a part of our spiritually and embodiment of the charism of the apparition. One can hear from good religiously-minded people a criticism of the message of Our Lady that it is overly negative. They sort of stop after reading about famines and grapes rotting, walnuts being worm eaten and children dying in their mother's arms and the heavy arm of my Son.

If you stop there, then the story is most depressing and hopeless. We are like Peter who wants to stop Jesus from dying as he goes to Jerusalem, the women of Jerusalem weeping for Jesus as he walks to his death, the finding of the empty tomb and interpreting that as they stole his body. We need to see the promise of the panacea and paradise in the second half of the message.

Let us look at some basic Christian Faith Realities:

### Creation:

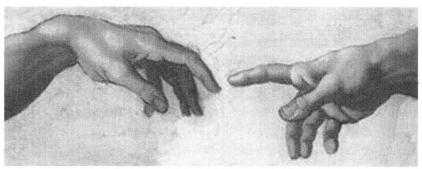

*Hands of God and Adam* by **Michelangelo (1475-1564)**

Genesis 1:1 –2-4 states: "In the beginning, when God created the heavens and the earth" (v. 1)... "God created (humankind) in his image; in the image of God he created them; male and female he created them. God blessed them, and God said to them: Be fertile and multiply;

fill the earth and subdue it. Have dominion over the fish of the sea, the birds of the air, and all the living things that crawl on the earth" (v. 26-28) ...and God looked at everything he had made, and found it very good" (v. 31). God created us to be a partner with him in creation. He walked with us in the Garden of Eden; he spoke to humanity in those early days; he shared the gift of freewill and allows us to choose the good if we so want. No matter what we will never lose our basic goodness, even though we sin.

## Sin Enters the World:

The sin of Adam was not about eating an "apple"; it was not even about disobeying God. It was much more fundamental it was wanting to be like God not a partner but a total equality that did not necessarily need the partnership. It was destroying the union between God and Humanity. Original Sin is the basic temptation in all things that we are God's equal, that we can do the things that he can do. We can live without him if we so choose. But God never gives up on us even if we give up on him.

## Sin versus Sins:

The two words can be distinguished as a matter of Attitude versus Actions. Sin is a lawlessness or Pride that tricks us into a conviction that we can do it on our own. We can prosper and survive without God; we can save ourselves. It helps to have God on our side when we fail miserably but most days, we can be self-sufficient. Sins are breaking the Law or Missing the mark. Sins are about the poor choices or the lesser good that we select. We know what God wants of us; we know what's best, but we accept less than the perfect. The early examples of Sin are seen in the stories of Cain and Abel Noah, the Tower of Babel it is the attitude not the action: we are the arbiters of life and death, of what is best in society, we can make our way to heaven by working together that leads to the ultimate divisions of tribe and language. Rebelliousness is the failure to accept the basic covenant: "You will be my people, and I will be your God" (Jeremiah 30:22).

## The Struggle Continues:

In the New Testament we see the use of the two concepts of Sin and Sins. The best examples of Sin are the Temptations of Christ: Create bread because you are hungry – Use your power for yourself – Turn the rocks into loaves of bread. At the Apparition Mary speaks of the stones becoming heaps of wheat. God's work - not ours, not Jesus for himself. The jump from the temple parapet –Test God and your relationship with him. Make him respond to you rather than responding to his will. Finally worship Power – Seek your own Kingdom: become the early Messiah, do not journey to Jerusalem to die; let the request in the Agony of the Garden be that the Father saves you from this hour and that your own will be done not the Father's will.

Sins are those actions that can be forgiven and that lead to the ultimate conversion in the mercy of God. The woman caught in adultery, Peter's denials at the place of Jesus' trial, Saul persecuting the Christians all lead to a complete fundamental change as they are forgiven. Love, commitment, covenant all come from God's generous acceptance of us as we are and calling us to something better.

## The Context of 1846:

People had lost sight of God in their lives. They did not go to church on a regular basis. They lacked a respect for God's Name. They went to meat markets during Lent like dogs. These three "sins" were symptoms of the more basic sin of abandoning God in their lives. Mary was weeping that her people were missing the bottom line: God was not important to them, respected by them, providing for them.

The three fundamental actions of a Catholic are: to keep holy the Sabbath day, to have a profound reverence and awe of God and to see that the gifts of the earth were gifts of God. Fasting is not about cutting back on food and drink; it is recognizing that God provides our food and drink – he nourishes us, and we do not let our appetites and needs control us. We instead control them. The actions of attending Mass, respecting God's name, and fasting make us his children. They are the new covenant being manifested by these simple activities; they make us his family, his people, his children.

## Mary's Invitation:

*"Come closer, my children; don't be afraid."* A crying, vulnerable Mother is reaching out to her children. Mary's tears and the purpose of the apparition were to let Melanie Calvat and Maximin Giraud know how disappointed she was in her people and us because she loved us and wants the best for us always. Invitations are offered to the children and to us to Come closer and do not be afraid.

The children were fearful. They approached the bright light and the sobbing woman hesitantly but her actions and words were reassuring to them and so they trusted in her and of course the shepherd's staffs they had at hand. They did not need the staffs. Their fears turned to compassion for a woman who may have been beaten or abused by her children (us through our sin of abandoning our faith in God.) Approaching her would forever change their lives and those of millions who would hear the message through them.

## Reconciliation not Reparation:

Mary invites us to let the power of God's love overwhelm us, once again, into becoming that people God made us to be. She states clearly that reparation or atonement are not the answer: *"however much you do, you will never be able to recompense the pains I have taken for you."* She looks for a change of heart and a new sense of belonging to God and one another. If we only submit to God's will and hopes and dreams for us, then greatness will be ours.

Remember the bottom line is that she has come to tell us *"great news."* The great news is not about famine and death and suffering; it is about restoration of the Kingdom of God in our midst. It is life being blessed with the joy of being loved by God, with his help and support, with the freedom of letting go of self-protection and independence and instead allowing God to be god in our lives.

## Famine vs. Prosperity:

The Old Testament is filled with promise at the time of adversity: in Exodus the story of slavery to freedom shows that God hears the cry of the poor his people in bondage. He sets them free, through forty years in the desert, and leads them into the Promised Land. First Isaiah shares the messianic vision of the restored nation from the age of false idols. The nation would be restored and blessed with the coming messiah. True peace and reconciliation would happen as the Lord sends true leadership for them. Second and Third Isaiah speak to a people on the way back from Exile. He speaks of a new restored nation and a suffering servant who would guide them. Suffering and hardship are redemptive. Jeremiah & Ezekiel speak of a new heart and new flesh that will be placed in his people making us once again the human beings that we were created to become.

## The God of Adversity:

Unfortunately we often assume or believe that the troubles we suffer in life are sent from God to us because we have sinned, we have not done what is right, or that God does not love us as much as he actually loves us. This is not the God of the Scriptures – Old or New Testament. Adversity is a part of living in a broken, sinful world where we do not live out our lives perfectly. When things go bad, we can easily blame God; he is powerful enough to take our reactions, but they lessen who we are.

Mary speaks about the people who drive their carts using God's name in vain (road rage of 1846). But there is no atheist in a foxhole; danger turns us to God. When we are not in control, then we turn things over to him. Look at the reaction to the deadly destruction of September 11, 2001 that led to heightened prayer and attendance at Masses and Church services the following weeks.

Turning to God in crises is perfectly normal for even the most in-active believers – when we face personal struggles (unemployment, sickness and death, broken relationships) or natural disasters (hurricanes, tornadoes, drought, wildfires, earthquakes, and famine) or

51

global problems (war and terrorism, crime and violence, injustice and oppression, climate change and ecological problems and pollution, racism and world hunger). We pray at these times and we also hopefully do what we can. Together we and God can conquer through our trust in the Paschal Mystery.

## The apparition prophesies:

Mary speaks of the possibilities of disaster coming our way if we do not change our ways. A great famine is coming, children will die in the arms of their mothers, the grapes will rot, the walnuts will be worm eaten, the wheat crop will fail, the warning of blight and the destruction in the potatoes. These things might happen, and some would, but they led many to change their ways. God is not punishing the world; Mary is not threatening us; they come from the world we live in and often our sinful responses. They can have the power to lead to conversion as we turn back to God.

*Pope St. John Paul II;*
**photo: Rob Croes**

John Paul II stated: "As I wrote on the occasion of the 150th anniversary, 'La Salette is a message of hope, for our hope is nourished by the intercession of her who is the Mother of mankind.'" The hope of Mary is for a better world, a better life, and our being overwhelmed by the mercy and love of our God.

## A Personal God:

The central point of the Apparition is: *"If they are converted, rocks and stones will turn into heaps of wheat, and potatoes will be self-sown in the fields."* To an agrarian world, Mary speaks of two marvelous changes: the rocks in the field, the enemy of planting and plows will be turned into the harvest. Instead of having to carry off the stones and facing a broken plow, the stones will become heaps of wheat. The backbreaking task of planting potatoes takes its toll on all who grow them. Down on their knees, dragging sacks of seed potatoes, planting one at a time was one of the most difficult tasks for the farmers of the day. These will be self-sown instead; the toil will be replaced by God's work for us. The point here is that we can struggle through life alone or we can trust that God is helping us and loving us in the difficult moments of life.

The Power of Love is transformative. Have you ever been in love before? What power does being loved and loving someone have in or daily life? What difference does it make when you know you are loved? How easy is it to act when you love your spouse, your children? Is life better when you love your job? When you do things that you like, that are satisfying, that enrich you it is natural to put better efforts into the task and often succeed easily and more completely.

## A personal relationship with Jesus:

Most Catholics do not believe that it is possible to have a personal relationship with Jesus Christ. Now that might sound very strange, but the way we relate to God through Sacraments and Sacramentals, can reinforce this false belief. Worship and liturgy are for many the way of practicing their faith. They go to Church on Sunday and can make statements that they are giving God his due, his hour for the week. But private prayer and meditation, reading and praying the Scriptures, faith sharing and activities of faith formation are also important.

Interestingly Mary asks the children if they pray well and when they say "not well," she invites them to say and *Our Father* and a *Hail Mary* in the morning and evening. Although she talks about the importance of going to Mass, she starts with personal prayer. The children did not say these prayers well and would have to learn them completely, but they would, and the praying would create this personal relationship with God and Mary. When that happens, then they will be capable of "Glorifying the Lord by their life."

## The Corner Field:

Jesus spoke in the Gospel of how the Father cares about the details of our life; the Father knows the amount of hairs on our head. He reminds us that he cares about the little things in our lives and not just the major events. Mary shares her remembrance of an incident in a corner field with Maximin and his father. This reinforces this reality for the two children that their every moment is precious to her and to the Father. The story eventually leads to the father's conversion as Maximin relates how she spoke about him. It reminds us of the way God cares about the details and intricacies of our life.

The Gospel is filled with examples: Nathaniel under the fig tree, Zacchaeus in the sycamore tree whom Jesus calls by name and invites himself to the tax collector's house, the wedding feast at Cana where Jesus saves the wedding day and the couple's reputation by making more wine; the man born blind who sees Jesus; he meets the widow of Nain whose son is raised from the dead for her; Mary at the Cross is entrusted to the beloved disciple's care and ours as well. In all these events and thousands of others throughout the Scripture, God provides for the needs of people *before* they ask.

## Our need for and consciousness of God's Love:

When we say the *Our Father* and the *Hail Mary* in the morning and in the evening, we dedicate our lives to the Lord. By a morning offering that recognizes God and what we can do together in our lives and reminds us of how blessed Mary is because she was God's lowly handmaid and filled with God's grace.

At the end of the day we do an examination of conscience or consciousness. Starting with a lookover of the day as it ends, we can see what did we do wrong, but then we go further and see what did we do right? We look at the promise we made to build God's kingdom, to hallow his name, to forgive those who have sinned against us and how we passed through the temptations to not do our best. We also review what did God do for us, how do we recognize God's action in my Life; what was the daily bread he fed us; how was God present in my day and bless us with his goodness. All this leads to the power of gratitude for our relationship with him and his place in our lives. We conclude the prayers of the day by asking Mary our Mother to pray for us this night and throughout our lives. With her intercession we are not alone, and we will be protected always.

# The Preface at Eucharist:

The introduction to most Prefaces in the Eucharist begins with a dialogue and then continues "It is right and just, our duty and *our salvation* to give you thanks...." We say those words day after day as we begin the Eucharistic Prayer and we cannot even hear the impact of the words we say or hear. We are saved by God's actions in our lives, but more particularly by recognizing his saving power. Faith is a gift that is freely bestowed upon us; the gift needs to be recognized. The recognized gift transforms us, our lives, and our world. Giving thanks to God for all that we receive, for what has been happening to us and our world is based on us noticing his loving actions and their importance to us.

## Sharing the Message:

Pope Francis and his
Papal Emblem

The "*great news*" of La Salette needs to be shared by word, by action, by transformation. Pope Francis reminds us of the "*Joy of the Gospel (Evangelii gaudium)*": the Good News is heard; the hearing leads to wholeness of spirit in us and leads to sharing it with others. It changes who we are and how we look at the world that is around us and this cannot be hidden under a bushel basket. The joy of our knowledge and relationship with Christ is kept alive but lets us share it with others. Come and rejoice with me because of what God has done for me.

Success, accomplishments, good fortune, healing, the birth of a Child, a new job, winning the lottery bring such joy that we want to shout the blessings from the mountaintop. Melanie and Maximin go back to the nearby hamlet of Les Ablandins that night and share the events of the day with excitement; the next morning they go to the village of

La Salette and share the story with the local priest. That would begin the task of "making this message known to all (her) people."

Records show that each time they shared the story of the apparition with pilgrims, the curious, detractors and critics they did it from their souls. They would be joyful sharers of the great news and hoped that all who would listened would be changed and transformed.

## La Salette – A Transforming Event:

The children's lives and future were changed by that short encounter on the mountain. The south of France and eventually Europe and the world heard the message of God's love through his Mother and millions of lives would be changed. The lives of people would be changed as they were reconciled to God and one another.

The charism – the gift – continues to be experienced in individual lives, in community and in the Church and the world today and it is effective. When someone goes to La Salette in France, the natural vistas are inspiring as you climb the mountain and then arrive at times above the clouds. One is tempted to take pictures and videos, to capture the wonders of the days.

To walk in procession, to chant the Angelus, to visit the site of the Apparition create lifelong memories. To pray, to be reconciled in the Sacrament of Penance, to hear the event retold – all touch the heart of the pilgrim. We need to see that it is more than an event of over 175 years ago; it is even an event that happens again in our lives today. Whenever we reflect on the memories of past visits or readings, or contemplate the message today and attempt to apply it to our lives, then we make real the words of Mary: "*If they are converted ...*"

### Reflection Questions:

• How has the message of La Salette transformed your faith life and your relationship with God and one another? How are you different because of this encounter with Mary?

• Share a way that God has specifically touched your life and blessed you with his love and mercy?

• How can you be a messenger of the apparition in the world in which you live? How do you share the message with others by what you say and do?

# Chapter 6 —
# Reflections on the La Salette Apparition
## By Fr. Roger Castel, M.S.

### Jesus Christ, Our Crucified Lord:

Mary speaking with the two children
during the La Salette apparition

On the Beautiful Lady's breast, Christ on the cross is the heart of the living light that shapes the entire Apparition and envelops even the two children, Maximin and Melanie. He is the Christ of glory (Matthew 25:31), the Crucified who already speaks as the Risen One, the Lord who entrusts to Mary her mission as mother of the believers and calls the disciple he loves to contemplate and imitate her, "taking into his home" the first and perfect disciple.

"If anyone wishes to come after me, he must deny himself and take up his cross daily* and follow me" (Luke 9:23). And Mary *stands* at the foot of the cross: her presence is a yes carried out in faithfulness, in watchfulness. And in the silence of a gift so complete that it no longer has need of words (John 19:25-27).

All the baptized are called to give such a response. Even more so are the religious, whose sale reason for being is to "follow after Jesus." The letter to the Hebrews presents Christ to everyone as the source, the growth and the fullness of our faith. In a striking summary we can affirm: "Christ is the rule of our life" (Hebrews 3:1-6; 12:1-4).

A dynamic view of the faith and of the religious life, the continual unfolding of a pedagogy Saint Paul described so well: "I have indeed been taken possession of by Christ [Jesus]... I for my part do not consider myself to have taken possession" (Philippians 3:12b-13a).

## We are people on the move:

And so, we are people in motion, people on the move. Nothing could be more unchristian than to settle in behind the walls of one's certitudes and habits. On page after page, the Gospel tells us that God's tenderness is made manifest for our sake through the humanity of Jesus, this Jesus of Nazareth who in no way seeks to distinguish himself from the people of his day except that he is ever on the move: the Son of Man has nowhere to lay his head (Matthew 8:20)... His every gesture, his every word, reveals.

Grasped by Christ, do we manage to devise deeds and words each day by which our contemporaries might come to know that they are truly loved, loved, even unto suffering and death, loved to the point where they are enabled to share in the life of God, who is love, passionate love, consuming love, exacting love, yet the only love that can satisfy the famished people we all are? "I am the way," Jesus tell us once again. Do we follow him? (John 14:6).

## Symbols displayed for us:

In this dynamic and pedagogy, the other elements of the Apparition yield their meaning. We can do no more here than evoke the paths to be pursued, the conversions to be experienced, the convictions to be "made known": in our own lives to begin with, then to others... "*To all my people.*"

The Beautiful Lady "displays" symbols (and this word is to be taken in its strongest sense: the very expression of reality). Her tears, first of all, tears of light and glory, but still the real tears of the One who never ceases to pray and intervene "for the brethren of her Son, who still journey on earth surrounded by dangers and cultics, until they are led into the happiness of their true home" (Vatican II, *Lumen gentium*, #62).

# Why her tears?

In our worship we sing: "Who then is this God who mourns our woes like a mother?" This should be enough to move us, not merely with sentimental and fleeting emotion, but in a way that gets us moving. These tears of Mary tell us how powerless God is when confronted by our refusals.

"Without him our lives fall into ruin!" as one of the liturgical prayers puts it. Should we wonder that a cry of distress be sent our way? God is love. He will not save us despite ourselves.

Symbols offer the advantage of evoking the manifold riches of a reality so intense that we could not otherwise grasp its total content all at once. They lend themselves, therefore, to several interpretations. But since we are concerned here with "the flow," why not ask ourselves how to go from the hammer that crucifies to the pincers that set free, from the chains of injustice to the roses of love.

The Council tells us that human beings are aware of their own powerlessness in the struggle against evil and feel as though "bound by chains." It reminds us too that Christ put hatred to death on the cross, bringing forth the human person according to God's own heart, the pattern of the new humanity in which all peoples are found, united and reconciled (Ephesians 2:14-16).

## Her peasant attire:

The Beautiful Lady presents herself in the attire of a peasant woman or Dauphine housewife. "We thought she was a lady from Valjoufrey, a mother who had been beaten by her children and who had run off into the mountains to cry." Maximin and Melanie would say later on. This lady, close and neglected at the same time, is Christ's mother and ours, weeping over her unappreciated Son and her undeserving children. How well they understood this, those early pilgrims who named the tearful Virgin the Reconciler.

Thanks to the Apparition, the area residents went from the notion of a faraway God, easily dismissed, to the experience of a familiar presence: the presence of this mother who cares about their faults, their anxieties, their children, their conversion and their faith life, as time goes by (John 19:25).

## Words:

Here again let us focus solely on the dynamic aspect of the *words* in the Beautiful Lady's discourse. Maximin and Melanie stand stock-still, stunned, on their guard. Mary sets them moving: "*Come closer, my children; don't be afraid ...*", like Jesus said to his first disciples: "'Come, and you will see.' So they went and saw where he was staying, and they stayed with him that day" (John 1:39).

"Come and see," Jesus had said. And we were no longer afraid, and we went down towards her. As the two witnesses commented: "We were so close to her that no one could have passed between her and us."

The opening sentences of the discourse disclose to us a whole pedagogy of conversion. On first hearing, they sound harsh; we hear and interpret them according to our own mindset and the hardness of our hearts, and, of course, we apply them to other people.

## "Submission:"

*Submission* means the obedience of the slave to the master. *Arm* means the arm that strikes. *Abandonment* means that God has lost interest in us. And we forget that each section of the discourse begins with "and *if*" or with a question, which means that we are directly challenged, either collectively as "*my people*" or personally as were Maximin and Melanie with her words, "*my children,... my child.*"

She who weeps over our misconduct and our misfortune comes to tell us once again: "We implore you on behalf of Christ, be reconciled to God" (2 Corinthians 5:20). Her language is the language of faith and she wishes to "have us see," to "move us" from our human vantage point to God's design (Isaiah 48:13). It is up to us to learn that submission means the submission of the heart, the surrender of communion, that of the Son to the Father: "My food is to do the will of the one who sent me" (John 4:34).

## "Arm:"

The Lord is saving his people "with a mighty hand and outstretched arm" (Psalm 136:12), unhappy are they who set themselves at cross-purposes with or outside that love. And when the prophet announces that the Lord will abandon his people (Leviticus 26:44); he does so because this people for too long a time has abandoned its God.

## "The Seventh Day:"

Mary speaks no other language than that of her Son. The language of love is demanding. It is no laughing matter. There can be no cheating

The Arm of My Son from a German La Salette Holy Card

where love is concerned. At a time – but it is not ours – when people were putting their faith in progress without regression and human labor was becoming a new form of slavery, Mary reminds us that it is on the seventh day (Exodus 20:8) that we assert our dignity as free beings and return to the Lord like children to their Father.

## "the Name:"

At a time – but is it not our own in another guise – when blasphemy was an anti-profession of faith, a stand against Christ and his Church, Mary reminds us that there is no other name but that of her Son "by which we are to be saved" (Acts 4:12).

Without this constant recentering of our life on Christ, how can his arm be deployed for our salvation, how can Mary's intercession be efficacious? God himself cannot save us in spite of ourselves. (Acts 2:21). At stake here are the dignity and the prerogative of the freedom he has given us as well as our responsibility. It is up to us to exercise it.

# Events:

The harvest is spoiling. The potatoes have been rotting for the past year (Jeremiah 12:13). And now the wheat is crumbling into dust. "Eat some bread while we still have it this year," concludes Mr. Giraud speaking to Maximin. "I don't know who will eat any next year if the wheat goes on like this!" Sad realization, and a desperate gesture of a father who hands his child one last piece of bread. There is no future, hope is dead; that raw fact blocks out every horizon.

## "The small children:"

Mary sees a father; she sees that a ruined autumn will jeopardize the grape and walnut harvests. She sees that people's sparse reserves will soon be depleted; she is aware that small children will be the first victims. Above all she "calls attention" to reality and unveils a future.

## "This passing world:"

She points out that this world is passing away and that what we consider to be our wealth is short-lived. Are not our very years numbered? "...this night your life will be demanded of you; and the things you have prepared, to whom will they belong?" (Luke 12:20).

## "Conversion and its rewards:"

Mary invites us to "move on" from a short-sighted, narrow, exclusively materialistic view of world events and of our lives to the infinite horizons of God's design (Jeremiah 29:11). in the midst of this passing world a new self can be born in us and a new world is in the making. It is a long inner journey, if we accept its challenge, and it leads to such a self and such a world (Luke 13:3). It is up to us, once again, to see and to see to it. *"If they are converted!"* (Ezekiel 18:32).

How well we know that the mounds of wheat and the self-sowing by the fields are a way of expressing the inexpressible: what the eye has never seen, what the ear has never heard (1 Corinthians 2:9), what one's mind cannot conceive; the future that God holds in store for those he loves and who welcome his will with trust. "If you then, who are wicked, know how to give good gifts to your children, how much more will your heavenly Father give good things to those who ask him" (Matthew 7:11).

And the Spirit of God is life, life in the here and now and life that extends beyond death (Matthew 10:20). Yet we must remain in contact with him: be plugged in on the same wavelength and respond each time he calls (Romans 8:9b).

## The Means:

"I give praise to you, Father, Lord of heaven and earth, for although you have hidden these things from the wise and the learned you have revealed them to the childlike" (Matthew 11:25). Jesus' thanksgiving comes to our lips as we realize the simplicity and effectiveness of the means proposed by Mary at La Salette. They are so basic, yet so easily forgotten or neglected. Faith is a gift from God, his flame burning within us, and it is up to us to keep it alive by burning there even the insignificant things in our lives.

### "simple prayers in the morning and evening:"

Here again, Mary shows the way: She brings us back to the starting point, the indispensable minimum: "*an Our Father, a Hail Mary, morning and evening,*" participation in the Sunday Eucharist "without mocking religion," the season of Lent not "lived like dogs." But then she immediately urges us to personal greater and community endeavor: "*when you can, do more …*"

### "Do more … the small things:"

More, she says: there is the word, the sign, and the rule of love. Its simplicity is attainable, an effort within the means of everyone but a demand that cannot be circumvented. "If anyone loves me… " (John 12:14). "…do you love me?" (John 21:16). The logic of love is contained in the word: more. And discovering God in daily, weekly, annual contacts, is to introduce him into our lives and sharing in his own life. "God so loved the world..." (John 3:16).

When we discover him at the heart of our prayer, he is asking: "Do you love me? All the way to the cross?" "In your struggle against sin you have not yet resisted to the point of shedding blood" (Hebrews 12:4). "Amen, I say to you, whatever you did for one of these least brothers of mine, you did for me" (Matthew 25:40).

## Notice God's presence:

We have already brought up the episode of the spoiled wheat at the "Terre du Coin," Well, each of us has his own piece of turf where we feel alone, where we feel abandoned. Mr. Giraud walked with young Maximin: they were going home, but for this man it was a dead end. Neither of the two disciples knew that on this road of despair, someone walked with them, just as the companion of the disciples of Emmaus (Luke 24:13-35). Mr. Giraud's words and the piece of bread they sadly shared were forgotten by Maximin and his father. But many months later, this gesture and these words were still echoing in Mary's heart and memory.

## "We are not alone:"

This revelation sparked the memory and heart of Maximin and of his father. "It is really true. Madame,... I had forgotten about it," the boy exclaimed. A few days later, "Papa, she spoke about you!" The one and the other, each in his own space and time, would be conscious of this invisible presence: they were not alone; from that moment on they knew it. We are not alone either. Do we know it? And what are the conclusions we can draw?

## The walk and the missioning:

Preceding then, Mary began to walk. She climbed a zigzag path to the crest of the Sezia where the horizon opened. "We followed closely," Maximin said. Then she rose high above the ground. Already, when she walked, her feet barely touched the top of the grass. Isn't this the way we should walk on this earth: in touch with but already detached? In touch with, while raising ourselves always to the point of discovering the horizons of God. "She looked towards heaven, then towards the earth; and then she began to melt into the light." The early pilgrims to the La Salette site erected simple Stations of the Cross.

## "The Way of the Cross:"

Early pilgrims erect first Stations of the Cross
on the Holy Mountain

The first pilgrims planted crosses on the sight of the apparition. Melanie with her shepherd's staff, then Maximin with a cross made by his father; others imitated them. In the spring of 1847, people were already making the way of the cross. This is the road of all Christians, walking in the footsteps of Christ, in the battle against evil, the evil in each Christian, the evil in the world. The Way of the Cross is the way of reconciliation, love and forgiveness, with light at its end, a light already there at each step, a light radiating from God's horizon.

## Words for My People—A Message for the Ages:

During the days following Easter one year, the chaplains gathered at the Holy Mountain of La Salette to pray, meditate and exchange views on the message of the Weeping Mother, which message will be in a very particular manner this year the theme of the summer pilgrimages. In the midst of a world on fire and dismembered, such a proposal may appear surprising. It seems only natural that those who believe in the Apparition should ascend in pilgrimage to this high place to pray to the Blessed Virgin in the solitude of these mountains.

## La Salette—A Biblical and Ageless Message:

But is not the message addressed to the two children, Maximin Giraud and Melanie Calvat, on the 19th of September, 1846 — half in French, half in the local dialect— and referring to rural situations of the mid-nineteenth century, out of date? If the Gospel criterion remains true — which tells us that a tree should be judged by its fruits — we can testify that the message of La Salette is more actual than ever. But in what does its actuality consist. That is what we are setting out to discover.

It would be easy to comment at length using the Beautiful Lady's discourse as a starting point, seizing on a word or image and expatiating on it at will, on the principle that everything is in everything, and vice versa. What we are planning is much more demanding and precise.

We intend, beginning with the *first phase* of our discussion; namely, reflecting on the critically established text of the Discourse, to strive to comprehend exactly the meaning of each phrase Our Lady spoke; to penetrate the profound reality it expresses, taking into account the context and the immediate and remote circumstances in which the message was delivered. It is then a matter of elementary intellectual honesty.

In our *second phase*, we will seek out in the Bible and especially in the New Testament the realities of the Faith which the attitudes and discourse of the Beautiful Lady emphasize. Finally, in our *third phase*, we will reflect in a constructive and positive way on our life and world, such as they are. We will endeavor to discover what the profound needs are, to which this message responds, to the point of attracting more pilgrims each year to this magnetic mountain.

It is our conviction that to bring out the profound cohesion of the Virgin's words, their complete harmony with "the things of faith", their urgency from the standpoint of the signs of the times as perceived in and by the Church, is the most pressing task we have to accomplish to be faithful to the ministry to which we Missionaries of Our Lady of La Salette have been called, and to respond to the hunger of the humanity of today who "lives not by bread alone, but by every word that comes from the mouth of God" (Matthew 4:4). That is the effort we shall attempt.

## Test the Spirits:

Of course, other approaches can be imagined. But this one seems to us the most apt for safeguarding an objectivity which is not, alas, the primordial concern of certain Christians today. Not everything that is said and done "in the name of the Lord" and in Our Lady's name (and sometimes under the title of La Salette) is necessarily true or sound. Between the poetry of some and the silence of others there is room for sound commentary. "...test the spirits to see whether they belong to God" (1 John 4:1).

We must likewise be aware that today there are certain authors and publishers who call themselves Christian but who give more proof of their good intentions and their good business sense than they do of discernment. They defend or attack a Church such as they imagine it is (or should be) or regret that it is not, rather than living humbly and faithfully in the Church just as it is.

## Heed Her Words:

The Virgin of La Salette speaks to the two children

The Virgin of La Salette invites us to give proof of such discernment in understanding and following the mind of the

67

Church. "*My Son ... my people*," she said referring to the Church. And as for discernment: "*I gave you warning… but you did not heed it!*"

In the life and ministry of the La Salette Missionaries – sisters, brothers, and priests – we have other wondrous events. I'd like to explore with you the mystery of passing on our charism of reconciliation, which the Church has affirmed, and others readily recognize in our work among the people of God.

**Reflection Questions:**

•Fr. Castel presents many different topics in these articles. Which topic was most impressive to you? What was new for you?

•How are you called to act differently or to adjust your thoughts and beliefs about the Apparition?

•When you tell the message to others, what Great News will you stress in talking with them?

# Section 2 —
# Scripture and Doctrine

# Chapter 7 —
# Our Lady of La Salette:
# Catechist and Model of Evangelization
## By Fr. Flavio Gillio, M.S.

**Mary, Our Lady of Evangelization**

In the present article, we will approach the Our Lady of La Salette as Catechist and paradigm of the New Evangelization. At La Salette, through her posture and words, Mary reminds us some of the main traits that should characterize every disciple of Jesus. For all those whose lives have been touched by the event that occurred at La Salette on September 19, 1846, the Our Lady also teaches how to evangelize in a way that reflects the La Salette Charism and Spirituality.

In order to better highlight the richness of the Apparition, we will be dialoguing, on the one hand with the Bible, and on the other hand with the Apostolic Letter, *The Joy of the Gospel*, written by Pope Francis, and published in 2014. Scriptures will allow us to better recognize the biblical background of the La Salette Apparition, Charism, and Spirituality (1) Pope Francis' *The Joy of the Gospel* will help us to appreciate the contemporary and prophetic value of Mary's words at La Salette (2). Even though *The Joy of the Gospel* was given to the Church 156 years after the events of La Salette, it echoes more than once Mary's apparition. *The Joy of the Gospel* is imbued with Marian spirituality, in line with what Pope Francis states when he writes that "there is a Marian 'style' to the Church's work of evangelization." In fact, many passages of *The Joy of the Gospel* reveal a Pope with a La

Salette heart.

Since it is impossible to include in this article all the relevant elements of the Apparition of Our Lady of La Salette in relation to the topic of the New Evangelization as explained in *The Joy of the Gospel*, I will take into consideration only the following points:

1) the context of the Apparition;

2) its purpose and goal;

3) the addressees;

4) Our Lady's dress;

5) Our Lady's tears;

6) the opening of Our Lady's message and

7) the end of Our Lady's message.

## 1-The Context of the Apparition of Our Lady of La Salette:

Both the Apparition of Our Lady of La Salette and *The Joy of the Gospel* did not happen in a vacuum. Even though they occurred in two very different historical, religious and cultural settings, they are framed by two similar contexts.

At La Salette, at the time of the apparition, people lived in a deplorable social, moral and religious situation. Indifference and unbelief were widespread and deeply rooted in the lives of the people. Indeed, Mary's words clearly point to a church in need to be re-evangelized. (3) To use Pope St. John Paul II's words, Mary hints to a Church whose members seem to have accepted a secular model of thinking and living, and thus "[...] live a life far removed from Christ and his Gospel." (4) Mary refers to her own people as men and women whose lives were shaped more by the secular world around them than by the Gospel. One hundred and fifty-six years later, and with the due differences, the context framing *The Joy of the Gospel* does not seem to have changed a lot from the one framing the message of Our Lady of La Salette. Indeed, as Pope Francis reminds us in *The Joy of the Gospel*, many people who have heard of Jesus, been baptized, share Catholic roots, and have some connections to the Catholic Church, are more influenced by the secular, individualistic, and consumerist culture than by the values lived by Jesus the Christ. (5) Pope Francis also makes us aware of the existence of large groups of people who do not have a profound Christian outlook even though they call themselves Catholic, go to Mass every Sunday, serve on a parish committee, sing in the choir, teach children's catechesis, or are Eucharistic Ministers. (6) The context outlined by *The Joy of the Gospel* helps us to better perceive why the La Salette Charism and Spirituality are so contemporary and relevant for today's world and Church.

Both the world and the Church are in need of men and women living the charism and spirituality that flow from the Apparition of Our Lady of La Salette. By looking at her we learn how to *re-propose* the splendor of the Gospel in meaningful ways to those who may have brushed aside their faith; we learn inspiring ways of approaching the current situation of the Church, where a growing number of its members, even if active in their parishes, might not have experienced an initial and radical conversion, or encountered the Risen Jesus in a life-changing manner.

At La Salette, the presence of Mary offers a paradigm for the New Evangelization because her posture, words and actions teach us relevant principles concerning how to re-propose the Gospel to our contemporary world that is experiencing a serious crisis of faith due to secularization. Not by coincidence, Pope Benedict XVI described, more than once during his Pontificate, the New Evangelization as an opportunity to re-propose the Gospel of Jesus the Christ to those for whom it holds no interest. The New Evangelization also requires the ability and creativity of retelling the Good News in order to engage and reignite the faith among all Catholics.

## 2 – The Purpose and Goal of the Apparition of Our Lady of La Salette:

Like *The Joy of the Gospel*, the message of Our Lady of La Salette is meant to encourage us to go in the streets of the world and to reach out to the new *Agoràs (marketplaces)* of today's society. (7) Following the Synoptic Gospels, the message of Our Lady of La Salette and *The Joy of the Gospel* ultimately sketch out our *radical* call to live as missionary-disciples, that is, Christians who walk in discipleship with Jesus each day, who are on a mission, willing to share the love of Christ with the people God has placed in our lives. They offer a pastoral roadmap.

Indeed, both of them have a paradigmatic value: on the one hand, *The Joy of the Gospel* is a paradigm for all the Church's activity and should "give shape to a style of evangelization to be adopted in every undertaken activity" (8); on the other hand, the message of the "Beautiful Lady" is meant to shape and mold our ways of spreading the good news delivered first to Maximin Giraud and Melanie Calvat. Her words and actions educate and equip us to be her apostles and missionaries.

Something very similar occurs in Pope Francis' *The Joy of the Gospel*, whose goal and purpose are clearly mission-oriented: his Apostolic Letter aims at encouraging us to rediscover our identity of missionary-disciples. Similarly, when the message of La Salette is not only read, but pondered, prayed, and meditated, it becomes an educational journey leading us from *being at the feet* of Our Lady of La Salette to *being on our own feet* as missionaries who make her message known. Mary's words forge and mold a mission-oriented Charism and Spirituality. Not by coincidence her last words are: "*Now, my children, make it known to all my people.*"

Even more: at La Salette, Our Lady articulates and organizes her message in such a manner that it recalls the way the Evangelists unfold Jesus' public ministry. Both Our Lady and the Evangelists offer to their readers a transforming journey from *discipleship to mission*. Both the Gospels and the message of La Salette unfold a journey that involves three relevant stages: invitation, formation, and mission. For example, at the beginning of his public ministry, Jesus, according to the version of Matthew, invites two couples of brothers to follow him: Simon, called Peter, and his brother Andrew; James, son of Zebedee and his brother John. (9) At La Salette, Mary starts her interaction with the two children by *inviting* them to come closer.

The second stage, transformation, occurs while the disciples (and the reader of the Gospels) are following Jesus of Nazareth in his public ministry. It is interesting to notice that Jesus' first followers, at the beginning of their discipleship, are simply identified through their personal names, family ties, and profession. Later on, the Evangelists relates to them as disciples, and by the end of the Gospels they are called apostles, from the Greek verb *apostello*, that means to send. They are missionaries. Similarly, at La Salette, by the end of Our Lady's message, a fourteen year old girl, Melanie, and an eleven year old boy, Maximin, will be the "new" apostles of Mary of Nazareth.

The third stage, mission, stands out at the end of both the message of Our Lady of La Salette and Gospels (especially Matthew and Mark). For example, at the end of the Gospel according to Matthew and the one according to Mark, the disciples-apostles receive their mission from the Risen Jesus(10); at La Salette, at the end of her message, the Beautiful Lady entrusts the two children with a clear mission: *"Well, my children, you will make this known to all my people."* La Salette Charism and Spirituality, anticipating the spirit of Pope Francis' *The Joy of the Gospel*, are meant to form committed missionary-disciples and apostles, rather than only and simply devout Christians.

## The Addressees:

A third relevant point related to Mary as catechist and paradigm for the New Evangelization concerns Maximin Giraud and Melanie Calvat. At La Salette, Our Lady did not appear to two adults well versed into the realm of God and religion, or to two well-educated and noble children. The people of the hamlet of La Salette were extremely ordinary people. Poor people. Moreover, Melanie Calvat and Maximin Giraud were two dysfunctional children, coming from two marginal and dysfunctional families. They were totally uneducated, and without any outstanding qualities or skills. Even after the apparition the two children kept on being marginal characters. They lived at the margins of the world, society and church of that time. In Pope Francis' language, the "Beautiful Lady" reaches out to the peripheries.

From a biblical perspective, Our Lady of La Salette mirrors both Adonai and her Son, Jesus of Nazareth. (11) For example, all the four

The two witnesses to the La Salette Apparition:
Maximin Giraud and Melanie Calvat.

Gospels offer various examples regarding how Jesus reached out to those left at the margins of his religious and cultural world. (12) Our Lady of La Salette continues this trend so rooted in the Bible. Both Maximin and Melanie were 'little' before the world; they were at the margins, but great before Our Lady of La Salette." (13)

At La Salette, Mary chooses two insignificant and uneducated children for a mission much bigger than their possibilities, abilities, and skills. The choice of Our Lady of La Salette encourages us to walk on the peripheries of our church and society, and to have real contacts with all those who are alienated members of God's people. As missionaries, Our Lady of La Salette leads us to the existential, cultural and religious margins of today's society. She mirrors the Son, whose ministry was a ministry of 'reconciliation', a 'restorative ministry' aimed at giving back *shalom*, that is, wholeness and fullness of life. (14)

## The dress of Our Lady of La Salette:

A fourth relevant point related to Mary as catechist and paradigm for the New Evangelization concerns the way Mary was dressed at the moment of the apparition. Indeed, she appeared dressed like any other women of the region: a long dress, an apron, a shawl and a cap or bonnet that were worn by peasant women of that geographical area. Some roses crowned her head and a second and third set of roses were placed at the edges of the white shawl, and around her shoes. She was so much like any other ordinary woman that during and after the apparition the two children never related to her as Mary, but simply as the "Beautiful Lady". Even in this instance, Our Lady of La Salette follows the footsteps of her Son, and foreshadows what Pope Francis writes in the Apostolic Letter *The Joy of the Gospel*. Like the Son (15), the Mother, at La Salette, emptied herself to the point of not being recognized.

Our Lady of La Salette reminds us that the Charism and Spirituality flowing from the apparition follow the dynamic of the Incarnation: Our Lady leads us to step outside of ourselves, to move beyond what is secure and familiar, to invest our lives in those of our brothers and sisters, removing our sandals "before the sacred ground of the other." (16) In this perspective, the La Salette Charism and Spirituality lead us to share the good news of Jesus the Christ not by withdrawing from the world, but rather by embracing it, in solidarity with it and with God's people. This trait of the La Salette Charism and Spirituality is further outlined by Mary's tears, one of the unique features of the apparition.

## The tears of Our Lady of La Salette:

When the two children first approached Our Lady of La Salette, she was weeping, sitting on a rock. According to the report of the two young shepherds, her tears were translucent, disappearing without touching the ground.

In the Bible tears bear more than one meaning. For example, Abraham's tears are an expression of sorrow for the loss of Sarah, his wife; Esau's tears express anger and disappointment; Joseph the dreamer, the great Prince of Egypt, weeps six times, out of deep emotion; David's tears express his deep pain before the dead body of his dearest friend Jonathan, and that of Jonathan's father, Saul . (17) Hannah's tears express the sadness of her heart for being a barren woman without children. (18) Even Jesus is depicted weeping. The Gospels tell us that he wept twice, once facing Jerusalem and once on the occasion of Lazarus' death. (19)

The meaning of Mary's tears at la Salette becomes clearer when it is paired with her words. Like in the Gospels, where Jesus' deeds bring to light the meaning of his words and vice versa, Mary's actions and words are deeply connected, and they enlighten each other. In this perspective, Our Lady's tears reveal her maternal heart and affection. They witness her loving attention and the pain she suffers seeing her children straying from the ways of the Lord. Her tears are tears of compassion and mercy. They reveal her deep communion with our world that needs to be reconciled, healed and restored to the original biblical *shalom* envisioned in the first chapter of the book of Genesis.

Like the Son, the "Beautiful Lady" of La Salette is not observing the broken world from afar, from a distance. Instead, she is with us and for us, moved to suffer with us. Like her Son, Mary is burdened with suffering out of love and for those she loves. Her tears say exactly what Scripture states about Adonai: "The Lord is close to the broken-hearted, saves those whose spirit is crushed." (20)

The La Salette Charism and Spirituality place us next to the weeping mother as ambassadors of reconciliation while collaborating with her for the healing of our broken world. The weeping mother encourages us to embrace a way of living that is able to bring to those who are left at the peripheries, or who feel to be left at the margins of the Church and society, the good news that in Christ they are unconditionally loved by the Father; the good news that the peripheries and margins are not meant to remain so forever. The world hunger for this good news, and opportunities to hear this message can bring deep transformation and healing.

## The opening of the La Salette Message:

Mary's message begins with a tender and maternal invitation addressed to the children to come closer to hear a great news. Her opening words overcome their fears, gaining their trust and confidence. Mary's opening words create the proper conditions that will allow the two children to experience a transforming encounter.

Mary's approach echoes what Pope Francis writes in *The Joy of the Gospel* concerning the importance of fostering and promoting a "culture of encounter" as a pre-requisite for a fruitful work of evangelization? Mary's words reveal an authentic "pastoral care", and promote an encounter. She acknowledges, recognizes, and welcomes the presence of the two children; she reassures them in such a way that they become ready to receive her message.

Zacchaeus receives Jesus, Church of the Good Shepherd, Jericho, Palestine; photo: Tango7174

Mary's attitude reflects and is aligned with the one of her Son, Jesus of Nazareth. Among the many instances in which Jesus promotes an encounter, the story of Zaccheus, the chief tax collector, is a good exemplification. Zaccheus' fear echoes the fear of the two children. Because of his fear, Zaccheus remains hidden among the big leaves of a sycamore tree: he wants to see without being seen. The turning point of the story occurs when Luke writes: "When Jesus reached the spot, he looked up and said to him, 'Zacchaeus, come down immediately, I must stay at your house today." (21) Please, notice how Jesus, like Our Lady of La Salette, gains Zaccheus' confidence and trust by acknowledging, recognizing, and welcoming his presence without asking anything back.

We should not underestimate the importance of cultivating and nurturing caring relationships as part of the process aimed at sharing the Gospel of Jesus the Christ. As Pope Francis points out, today's society is thirsting and hungry for gratuitous and caring relationships. There is, without any doubts, an overflowing of immediate communication, and yet little communion, few opportunities to encounter the *other* personally. As Pope Francis underlines more than once, our culture is marked by a deep thirst for true life-giving relationships.

Life-giving relationships, such as the one experienced by Zaccheus with Jesus, and by Maximin and Melanie with Mary, can open unexpected doors to welcome *The Joy of the Gospel* of Jesus the Christ. Indeed, when we sincerely enter into other people's lives, listening to their hopes and dreams, to their fears and sorrows, we discover opportunities to show how God's Word can shed light on their situations. The way Our Lady of La Salette decided to begin her dialogue with the two children, functions as a paradigm to evangelize with a La Salette flavor: getting gently and respectfully involved with the lives of those around us by acknowledging them, recognizing them, welcoming them, and in so doing by building, in an intentional way, a culture of encounter. At La Salette, Our Lady teaches us how and why to go out of ourselves and truly meet the other person.

## The end of the La Salette Message:

Mary's last words echo Jesus' last words to the disciples before his ascension to heaven. (22) Both the message and the Gospels are meant to build our identity as missionary-disciples. The final words of Our Lady of La Salette challenge us to consider how well we live out our mission in the world, and how much our communities, parishes and groups, are animated by a missionary zeal aimed at sharing *The Joy of the Gospel*. The mission that Mary entrusts to the two children, like the one that Jesus entrusts to the disciples-apostles, is not an option.

La Salette Spirituality and Charism, like the Church in the Book of Acts, come into being thanks to the mission, and they exist and grow as long as this missionary zeal is alive. The mission given to the children at La Salette is today our mission: it is a call/invitation to participate in the Church's evangelizing mission; a call to go beyond our own comfort zones in order to reach the marginal in need of the light of the Gospel. (23)

Mary's last words imply another important element which is related to the theme of New Evangelization. It is beautifully recalled to our attention by Pope Francis when he talks about the kind of Church he dreams to see in action, that is, a church whose doors are always open. At first, we may assume that Pope Francis is referring to a more welcoming, warm, and friendly Church. But this is not the case.

Yes, because when Pope Francis speaks about a church whose doors are always open, he isn't always thinking about how we let people come in, but mostly how we step outside the safe and comfortable walls of our churches, communities and groups to bring to the world the saving love of Jesus the Christ. The evangelizing style that both Our Lady of La Salette and Pope Francis envision for a truly missionary church is the one whose focus is on "go out" approach, rather than on a "come to me" approach.

## Conclusion:

Pilgrims at La Salette gather around Mary's Assumption statue after processing, singing and praying the Rosary

La Salette Charism and Spirituality are all about waking up the world to the Good News of Jesus the Christ. They represent a way of being and living that, inspired and guided by the apparition of the Beautiful Lady of La Salette, strive to bring forth the fruits of the work of reconciliation accomplished by Jesus the Christ. At La Salette, Mary teaches us how to let this gift flourish and blossom. She inspires us to embrace with tenderness our broken world; she encourages us to be in solidarity with God's people and her children; she teaches us how to promote an encounter with those at the margins of our world and church in order to share with them gentleness, respect, and the Good News of Jesus the Christ.

Being men and women who drink from the sources of La Salette means to journey through life as ambassadors of reconciliation by bringing healing, new life, recreation. It means to make visible God's unconditional love as reflected through the Son, Jesus the Christ, and through the weeping mother of La Salette. It simply means to be missionary-disciples who take on the heart of "the Beautiful Lady of La Salette," who mirrors the heart of her Son.

## Reflection Questions:

• The article speaks of the journey "from discipleship to mission": How do we appreciate and live out this movement to action?

• The details of the apparition have an importance in its being understood. What detail of the event stick out for you and help you better understand the impact of Mary on your life?

• Pope Francis describes *The Joy of the Gospel* as a force in life; how do you find the power of great news of Mary's message at La Salette exciting you to joy and happiness?

## Endnotes:

(1) Cardinal Carlo Maria Martini, former Archbishop of Milan, Italy considered the Apparition of Our Lady of La Salette the most biblical among the major Marian Apparitions. He shared this thought with me when, while living in Jerusalem, he introduced me to Our Lady of La Salette through the book, *Les Larmes de Marie*.

(2) In relation to its setting, content and addressees, *The Joy of the Gospel* is eminently "catholic", i.e. universal. Indeed, this Apostolic Letter followed up on the extraordinary Synod of Bishops held in Rome in October 2012. As far as the content is concerned, *The Joy of the Gospel* is an inspiring roadmap to implement the New Evangelization in our Christian communities and parishes. *The Joy of the Gospel* is "catholic" also in relation to its addressees: it is addressed to clergy, religious, pastoral workers, and ordinary lay people. It has been rightly considered to be a kind of "*Magna Charta*" for the New Evangelization for the following reasons:

• it brings together key insights from the 2012 gathering of all the Bishops of the world;

• it outlines what kind of approach Pope Francis desires the Church to embrace in the work of the New Evangelization, and

• it invites every disciple of Jesus to re-discover, at the center of his or her faith, a missionary heart

(3) *"Those who drive the carts cannot swear without introducing the name of my Son...", or "On the contrary, when you found the potatoes spoilt, you swore, you took the name of my Son in vain..." or "There are none who go to Mass except a few aged women. The rest work on Sunday all summer; then in the winter, when they know not what to do, they go to Mass only to mock at religion. During Lent, they go to the meat-market like dogs."*

(4) *Redemptoris Missio*, 33.

(5) For a more detailed analysis, we suggest to read the studies conducted by CARA (Center for Applied Research in the Apostolate) and the book, *Forming Intentional Disciples*, written by Sherry Weddell, one of the leading figures at St. Augustine Institute.

(6) A similar thought is also expressed by the distinguished Christian philosopher Dallas Willard who, more than once in his books, speaks about "Christian without Jesus the Christ".

(7) See Acts 17:16-34.

(8) See *The Joy of the Gospel*, §15 and §18.

(9) See Mark 1:16-34 and Luke 5:1-11.

(10) See for example Matthew 28:19.

(11) See 1 Samuel 16, an exemplary text concerning the anointing of David, the youngest of Jesse's seven sons, and the less fit to be anointed by the prophet. This episode is perfectly in coherence with what, many centuries later, Paul will write to the community in Corinth: "Consider your own calling... Not many of you were wise by human standards, not many were powerful, not many were of noble birth. Rather, God chose the foolish of the world to shame the wise, and God chose the weak of the world to shame the strong,

and God chose the lowly and despised of the world, those who count for nothing, to reduce to nothing those who are something,

29so that no human being might boast before God. [...] [A]s it is written, "Whoever boasts, should boast in the Lord" (1 Corinthians 1:26-29,31).

(12) See for example Matthew 9:9-13 that parallels Luke 5:27-32, and

Luke 19:1-10, the encounter between Jesus and Zaccheus.

(13) See for example Psalms 34 and 140.

(14) See 2 Corinthians 5:18-21.

(15) See Philippians 2:6-11. See also 1 Corinthians 9:19-23.

(16) See *The Joy of the Gospel*, § 169.

(17) See Genesis 23:2; 27:38; 42:24; 43:30; 45:2.14; 46:27; 50:1; 2 Samuel 1:12

(18) 1 Samuel 1:8.

(19) Luke 19:41; John 11:35.

(20) Psalm 34:19.

(21) Matthew 19:5.

(22) Matthew 28: 19–20.

(23) See *The Joy of the Gospel*, § 20.

# Chapter 8 —
# A New Heart and A New Spirit
## By Fr. Phil "Skip" Negley, M.S.

*The Prophet Ezekiel's vision of God in Majesty* by Raphael (1483-1520)

Within the holy ground of the books of the Old Testament there lies the seeds of a theology of reconciliation. One passage that is most germane is found in the Ezekiel, chapter 36. God's own chosen People had experienced disobedience, infidelity, and the lack of moral integrity from within the leadership and the stewardship of the covenant community. Ezekiel will be faithful to his commission to announce God's justice and mercy no matter who will listen. He will call this remnant back to the holiness of a God who will, once again, reach out with the promise of repentance, healing, and restoration. Yahweh will act swiftly. In a remarkable manner of forgiveness God's capacity to punish will be tempered by God's desire to renew. God will be faithful to the divine zeal of covenant-love, restoring light and life where there appeared darkness and death. The prophet's words are steeped with tenderness as he writes:

> "I will sprinkle clean water over you to make you clean; from all your impurities and from all your idols I will cleanse you. I will give you a new heart, and a new spirit I will put within you... I will put my spirit within you... you will be my people, and I will be your God" (Ezekiel 36:25-27a,28b).

In an earlier but similar passage found in the Psalms we hear the sorrowful prayer for cleansing and pardon from the lips of Kind David, "A clean heart create for me, God; renew within me a steadfast spirit" (Psalm 51:12). Reconciliation is attested by a new heart and a new spirit.

## A new heart and a new spirit:

In Scripture the heart is the center of personhood, of thinking and of all loving. The heart is the core of consciousness, free personality, and decisive choices. It is the place where God encounters the person. To bequeath a new heart is to summon the hope of new ways of being and of relating to all creation and life. The spirit is that indiscernible force of a being, which brings freshness and life, and which flows outward beyond one's charge. It is breath and power, which activates and animates a living soul and body. When the Spirit of God joins to our spirit, we are reborn with new identity, purpose, and direction. Ezekiel proclaimed that God is actively and intimately involved in the lives and events of humankind.

A theology of reconciliation flourishes with the promise of repentance, healing, and restoration. This is the reconciliation of which St. Paul knows firsthand when he writes, "All of this is from God, who reconciled us to himself through Christ and has given us the ministry of reconciliation, namely, God was reconciling the world to himself in Christ" (2 Corinthians 5:18-19a). We know all too well the charism of reconciliation which is at the heart of our mission and our ministry as members of the Missionaries of Our Lady of La Salette, the Sisters of Our Lady of La Salette and the members of the La Salette Laity. More than an inspiration or the founding grace guiding our lives reconciliation is the living organism giving purpose and priority to our past and our present and providing the promise to our future. Our ministry obliges our fullest commitment to participate in preserving the heartbeat of this reconciling action of God alive and beating. In union with Christ and as La Salettes we vow/promise this charism as our defining mission within the Church.

Robert Schreiter, C.PP.S. reminded us of the meaning of reconciliation from our Assembly 2009 (Orlando, FL; October 26, 2009).

Our understanding of reconciliation in all its different forms is always grounded in God's work of reconciliation – the bringing about of healing and return of all people and indeed of all creation to Himself though Jesus Christ...We are participants in God's great work. The ministry of reconciliation has been entrusted to the Church in a special way to be both a sign and an instrument of God's reconciliation. Mary, as the model Reconciler, guides and accompanies us in this ministry. ("The Charism of Reconciliation and Its Practices." p. 2.)

With all its citations and theological references, this is as fine a definition of reconciliation for the purposes of this presentation: *the bringing about the healing and return of all people and indeed creation* to God through Jesus Christ. In cooperation with the Holy Spirit as La Salette Missionaries, Sisters and Laity "we enter more deeply into the mystery of reconciliation" (*Rule*, 1 cp) with Christ in this divine plan of God.

## Become accountable:

The apparition of the Blessed Mother Mary at La Salette is a grace, a charism, given to the Church. Theologians will remind us that apparitions are not a new revelation. The appearance and the message of Our Lady of La Salette certainly manifests a brilliant light and a fresh enthusiasm, inviting all of God's people to renew their faith journeys in the healing grace of reconciliation. This is the perpetual "good news" of Jesus Christ. God desires to restore the original divine "we-thou" relationship with God's self and with all creatures, even creation itself, through the words, the tears and the maternal prayers of the Mother of God, made our mother at the foot of the Cross.

Her means of revealing this healing invitation are nothing less than those of her Son who in his humanity walked the face of the earth as the divine physician in search of the sick, the lost, and the castoff. At La Salette Our Lady embraced, encountered, engaged, enabled, and enthused two chosen children to be her first ministers (*and missionaries*) of reconciliation. In in their budding discipleship Melanie and Maximin became accountable to every word, every detail, and every memory.

As contemporary missionaries of reconciliation, as La Salette priests and brothers, as La Salette sisters and as La Salette laity, we are invited and called to share in this same healing grace, this charism of reconciliation. We are to foster a universal budding discipleship; we are to become accountable as ambassadors of Christ and ministers of reconciliation. As collaborators in the community of the Church we are called to servant-ministry, to contribute. We are constantly challenged to balance certain paradoxes inherent in our common vocation. We must strive to be bold yet prudent, creative yet humble, heroic yet obedient, flexible yet grounded, prophets yet listeners, leaders yet servants.

Our vocation always involves a "spirituality of limitations," walking along the hard road, entering through the narrow gate, taking nothing for the journey, befriending the stranger, and proclaiming a message not our own. How do we witness, search, and proclaim and not lose heart? Become accountable. Inherent in our baptismal covenant is the privilege and the responsibility to "become accountable" to one another. We are a covenant community, and this demands a mutual interdependence. To become accountable is to freely place ourselves in the bonds of communal discipleship with fellow priests, religious and laity, with all the People of God in three special ways: *presence, persons, and principles.*

## Accountable to Presence:

Our primary accountability is to the God who calls each of us by name. God first summons our full attention. "Be still and know that I am God!" (Psalm 46:11). The merciful message of Our Blessed Mother at La Salette echoes the thoughts from Revelation, "Yet I hold this against you: you have lost the love you had at first" (Revelation 2:4). From our earliest moments of faith/vocation/formation we have reserved a special time and place for *presence.* Acts of meditation and prayer, the Eucharist and adoration, the journeys into the stillness of contemplation assure the sacred presence of the Holy. In the all-too-demanding regimen of contemporary daily ministries many times we long for this presence yet we indulge less and less in the "tent of meeting."

Like the woman at the well, Jesus invites us to drink deeply from the source of living waters, which quenches all thirsts. To be accountable to *presence* is to be "response-able" again and again to our baptismal calling, to be obedient (faithful listeners) to the sending in zealous discipleship, and to be open to the power of the Spirit at work in our lives, our Church, and our world. We have been taught the value of sacred environments, holy times, and holy spaces where our traditions hold to the *presence* of God. Our recommitment to these chapels and communities of the Spirit offers a reconciling and transformative grace to our ministry, personhood, and call to make known the Good News of Jesus Christ.

## Accountable to Persons:

"You will make this known to all my people."

Mary's final words at La Salette from window
in Mary Keane Chapel, Enfield, New Hampshire

To be accountable to *persons* is to affirm the conviction that the God of creation is a God of intimacy and love, actively involved in the lives and events of humankind. The call of the gospel is always to

88

become a new creation "here and now." This invitational command to "make this message well-known" is inherently a communal experience. God calls in faith and always within the community. If intensely private and uniquely intimate, our accountability as messengers of reconciliation is never so personal as to be solitary. Our discipleship must always be interdependent within the community of faith.

If others' joy and hope, grief and anguish, and especially of the poor or afflicted, the victimized, the abused, and the accused, are to be fully ours, if healing is to ever saturate the Body of Christ, then we must determine to be accountable to one another, to be in dialogue with one another, and to be in collaboration with one another. Our conversations must be understood as "helping," "healing," "instructing," "modeling," "companioning," "shepherding," "discerning," "reconciling," "uplifting," "sacramental," "charismatic," and "incarnational" so that they foster intimacy, restore trust, assure justice, and seek to dispel the natural tension between reason and grace in the world.

History and scripture have always recorded the significant role of special persons whose primary vocation was to guide, befriend, confront, challenge, interpret, and/or awaken the human heart/will to the divine heart/will. Socrates called these figures "healers of the soul." They are the sages and shamans, friends, and favorites. From the Book of Sirach, we are reminded:

> "If you are willing to listen, you can learn; if you pay attention, you can be instructed. Stand in the company of the elders..." (Sirach 6:33-34a). "...If you see the intelligent, seek them out; let your feet wear away their doorsteps!" (Sirach 6:36).

Our tradition of Christian spirituality acknowledges abbas, ammas, mentors, soul keepers, spiritual directors, physicians of souls, ushers of God, pilgrim companions, carriers of the Spirit (*pneumatophores*), and the unique title from Gaelic (and my favorite), *anamchara*: soul friends. As co-missionaries we would be wise witnesses to seek, and to be sought in, these sacred roles.

## Accountable to Principles:

Before charters and norms, canons and decrees, from our baptism we are accountable to the gospel and the law of love. It was Christ who first counseled this supreme law in the legal inquiry found in the parable of the Good Samaritan (Luke 10:27) and again in words of "The Golden Rule" of Matthew's sermon on the mountainside. "In everything do to others as you would have them do to you, for this is the law and the prophets" (Matthew 7:12). Accountability to *principles* is to be "response-able" to commandments, constitutions, beatitudes, virtues, vows, resolutions, reviews, norms, laws, promises, policies, and pledges.

We might reflect on the proportionality and abundance of these synonyms and systems to the necessity and need within the framework of societies to adopt and to live faithfully by codes of discipline. Presbyters, Religious, and Laity live by sacred words freely proclaimed and repeated at the moment of ordination, profession and promises. "I do with the help of God." In our own unique manner and with the divine assistance of the Holy Spirit we pledge to make the merciful message of our Mother Mary and our Mother Church known to all her people.

In the heritage of our religious congregations, societies, and those sacraments of commitment we covenant to live freely and willingly by "Rules of Life," "Rules of Saints," fidelity to founders and charisms, "First Principle and Foundation," Twelve Steps and Promises, effective habits, mission statements, and especially unlimited reconciliation seventy times seven times. Ours is an accountability to *principles* that flows from the first primacy, one of binding and loosing here and hereafter. In summary, my co-missionaries, become accountable to *presence, persons, and principles.*

## Promises of joy:

I have tried to choose words and phrases with great care. They are first meant to reconcile and renew our love for God. As with those of the Lord, our words and actions must always be placed at the service of those who are voiceless that they might find the healing grace of reconciliation and the peace of Christ that our mission and ministry are called to make known. The apparition and the message of the Beautiful Lady of La Salette must also preach the *promise of joy.* With the presence of flowing tears and words of submission and suffering we may ask, where is this joy? A reconciler knows when making the message of La Salette known, our words and witness will also preach the *promise of joy*. Conversion from sin and reconciliation with God will always provide a threefold promise of joy. There is always joy, sometimes hidden, sometimes overflowing in the ministry of mercy. La Salettes know this to be true.

When using all our God-given talents in service to the Lord we are promised the reward, not of earthly treasures, but of "greater responsibilities" accompanied with Jesus' pledge to "Come, share your master's joy" (Matthew 25:21; 23). If the "making known" assures a share in Mary's tearful eyes, the hope of healing ensures the reward of joyful hearts. "Those who sow in tears will reap with cries of joy" (Psalm 126:6).

In the words of Pope Francis, the joy of our witness is rooted in love.

"All pastoral ministry is born in love... a sign of Christ's reconciling love... in the variety of our vocations [*La Salette Missionaries, La Salette Sisters, and La Salette Laity*], each of us is called, in some way, to be love in the heart of the Church. St Paul tells us (2 Cor. 5:14) that the love we are called to proclaim is a reconciling love, flowing from the heart of the crucified Savior. We are called to be "ambassadors for Christ" (2 Corinthians 5:20). Ours is a ministry of reconciliation..." (Homily during Mass for Bishops, Priests, et al., Manila, Philippines, January 16, 2015).

THE SECOND PROMISE OF JOY will always be evident in the one(s) reconciled.

St. Paul knew this firsthand when he encouraged Christ's followers to always trust in God's fidelity and mercy. "May the God of hope fill you with all joy and peace in believing..." (Romans 15:13a). We are sent to remind God's people that the grace of reconciliation is an overflowing cup which will never run dry and that the Son of God did not fail in his math when he told his disciples to forgive "seventy-seven times" (Matthew 18:22). This is the forgiveness that turns tears of sorrow into tears of joy.

Jesus spoke other parables that deserve a deeper reflection on the grace of reconciling love and the redemption of all people, saints and sinners. In Matthew 13:44-46 we read of the "treasure buried in a field" and the "pearl of great price." Once again, the motive for "selling all" to purchase the field or the precious gem is *joy*. Who is the finder and who is the merchant if not Jesus himself who sells "all that he has" – his birthright, his "equality with God" yes, even his life "emptied" (Philippians 2:6-7) in obedience to the Father's will? Do we see ourselves, in all our broken humanity and abused freedoms as the discovered treasure and the pearl of great price? In these parables sacrificial love is the cause and reconciling mercy is the effect. We are the sons and daughters honored to celebrate and to rejoice with the feast. We must rejoice for we were dead and have come to life again; we were lost and have been found.

**THE THIRD PROMISE OF JOY** within the grace of reconciliation may be beyond our capability to comprehend. For as St. Paul reminds us:

> "For who has known the mind of the Lord or who has been his counselor? Or who has given him anything that he may be repaid?" (Romans 11: 34-35).

Ezekiel on the ceiling of the Sistine Chapel in the Vatican by Michelangelo (1475–1564)

We turn to the parables of mercy in Luke chapter 15. If the promise of joy is within the hearts of all reconcilers and this gift of joy is rooted in the responses of all the reconciled, the manifestation and the greatest rejoicing will echo from the halls of heaven themselves and among the angels of God "over one sinner who repents" (Luke 15:7,10).

Whether the lost sheep, the lost coin or the lost son, Jesus confirms the promise of divine joy within God's very Self. Through reconciliation and by sharing our Master's joy we experience not just conversion but the hope and the promise of indwelling in the divine life of God. This is the Good News of Jesus Christ. This is the message Our Lady of La Salette came to announce and calls to make known to all her people. By our reconciliation in Christ, by our conversion and by our witness the prophecy of Ezekiel is also our joy. "A new heart I will give you and a new spirit I will put within you..." (Ezechiel 36:26). "... you shall be my people and I will be your God" (Ezekiel 36:28).

**Reflection Questions:**

• The article calls us to accountability to God, ourselves, others, and principles. How easy are these to do? Which cause me the most struggle?

• The promises of Joy are offered to us as we follow the path of accountability and reconciliation. Reflect on a time of joy and satisfaction following a reconciling situation.

• Can we be reconcilers in the world? What prevents or inhibits the work of reconciliation for us personally?

# Chapter 9 —
# Keys to the Meaning of the La Salette Message

## By Fr. Jim Henault, M.S.

*Editor: This is a reflection on several phrases in the Apparition message translated into our current lives and our world. It attempts to add some theological perspective to our view of who God is, who we are as humans and especially as his people.*

### "No Matter What You Do...":

Mary holding back the arm of her Son; Our Lady of Sorrows Church, Hartford, Ct.

Mary speaks these words reminding us that we are not able to do anything to make up for her pain and suffering, to repair the brokenness of our lives and world. It is not about us. God died for us while we were still sinners. As sinners we do not have to earn his gift of reconciliation and mercy; we merely must accept the gift freely offered to be saved. This hopefully leads to a true conversion – a *metanoia* – that will naturally flow from the love that God has for us and that we feel in the depth of soul.

Believing that we are loved, that we are forgiven, and that we are made worthy by the pure gift of Jesus' death and resurrection enables us and compels us to better our lives and follow his example. When we are loved and are overwhelmed by that love, we are capable of great things. We are inspired to follow in Jesus' footsteps, to adopt his values, to obey his commands and walk in his ways.

This does cause a conflict with the traditional notions of atonement and reparation. Too often they stem from a sense that we must do something to deserve what we have received and to make up for our sinful past. These seem to be reasonable actions to adopt and can lead to a better way of behaving. But it is basically a way of us trying to hold on to control of the relationship. A gift is not freely received if we keep the perspective that we do not deserve it and so much pay God back for salvation. The past is not truly forgiven if we feel that we must pay the price for our sins.

True reconciliation is based on us allowing ourselves to admit our wrongs, know that the love of God and his mercy are gifts unconditionally given to us, and we have to let go of the need to do anything except welcome God's invitation into our renewed relationship. The Parable of the Prodigal Son in Luke's Gospel show clearly how this works. The son having wasted the gift of his inheritance, having abandoned the family and his loving father, comes to his sense during a great famine and his inability to rely on his own devices. He sees his sin and goes back home to ask for his father's forgiveness as he admits the errors of his way. The father is already to welcome him home before a word is said.

While he was on his way the father, ever watching and hoping, sees the son and runs to him. Without any words said, the father rightfully interprets the return as the most significant action his son could do. While they embrace, the son asks forgiveness but before he can even utter the first syllable of being unworthy to be a son, the father restores the relationship. His son is alive, welcomed and treated with dignity and respect.

It is also important to recognize that there are no easy fixes in reconciliation. The second part of the story is what happens the next days in the parable. How does the son deal with his future relationships in the family? Can he repair the rejection of his older brother? Can the three family members become a family once again? Will he actual be a son again and all that he does? How does he change his life, abandoning his past values or lack thereof and act in better ways?

The relationship of humanity and God begins with God. His need to express his love led to the creation of the universe. His fullness of generosity, compassion, openness, all lead to him become the Creator. In the beginning God created the world. During that creative process we human beings are created in his image and likeness. We are charged to be co-creators, partners in the family of God and are charged to build the world and subdue all of creation to God's purposes and ways.

Sin enters the world as we attempt to push God out of the picture. The sin of Adam and Eve is not disobedience, it is rebellion. It is rejecting the partnership with God and doing a hostile takeover. They are now God's equals in such a way that they no longer need him and can be his competitors instead. Original sin will be pervasive throughout the world and throughout the history of humanity. The temptation to go it alone is found in reality in every century and in every corner of the globe.

In contrast, Salvation History is the journey of Humanity and particularly of Israel recognizing who God is and who they are. The covenants that are offered are ones of relationship in which we acknowledge who we are, that we need God's love and mercy, that he empowers us to great things and that following his will is valuable and life giving. Jesus is the paradigm in his death and resurrection. Dying to self and ultimate our physical death lead to the fullness of life for eternity. We continue the pilgrimage together with the support of one another and most especially with the blessings of our gracious God.

## "If my people refuse to submit…":

Submission is one of the strange words that immediately cause unease. As Americans we have always contrasted submission to freedom, self-reliance, independence, personal dignity. Slaves submit to their masters. In the past and in the Scriptures, we heard that wives should submit to their husbands. Teenagers in their struggle for autonomy and the freedom to make their own decisions want to break the chains of submission to parents, teachers, and societal norms. We want to be free from the oppression of imposed rules that make us wear masks during pandemics, of taking vaccines so we protect ourselves and others (even the ones that are effective and safe), we want guns that are meant for war and killing in the name of self-protection, we want our religious beliefs protected even as we denigrate those of other faith.

Submission is not a bad word; it is not a negative reality. It is the ultimate freedom that we admit that we are not the masters of our own destiny; we do not have to make all the decisions for ourselves and others; it does not have to be our way always. Letting go and sharing responsibility with God, with our spouse, with our brothers and sisters, with our employees and fellow workers, with our parents and children, enriches our lives as it eases the burdens, frees us for other adventures, ends useless struggles that have no real simple answers. Following God's will, his hopes, and dreams for us, living in his love make our lives so much easier to live. Have you ever fallen in love? Is that a snare that restricts us and limits us? Or rather is it a powerful enabling force (grace) that permit us to exceed in life by giving our best. Whenever we are united in a task through a loving supportive relationship we are bound to succeed and to accomplish great things. The burden disappears as we do not act out of obligation but out of commitment and reasonability in our relationships. When we accept a cause and see it as personally valuable then great efforts are easily made.

Submitting to God is where it all begins as we let go of those things that we cannot change or control and guess what we do not have to live that way. As Catholics we are good at wanting to control our relationship with God. We all know people who want to just get into heaven through the back door or speak of purgatory as alright for a while. We convince ourselves that we will never be Mother Teresa and so if we try to be a little better than mediocre, we are fine. We cannot help everyone and that can be the excuse for not helping anyone. We can often adopt a cause that touches our hearts. Look at all those commercials with beaten and abused dogs, children who have constant operations to help restore their health, starving children dying in their mother's arms with bloated bellies, or wounded warriors who all can be saved with your donation of just $19.00 a month. Having our hearts moved and making a long-term donation are good and wholesome things. They do not free us from responding to other needs outside our favorite charity, or worse they do not constitute so many need that we respond to none of them.

We do not take seriously the words of the Gospel when Jesus says:" Be perfect as your heavenly Father is perfect." Instead, we give God His due as we dedicate an hour or so to Sunday Eucharist. We pray when we are needy or when the occasion inspires us.

When we have hurt someone, we try to make up for what we have done. We apologize to others. We send cards or flowers; we offer promises that it will never happen again. We expect to be forgiven and we can even get angry when someone refuses to forgive because they are still hurting from the damage that we have done. They want to repair things in their own time and in their own way. We cannot erase the past we can only act differently in the future. We cannot make people forgive us; even more be reconciled with us. That is a partnership decision.

God's constant love and mercy are his free gifts to us. We do not deserve them; we do not earn them. Jesus did that. As St. Paul reminds us: "He died for us while we were still sinners." Jesus shows us the way to true submission and doing God's will. We see this: In the Agony in the Garden when Jesus honestly prays with the Father asking that the burden he is about to endure be taken away from him. After expressing his fears and reluctance and knowing that he has been heard he then accepted the father's will and not his own. On the Cross Jesus speaks words of hope and forgiveness; he reached out to his Mother with loving compassion to see that she is cared for in the future, but he also expresses words on the Cross of being abandoned and yet with his dying breath he trustingly says: "Into your hands I commend my spirit."

## Philippians 2:5-11:

The kenotic Hymn of the letter of Paul to the Philippians show this fundamental attitude of the Incarnation itself and of Jesus' relationship to us and the world of earth and heaven.

"Have among yourselves the same attitude that is also yours in Christ Jesus, Who, though he was in the form of God, did not regard equality with God something to be grasped. Rather, he emptied himself, taking the form of a slave, coming in human likeness;

and found human in appearance, he humbled himself, becoming obedient to death, even death on a cross. Because of this, God greatly exalted him and bestowed on him the name that is above every name, that at the name of Jesus every knee should bend, of those in heaven and on earth and under the earth, and every tongue confess that Jesus Christ is Lord, to the glory of God the Father" (Philippians 2: 5-11).

## Submission Demands that We Let Go of Control:

I want to stress a few points in this discussion for the sake of clarity.

- Atonement is something I do to make up for what I have done. I do penance, I give flowers or candy, I take someone out to supper, I apologize profusely. The key word there is "I".

- We cannot make up for our sins, for our failures, for our blindness, for our judgments, for our harsh words, for the injuries that we cause.

- Guilt, unease, carefulness, insecurity, doubt are all part of the earthly reality that can be extrapolated into the eschatological reality we call purgatory.

- Reconciliation on the other hand is in the hands of the Other; God forgives, forgets, and helps us to start over.

- Reconciliation with God begins with God. He graces us towards repentance, to coming back to him and forgives us long before we ask. We never stop being his sons and daughters even when we do not act like his children.

*"Do you say your prayers well, my children?... You should say them well, at night and in the morning, even if you say only an Our Father and a Hail Mary":*

When I first heard this request as a child growing up in a La Salette Parish, I thought Mary was generously caring for her children. She did not chastise them for not praying well nor even mentioning that they did not go to Church on Sundays. The message applied to them as it applied to millions of others of that age and of every age before and after. It seemed so easy to do.

I knew how to say the prayers in English, French and Latin and more recently in Spanish. (Coming from a French-Canadian heritage we learned the prayers in school and used the first two languages daily.) It is only recently that I became more aware of that fact that the two children really did not pray well. They did know those two prayers by heart. They barely spoke French, only speaking the local patois. Mary's request included that they had to better learn those two prayers and understand them well. These two prayers would gradually shape their lives and their relationship to God and her.

## Our Vision Statement as Christians:

The two prayers speak of God's relationship to us and to Mary as an example. The Our Father speaks of the profound mystery of salvation and the relationship between the God and us. He is the Father who shows himself ultimately in the Word made flesh and continues to guide us through the Holy Spirit. He shares his mission with us. In the Hail Mary we hear of God's special love for Mary, but also the love that he has for all his people. We recognize that Mary intercedes for us her children knowing that a mother's care is so valuable for us.

The two prayers offer a tripartite view of Reconciliation, Offering, and Consciousness. They speak of our true relationship with God our loving Father and how we can respond to his love in such a way that we too are blessed. They speak of offering our lives by building God's Kingdom, making His name and reputation, and following his will here on earth. The role of the lowly handmaid is to show that we too are blessed, because the Lord dwells within us and thus are blessed. They are prayers of offering especial when we say them in the morning: we pledge our day to God as he feeds us by meeting our needs and inspiring us to follow is way of reconciling love.

We see in Mary how she too walked in his ways and in fulfilling his call to her she is greatly blessed. At the end of the day as we repeat the two, we should be calling to mind what the Lord has done for us and how we forwarded the establishment of his Kingdom. What was the daily bread that we received, how did our commitment and actions build the Kingdom and so are deserving of God's blessing that we have received throughout the day?

# The Our Father: A Family Affair:

The Our Father has two parts:

• The first section is about the world we are building with the help of God.

> » **"Our Father"**: we are his children and it is a family business. It is not the master-slave concept of God commands and we must obey. It is not even the Old Testament covenantal relationship of God/Creator/Source of Grace and his People. It not teacher and disciple either. It's the intimate relationship of daddy and child; we are the cherished children of the perfect Parent, the apple of his eye. God wants us to grow in his image and likeness, supported by his example and blessings. He wants us "in the family."

> » **"Hallowed be thy name"**: this means much more than not us-ing the name of God's Son in vain. It is the upholding the family name, the God-Brand. Just like employees and executives of cor-porations like Coca Cola, M&M's, Rolls Royce, McDonald's, the Catholic Church are called to image the values of their job, so too must we respect and manifest who God is by our lives. Much more than using God's name in vain. I am always impressed by that word "hallowed" as it is reserved for special things: at Gettysburg Abraham Lincoln spoke about the cemetery that was being dedicated was hallowed by the death of those who gave their lives for freedom and unity, FDR used the word to speak of the Hoover Dam as hallowed by the efforts of those who strug-

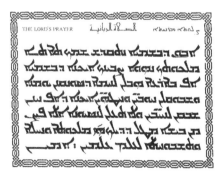

The Lord's Prayer written in Syriac

gled to be build it and those who died in the construction, and finally at a Committal Service we speak of graves being hallowed by Christ three days in the tomb and the faith of all who believe in him. Hallowing demands active witness to the truth of who God is for us.

» **"Thy Kingdom... thy will be done on earth as it is in heaven."** The reign of God is in our midst being formed each day, even though the ultimate equality of earth and heaven are so very future. The movement to perfect happens whenever we make God's ways our ways.

• The second part is about God's gifts to us so we can work towards fulfilling the vision and the promised commitment we just made.

» **Give us this day our daily bread:** the nourishment, the energy, the grace, the inspiration, the love, and the talents we need. Help us to conquer our fears, to meet the difficulties of the day, the ability to live out our pledge of the first part

» **Forgive us:** we are sinner but with your help we can be holy as you are holy. Having become aware of God's forgiveness we can then say the next phrase

» **As we forgive:** help us to act like you do, so that your best is also our best. Let us reconcile the world with you and in your way. Forgiveness band reconciliation are the groundwork of the kingdom.

» **Lead us not into temptation but delivers us from evil:** In other words, save us from temptation and from giving up the quest. We admit that we need God if we are going to succeed. We need to avoid the temptation to try to go it alone, or to not do our part this day to build the Kingdom and build our own kingdom instead. Keep us true to who we are and to the covenant that guides us.

## The Hail Mary: A Woman Blessed:

There are two parts to the Hail Mary as well:

• The first part is based on the Gospel of Luke and the words of the angel and Mary's Cousin Elizabeth.

» **Hail Mary, full of grace:** A woman, a human being, is filled with the grace of God that will empower her fiat. It is the same for us that when God's love, mercy, grace, and spirit fill our lives we too are made whole and enabled to respond to our calling.

» **The** Lord **is with you:** God dwells in her heart. This is the chief greeting of St. Paul in his letter and of the Church in its sacraments.

» **Blessed are you among women:** In other words, we thank Mary for saying yes to God. Our yes to God to accept his call always lead to blessing. Here the meaning is being filled with his love and goodness. Blessed are the peacemakers, the thirsting, the merciful, the sorrowful etc. They are richly rewarded for their actions. We are richly rewarded.

» **Blessed is the fruit of your womb, Jesus:** Above all, blessed is the child you bore as Mother of God. Accepting to be the Mother of God through the power of the Holy Spirit was a mystery for that moment and for Mary's whole life. When we accept our call, we often do not realize the implications of our "yes" rather we enter the mystery of our life journey.

The second half of this prayer reminds us that the Mother of God has a special relationship to us and we to her, established by Jesus on the Cross: "Woman, behold your Son... Son, behold your Mother" (John 19:26-27).

• **Pray for us:** Mary intercedes for us just as she did at Cana and other times in Jesus' life. The nature of a mother. She is the protective Mother and we are her beloved children.

• **Sinners:** Mary loves us just as we are. The same as the Father. The same as her Son.

• **Now and at the hour of our death:** She watches over us always – today and every day until our dying breath.

### "Lex Orandi, Lex Credendi (The law of praying is the law of believing)":

There is a principle in the Church that has guided us over the centuries; namely that there is a relationship between prayer and belief. This demands that our liturgical life and our theology and doctrinal teachings must be sympatico. It makes clear that there is a back and forth relationship between the two and what we pray shapes what we believe and what we believe belongs in prayer.

The presence of the Nicene Creed in the liturgy is just such a reality: as the creed was developed it was placed into the Eucharist on Sundays and Solemnities so that we all could be clear about God as Trinity and the purpose of the Church. If we prayed it enough, the phrases could sink into our psyche and we could begin to believe what we say. The same is true with the Our Father and the Hail Mary.

In Morning Time, these two prayers serve as an Offering of our day and a recognition that we are helped, guided, and protected by the Father and Mary our Mother. We will be graced. We commit ourselves to the process of living a holy life and we know that with God's help and Mary's example, that this is possible for us.

In the Evening Time, the two prayers serve as an Examination of Conscience. We pause to reflect on our day and the role that God and Mary played in it. Did we live up to our commitment that we made and how did God help us in that work; where did we receive our daily bread; how did Mary inspire us?

The more we do pray in this way, the more we grow in awareness of God's presence in our lives. We see that we are in need of strength and blessings and the example of others: the Father, Son and Spirit as well as Mary and the Communion of Saints. We are not left to our own devices but instead journey as God's Family, building the Kingdom of God in all we are and do.

**Reflection Questions:**

•Can we accept that God has done it all for us; that he has saved us and we need to be overwhelmed by the gift? Can we stop trying to be in control of God's mercy?

•Do we accept God's will in our life and seek to put it into practice? Can we submit to him and to the events of life that come our way? Can we be a true partner with others and not insist that all must go our way?

•Do we offer our life to God each day and ask Mother Mary for her help and guidance? Do we stop and reflect on God's action and Mary's help at the end of our day? Do we have "field of Corn" moments when we know that God is truly watching over us?

# Chapter 10 —
# Accompaniment: La Salette
# and the Ministry of Reconciliation
## by Fr. Cyriac C. Mattathilanickal, M.S.

Pope Francis in his first encyclical, "*The Joy of the Gospel*," writes, "In our world ordained ministers and other pastoral workers can make present the fragrance of Christ's closeness and his personal gaze. The Church will have to initiate everyone — priests, religious and laity —into this 'art of accompaniment' which teaches us to remove our sandals before the sacred ground of the other".

To me accompaniment is not just an art to be learned or acquired but a theological and pastoral pedagogy to be utilized as a tool for evangelization. The hallmark of a Christian and in fact every La Salette religious must be an ability to draw close to the 'other', the stranger among us, and pay particular attention to stories of his or her journey through the dark valley of fear and travesty of life. This spiritual accompaniment being a sacred task, operates in the realm of grace. Grace gives accompaniment its force.

Members of 2012 La Salette General Chapter
in House Chapel, Hartford, Connecticut

"Accompaniment is help given by one Christian to another which enables that person to pay attention to God's personal communication to him or her to respond to this personally communicating God, and to live out of the consequences of the relationship i.e. to be oriented to the heart of the Lord", says William Barry, S.J., in his book, *The Practice of Spiritual Direction*.

I believe that Mary our Mother, Our Lady of La Salette in a special way, has shown us the way of accompaniment through her apparitions, messages, and witnessing as a perfect disciple of Jesus, the son of God and Son of Mary. Mary meets us where we are and who we are and then guides us, draws us and invites to '*Come closer my children*'. The ministry and life of every Christian, every religious and every La Salette is to embrace a pastoral theology of accompaniment and bring the last, the least and the lost to the bosom of God so that they may experience the 'fragrance of God's love' and mercy.

## Accompaniment in the Scriptures:

From the story of creation, we hear "God created mankind in his image; in the image of God he created them; male and female he created them" (Genesis 1:27). The human person was the crown of God's creation but through original sin that glory was lost. Although banished from Paradise, the desire of God for the human person to return to the Creator was initiated by God by the sending of the prophets. God can never fully give up on God's own creation. All through the Hebrew Scriptures, we see the constant accompaniment of God of the chosen people of Israel. During the time of exodus, exile, war, poverty and misery, we see God accompanying the people of Israel through the mission of his prophets, Moses, Joshua, Elijah, Jeremiah many more.

In Leviticus 26:12-13 God says: "Ever present in your midst, I will be your God, and you will be my people; for I, the Lord, am your God, who brought you out of the land of Egypt to be slaves no more, breaking the bars of your yoke and making you walk erect." In Isaiah 49:15 we read, "Can a mother forget her infant, be without tenderness for the child of her womb? Even should she forget, I will never forget you."

This everlasting desire of God is reiterated by Jesus in John 14:18: "I will not leave you orphans; I will come to you." The incarnation of Jesus for me is the ultimate fulfillment of the prophecy of God to walk with God's children personally here on earth. When Jesus came he healed the leper (Mathew 8:1-4), taught the disciples (Mathew 13:18), calmed their fears (Mathew 8:26), wept with them (John 11:35), encouraged them to pray (Mathew 26:41) and predicted that he would die and rise (Mark 10:32-34). Christ therefore was a constant companion to his disciples.

Jesus sends the disciples two by two. In Luke 10:1 Jesus "appointed seventy [-two] others whom he sent ahead of him in pairs to every town..." "Three reasons for pairing are involved: mutual support; bearing witness to the truth of their testimony; living embodiment of the gospel of peace." (1) "The missionaries are sent in two's in order to give a witness that can be considered formal testimony about Jesus and the reign of God." (2) Jesus continues to journey with these two as he promised them that "for where two or three are gathered in my name, there am I in the midst of them" (Mathew 18:20).

The account of Jesus walking with the two disciples on the road to Emmaus (Luke 24: 13-35) gives a clear indication that Jesus never leaves us orphans, that he will comfort, console, teach, walk and break bread with us especially when we move away from our own 'Jerusalem' which is the true center of our lives. When we are caught up in our grief and emotional burdens and desolations God draws near and walks with us. Ekman Tam Ph.D. defines spiritual direction, one of the ministries that I enjoy doing, as "accompanying guests on the road to Emmaus" and its key elements being conversation, discovering, appreciating and responding, "with heightened awareness of love and a deeper commitment to love." (3)

In the farewell discourse of Jesus especially in John 17: 9b-10a, we see him praying for his disciples: "I do not pray for the world but for the ones you have given me, because they are yours, and everything of mine is yours and everything of yours is mine..." True accompaniment of God means that God in Jesus has kept all God's beloved in their hearts. Jesus consistently revealed that the disciples are his friends and not slaves (John 15:15). Jesus said, "No one has greater love than this, to lay down one's life for one's friends" (John 15:13). This defines a truly committed relationship.

## A Theology of Accompaniment:

The development of a theology of accompaniment is fairly new and owes its origin to the Latin American liberation theologians. Among them would be John Sobrino, Gustavo Gutierrez, and the United States Latino theologians, especially Roberto Goizueta. These theologians have woven together a theology from the experiences of suffering, pain, poverty, violence and hopelessness in Latin America.

The word "accompaniment" and "companion" both stem from the same Latin root *ad cum panis* which means "to go with bread." According to Webster's Dictionary 'to accompany' is to 'go with another on an equal basis', to go with or attend as a companion. Rev. Jim Barnett, a Dominican priest and missionary to El Salvador says, "accompaniment has to do with a companion who attends to a friend with bread, who "goes with" a friend with bread, who "breaks bread" with a friend, who "shares food", who shares life." (4)

Christ, who broke bread with the two disciples on the road to Emmaus, not only is a model for all on a spiritual journey but shows us the way to accompaniment, for Jesus is "the way and the truth and the life" (John 14:6b). Jesus who bore all the sufferings for the sake of humanity, and endured crucifixion and death has enormous significance for anyone who faces similar conditions in their own life. It simply means, "no matter what, God accompanies us. This is the "sine qua non" of all interpretations of the cross: if God is Love, then like any true love, this Love desires to become completely one with the beloved, sharing with and accompanying the beloved in everything." (5)

I believe that experience of cross, suffering, pain and violence are universal. For a non-poor like a North American, experiences of sexual abuse, divorce and separation, abortion, losses of any kind, be it job, home, death of a significant person in the family, terminal diseases like cancer etc. cause so much suffering and pain that they are constantly looking for God in the midst of them. In my own experience of pastoral ministry and spiritual direction, the directees that I have, clearly feel the accompaniment of God in their own life-situation of abandonment and divorce. So God is always present and especially where there is brokenness and pain.

Archbishop Oscar Romero, who laid his life for the poor farmers of El Salvador, reminded American missionaries: "What the people really need is that you simply *walk with them* in their lives, that you *accompany* them on their own faith journey that you are *there with them* as they struggle to work out their own historical destiny. If you do that you will discover a wonderful faith, and *your* faith and *your* lives will be transformed." (6) The witness and example of Oscar Romero has indeed influenced the growth and development of a theology and spirituality of accompaniment.

Therefore, a theology of accompaniment can be defined to mean the study of the accompaniment of God in the lives of God's children always and everywhere through joys and sorrows, success and failure, sickness and health, poverty and riches, suffering and pain and death. Pastoral ministries are avenues where we can explore this accompaniment of God in one's life and celebrate and live life to the fullest.

## A brief review of Salesian Spirituality:

Salesian Spirituality is a practical everyday spirituality for living in the modern world as learned, lived and shared by St. Francis de Sales (1567-1622) and St. Jane Frances de Chantal (1572-1641), spiritual friends. Salesian spirituality gives expression to a way to journey in the spiritual life as we embrace the duties of our responsibilities in response to the universal call to holiness - in the words of St. Francis de Sales to "bloom where you are planted." "Clerics, vowed religious,

Medals of Sts. Francis de Sales and Jane Frances de Chantal, 1867; photo: Defranoux

109

lay persons, men and women in all walks and states of life were intended to exercise their deepest human capacities in a unique marriage with the God who created them." (7) So all are called to holiness and live the "devout life" by passionately and joyfully meeting the demands in one's state in life for the love of God.

It is not so much what you do in your life but how and for whom you do it. This spirituality is relational and it is in the living out of our relationships in love that one lives the devout life. St. Francis says, "The measure of our love is to love without measure." One must strive to live according to the will of God. "So let us live courageously between the one will of God and the other" (Francis de Sales, *Treatise on the love of God*, Book 9).

Salesian spirituality is primarily a matter of the conversion of the heart. The devout life is a "process" and it only happens with grace, perseverance and patience over a lifetime. Francis says, "heart is the source of actions... engrave on your heart this holy maxim, Live Jesus!" (8)

Pastoral ministry of accompaniment in this spirituality is "not to instruct but to appeal to the whole person through the vital center, to make Jesus live by winning the heart through persuasion and gentle encouragement." (9) Salesian spirituality is lived out through the practice of gentleness, peace, humility, simplicity and in the little occasions that present themselves every day. As St. Jane Frances de Chantal says, "We cannot always offer God great things, but each instant we can offer him little things with great love." (10) By this way you discover the accompaniment of God in the day-to day life.

## Christ our Companion:
## Roberto Goizueta's view of accompaniment

How can one find meaning, purpose, hope and future when life is full of suffering, pain, poverty, violence, and 'diminishment'? Pope John Paul II says to the youth of the world reflecting on the Gospel of Mark 10:21, "'Jesus, looking upon him, loved him...' When everything would make us doubt ourselves and the meaning of our life, then this look of Christ, the awareness of the love that in him has shown itself more powerful than any evil and destruction, this awareness enables us to survive." (11)

Roberto Goizueta developed his contextual theology focusing on the lived religious experiences of Latinos. The poor, the marginalized and the sick have discovered that 'life is worth living no matter what in Christ crucified' says Roberto Goizueta. He is convinced that "the fundamental practical significance of the Crucified is that, no matter what, God accompanies us... if God is Love, then, like any true love, this Love desires to become completely one with the beloved, sharing with and accompanying the beloved in everything." (12) The Love that God has for his beloved is 'acute' when experiencing pain, struggle, loss, grief etc. Therefore, "this experience of God's presence with us, especially in our struggles, is what makes God's love believable, Christ's message credible, and life livable." (13) Goizueta continues to say, "Because Jesus accompanies us, he is real, and because he is real, he liberates. And the Cross is the guarantee that he does, in fact, remain with us-that he walks with us even today." (14) The Christ who accompanies us is the source of our hope. In our ministries of compassion and genuine friendship we must be able to bring to people the nearness of God.

## Mary Mother of Accompaniment:

At the annunciation angel Gabriel declared to Mary, "...The Lord is with you... the Holy Spirit... will overshadow you" (Luke 1:26-37). Here we see how God in the Spirit accompanies a simple of maiden of Judea in her role to be the Mother of the Son of God, Jesus. It is evident that Mary is apprehensive, fearful, and anxious and yet the assurance of the angel was one that of grace accompanying- companioning Mary at her most vulnerable moment. Grace gave her the force to accompany her cousin Elizabeth who was pregnant in her old age.

Mary was spent six months of her time serving and being with her cousin. At the age of 12, when Jesus was 'lost' in the temple and 'found' among the elders, Mary silently follows her Son gracefully and often wondering what all these mean but keeping all these things in her heart. Jesus grows in wisdom and age being accompanied by his Mother Mary and Joseph the foster father.

During the public ministry of Jesus, we seldom see Mary barring the miracle of Cana and a visit with Jesus' brothers. In all these Mary faithfully, obediently, silently follows and accompanies the redeemer in His ministry of preaching, teaching, healing, and miracles. At the passion, suffering and death of Jesus, we see Mary's most excruciating and painful time of accompaniment. "Standing by the cross of Jesus were his mother..." (John 19:25a).

Being with her son while being nailed, crucified, pierced were heart-wrenching moments, like a sword that pierced her heart. Compassion means 'to suffer with' and yes Mary accompanied and suffered with her Son when he needed her the most. Just as God never abandons her children, Mary the Mother of Jesus stands by her Son and never abandons him to the domain of death alone. Therefore, Mary is the perfect disciple who follows – a disciple par excellence.

We see Mary again at the 'upper room together with the apostles immersed in constant prayer before the Pentecost. There were present "...some women, and Mary the Mother of Jesus, and his brothers" so we read in Acts 1:14. We see Mary journeying with, consoling, comforting, grieving, and praying with the apostles. We will never fully capture the breadth and width of her compassion, care and accompaniment in the life of the disciples especially before and after the Pentecost.

Over the course of the history of the Church, there have been 26 Church approved apparitions of the Blessed Virgin Mary often paired with some type of message Our Lady wants to communicate to the Church. Mary's interventions in the history of Church were crucial turning points and life changing at that. They were graceful moments for Mary to help her children to find the Lord and draw them closer to her Son Jesus. Mary meets them where they are and who they are often clothed in native attire as if one of their own. The pattern of Mary's appearances clearly communicates her intimate desire to draw people ever so gently to God through a process of conversion.

### Apparition of La Salette a Moment of Grace:

At the apparition of Our Lady at La Salette, we hear her say to the children Maximin and Melanie: *"Come closer, my children; don't be afraid. I am here to tell you great news."* (15)

This is a gentle and maternal invitation extended to the children and to us. If you are a reconciler, if you are a true accompanist, a companion, you would respond generously to this beckoning of Mary. It is important to note that Mary met the children in their own home turf – in the pasture where they were grazing the cows, and in their poverty and meager education. From the apparition account of Melanie, we hear: "She wept all the while that she spoke to us. I did see the tears flow from her eyes- they flowed in steady stream." (16)

These tears of Mary are profoundly meaningful as it manifests the heart of Mary in solidarity with the hurting, suffering and sinful humanity. Cardinal Carlo Maria Martini, SJ in reflecting on the tears of Mary at La Salette writes, "In heaven God and Mary suffer because of our blindness and the paths of destruction that people are following... and that God and Mary are intimately aware of the suffering people on earth." (17)

Cardinal Carlo Maria Martini (1927-2012) in 2006; photo: Mafon1959

Mary as the Mother of the Church calls her children to accountability, warning them of the consequences of their rejection and alienation from God. Mary's true compassion is manifested in her tears that flows from her maternal heart that aches for her wayward sons and daughters. Mary accompanies her children and draws close to us even shedding tears of compassion. Cardinal Martini continues,

"First of all, La Salette reminds us of our relationship with God and the need for conversion and reconciliation, but it also shows us the needy, suffering and vulnerable face of God, as Jesus did in his agony and death."

It is out of compassion for each one of us that Mary accompanies the Church in her moments of sins, failures, woundedness and suffering. "The weeping of Mary and Jesus activates the dynamic that orders and redeems our emotional life, which is often disordered and distracted and focused on ourselves." (18) Pope Saint John Paul II in his message on the feast of La Salette remarked: "La Salette is a message of hope, for our hope is nourished by the intercession of her who is the Mother of mankind."

In her message to the children at La Salette, Mary clearly manifests how well attuned she is to the simplest details of their lives and us. Mary calls us from the locus of own poverty and sin and challenges to receive forgiveness and reconciliation and thus bask in the mercy of her Son Jesus. Therefore, Mary is not only the Mother of reconciliation but also Mother of accompaniment in the economy of salvation.

## Conclusion:

As the Missionaries of La Salette mark 175th anniversary of the merciful apparition of Our Lady, it is my desire and hope that we learn to embrace a spirituality of accompaniment inspired and empowered by the message and grace of La Salette. The Church today and world at large face pandemic, violence, war, political unrest, economic uncertainty, homelessness, poverty, and loss of every kind. Families are facing unprecedented crisis from broken marriages, relationships, and abuses of every kind. There is so much fear and anxiety in the air.

Pope Francis continues to challenge the church and community to get involved and be engaged in the struggles of humanity. Our ministry and evangelization must be "that gets involved by word and deed in people's daily lives; it bridges distances, it is willing to abase itself if necessary, and it embraces human life, touching the suffering flesh of Christ in others." (19)

As reconcilers our way of ministry must be inspired by the way Mary approached the children at La Salette. It was that of gentleness, compassion, respect, earnest desire to meet them where they are and invite them to see for themselves what the great news is: the mercy and love of God. It was indeed a ministry of accompaniment. Mary communicated the caress of God and mercy of God. The ministry of accompaniment that we undertake today may stem from our desire to walk with each other in life and that no one is left behind and that every one may feel the tenderness of God's love through our ministry of accompaniment and reconciliation.

Mary, Mother of Reconciliation, Pray for us. Amen.

## Reflection Questions:

• This essay speaks of the Theology of Accompaniment. How much easier is it when we have a partner on the journey? Give a personal example.

• La Salette is a moment of grace. How has your life been graced by the message, the spirituality, the charism of La Salette? Be specific.

• How do we bring the message of promise and hope to others? What can we do to move it forward in the world today?

## Endnotes:

(1) Brown, Raymond. *The New Jerome Biblical Commentary*, Prentice Hall, 1990, p. 701.

(2) Karris, Robert. *The Collegeville Bible Commentary*, The Liturgical Press, 1992, p. 956.

(3) *Presence: An international Journal of Spiritual Direction.* vol. 12, p. 65.

(4) http://www.domcentral.org/preach/accomp.htm#archbishop.

(5) Goizueta, Roberto S. *Christ Our Companion.* Orbis Books, 2009, p. 9.

(6) http://www.domcentral.org/preach/accomp.htm#archbishop.

(7) Wright, Wendy and Power Joseph. *Francis de Sales, Jane de Chantal.* Paulist Press, 1988, p. 35-36

(8) *Ibidem*, p. 55.

(9) *Ibidem*, p. 59.

(10) *Ibidem*, p. 62.

(11) Goizueta, Roberto S., p. 8.

(12) *Ibidem*, p. 9.

(13) *Ibidem*, p. 11.

(14) *Ibidem*.

(15)Ladouceur, Fr. Emile, M.S., *The Vision of La Salette: the Children Speak.*, La Salette Communications, 2016, p. 35

(16) *Ibidem*, p.36.

(17) Martini Cardinal, *The Gospel Way of Mary*. The Word Among Us Press, 2011, P. 94-95

(18) *Ibidem*, p. 103

(19) Pope Francis, *The Joy of the Gospel*. USCCB, 2013, p. 13

# Bibliography

Barry, William A. *Spiritual Direction: Recovery of a Tradition*. Tulsa, OK: University of Tulsa, Warren Center for Catholic Studies, 1994.

_____. *Spiritual Direction and the Encounter with God: A Theological Inquiry*. New York: Paulist Press, 1992.

_____. *With an Everlasting Love: Developing an Intimate Relationship with God*. New York: Paulist Press, 1999.

Barry, William A., and William J. Connolly. *The Practice of Spiritual Direction*. New York: Harper Collins, 2009.

Brown, Raymond. *The New Jerome Biblical Commentary*. New Jersey: Prentice Hall, 1990.

_____. *The Gospel according to John*. The Anchor Yale Bible Commentaries. New York: Doubleday, 1966, 1970.

Chittister, Joan D. *Scarred by Struggle, Transformed by Hope*. Michigan: WM.B. Eerdmans Publishing Co., 2003

Dunne, Tad. *Spiritual Mentoring: Guiding People through Spiritual Exercises to Life Decisions*. San Francisco: Harper San Francisco, 1991.

Dyckman, Katherine Marie, and L. Patrick Carroll. *Inviting the Mystic, Supporting the Prophet: An Introduction to Spiritual Direction*. New York:

Paulist Press, 1981.

Edwards, Tilden. *Spiritual Friend*. New York: Paulist Press, 1980.

Guenther, Margaret. *Holy Listening: The Art of Spiritual Direction*. Cambridge: Cowley Publications; London, Darton, Longman and Todd, 1992.

Gittins, Anthony J. *Encountering Jesus*. Missouri: Liguori/Triumph, 2002.

_____. *Come Follow Me*. Liguori/Triumph, 2004

Harrington, Daniel. Meeting St. John Today. Chicago: Loyola press, 2011

Karris, Robert. *The Collegeville Bible Commentary*: New Testament. Minnesota: The liturgical Press, 1992.

Kelsey, Morton. *Companions on the Inner Way: The Art of Spiritual Guidance*. 2d ed. New York: Crossroad, 1996.

O'Meara, Thomas. *Theology of Ministry*. New Jersey: Paulist Press, 1999.

*The New American Bible*. New Jersey: Catholic Book Publishing Corp., 1992

Martini Cardinal Carlo Maria, *The Gospel Way of Mary*. Maryland: The word among us press, 2011.

Ladouceur, Emile, M.S. *The Vision of La Salette: the Children Speak*. Attleboro: Missionaries of La Salette Corporation, 2016.

Pope Francis. *The Joy of the Gospel*. Washington D. C., United States Conference of Catholic Bishops, 2013

# Chapter 11 —
# La Salette and Our
# Ecological Well-Being:
# A Reflection on "Laudato si"

## By Fr. Ron Beauchemin, M.S.

St. Francis of Assisi prayed:
"Praise be to you, my Lord, through
our Sister, Mother Earth..."

"Then God said, 'Let the earth bring forth vegetation: every kind of plant that bears seed and every kind of fruit tree on earth that bears fruit with its seed in it.' And so, it happened: the earth brought forth vegetation: every kind of plant that bears seed and every kind of fruit tree on earth that bears fruit with its seed in it. God saw that it was good" (Genesis 1: 11-12).

"Praise be to you, my Lord, through our Sister, Mother Earth, who sustains and governs us, and who produces various fruit with colored flowers and herbs" (St. Francis of Assisi).

*"If they are converted, rocks and stones will turn into heaps of wheat, and potatoes will be self-sown in the fields..."* (Our Lady at La Salette)

All life depends on what we call "nature," that tremendous living environment that sustains us, as well as all living creatures or rather all living creation: plants, animals, birds, fish, insects, microbes and I could go on and on! We are all interconnected and interdependent!

The Story of Creation in Genesis is so beautifully and poetically put. After each phase of creation, God sees that his work is good that it is beneficial, it's essential to his entire plan. Each element fits in with the next, sustains it, becomes part of it, and contributes to the entire picture, the entire plan!

St. Francis of Assisi recognized the beauty of this divine plan of creation and penned a hymn of admiration for the beauty and harmony of creation surrounding him, "Praise be to you, my Lord!"

The Apparition of Our Lady of La Salette is mostly seen as an apparition dealing with "disobedience and callousness". It touches upon the first three Commandments of God:

1. You shall honor no other God but me.

2. You shall not misuse the name of the Lord your God.

3. Remember to keep holy the Sabbath. (Exodus 20: 2-11)

The beginning of Mary's message at La Salette speaks of these Commandments:

> *"If my people refuse to submit...I gave you six days to work; I have kept the seventh for myself, and no one will give it to me... And those who drive the carts cannot swear without throwing my Son's name. These are the two things that make the arm of my Son so heavy."*

The catechism used in France at that time had been composed under Napoleon after a Concordat (an agreement between the Holy See and a country) had been signed in which the Catholic religion was reinstated as the official religion of France. The catechism that was promulgated by Napoleon stressed the fourth to tenth Commandments which were seen as the social Commandments and of benefit to good citizens of the State. Our Lady, in her Apparition, stresses the first three Commandments as being essential to one's whole well-being and on which the others depend. Our relationship with God is paramount for smooth relationships with others and nature.

Our Lady, in her magnificent Apparition at La Salette, touches upon the reality of creation as well as the interdependence that exists in this creation. She lets it be known, in Biblical terms, that the sin of humanity affects not only ourselves but has repercussions on all of nature: *"If the harvest is ruined, it is only on account of yourselves."*

We do not often think of the world around us as a "blessing"; we're taken up with the problems and challenges that everyday existence places before us and at times, we're overwhelmed by the complexity of life. Repetition, doing the same thing every day, deadens our sense of well-being and limits our appreciation of the world around us. Our technological advances, as beneficial as they are, also have negative repercussions on our well-being. For instance, our cell phones make communication possible wherever we are and whenever we want to. Unfortunately, instead of strengthening our relationships, they often tend to isolate us from one another through an artificial sense of togetherness.

Our young people, who are engrossed in this technology, find themselves isolated from any meaningful face-to-face relationships to the point that some cannot communicate except through their iPhone or iPad. They become strangers to themselves as well as to others including those with whom they live!

We often hear, "stop and smell the roses." This is a challenge to our ability of appreciating nature around us as we try to earn our livelihood and cope with the demands of life in the post-modern world; a world of ever accelerating change and complexity. As we often say, "it's difficult just to keep up!" Have we, in this "trying to keep up" overlooked an important area on which our very existence depends - the world we live in?

We need to look at what St. Francis of Assisi shares with us:

I quote from Pope Francis' encyclical: *"On Care for Our Common Home (Laudato si)"*, #11:

"Francis helps us to see that an integral ecology calls for openness to categories which transcend the language of mathematics and biology and take us to the heart of what it is to be human. Just as happens when we fall in love with someone, whenever he would gaze at the sun, the moon, or the smallest of animals, he burst into song, drawing all other creatures into his praise. He communed with all creation... His response to the world around him was much more than intellectual appreciation or economic calculus, for to him each and every creature was a sister united to him by bonds of affection. That is why he felt called to care for all that exists."

Due to the devastation the world has suffered during the past years

– wild fires in the west of the United States and parts of Australia; tremendous flooding in the mid-west, England and other parts of Europe; erosion, landslides and damage to infrastructure and crops as a result of these catastrophes – we have begun to take notice of the abuse our planet and environment have suffered at our hands over past decades.

It's not easy to take responsibility for abuse and outright destruction of land, and environment that we feel is beyond our control and often the result of mega-industry's avarice and disregard for the well-being of the planet on which we live and government ineptitude or short-sightedness. Yet, down deep, we know that we are implicated because we profit from this disregard in the form of employment and our standard of living.

We know that we do have the power to change things if we have the will and the spiritual strength to confront this goliath of destruction and irresponsibility. It took only one woman (Candace Lightner) to found MADD (mothers against drunk drivers) and to change our justice system, across the country in dealing with the problem of inebriated drivers! This is only one example of a dozen that I could cite dealing with determination rather than numbers or political clout!

I mentioned above, "spiritual strength" which is certainly one important element in coming to terms with the problem we face.

We do not often think of La Salette as a message of environmental concern; yet, of all the Apparitions of Our Lady, it is La Salette that is most concerned with the physical well-being of God's children:

> *"If the harvest is ruined, it is only on account of yourselves. I warned you last year with the potatoes... when you found potatoes spoiled, you swore... (The potatoes) are going to continue to spoil, and by Christmas this year there will be none left... If you have wheat, you must not sow it. Anything you sow the vermin will eat, and whatever does grow will fall into dust when you thresh it... The walnuts will become worm-eaten; the grapes will rot... Have you never seen wheat gone bad, my children?"*

When the children shook their heads no, she reminded Maximin of the time he and his father were visiting a farm and the farmer invited his father to come and see his ruined wheat. She is even able to

"A famine is coming...potatoes and wheat... walnuts and grapes..."

A Famine is Coming, window from
Mary Keane Chapel, Enfield, New Hampshire

reconstruct their dialogue on their way home. This is how concerned she is about the wellbeing of her children.

At the time of the Apparition, France was still very much an agricultural country. Therefore, the Blessed Virgin spoke a message of penance in agricultural terms that could be easily understood by the children and by the people of France. We are all aware of the terrible potato famine in Ireland during the time of the Apparition. We are less aware of the fact that this crop failure touched other countries as well. Our Lady mentions precisely spoiled potatoes and the devastating effect this will have:

> "I warned you last year with the potatoes. You paid no heed. Instead, when you found potatoes spoiled, you swore, and threw in my Son's name. They are going to continue to spoil, and by Christmas this year there will be none left."

This is a dire warning tied to the disregard of the first three Commandments which deal with our relationship to God. La Salette is prophetic because it reflects on the Gospel message for us today. Like the Gospel message, it is down to earth. And like the Gospel, it reminds us that our actions or lack thereof have repercussions, not only in our lives, but in the world in which we live.

What Our Lady is challenging us to see, at La Salette, is our co-responsibility in the well-being of the world in which we live. John Donne's famous declaration, "no man is an island" stands before us today and challenges our sense of independence and individualism.

As Americans, freedom is an ingrained value that we need to better understand and confront. For St. Augustine, one of the great early church writers, freedom was seen as an empowerment. Through *freedom*, I am able to achieve the *good*. In other words, freedom is the ability to choose well; to choose what is right.

He did not see freedom as autonomy but that the value of freedom was the possibility to participate in God's creative action; in what will bear fruit, not only for the benefit of the individual but also that which benefits others, the entire community. This is what makes action and doing, truly human.

Early humans did not have a concept of themselves as "individuals" but were a member of a tribe, a community. Their identity was tied to "belonging" or being a part of something larger. Their actions benefited not only themselves but all the members of their tribe or community. All benefitted or all suffered from what they did or did not do.

Today, in our post-modern society, freedom is seen as autonomy. It is tied to the individual in disregard for others or to a sense of responsibility or obligation. And in our society, freedom and individualism are *idolized*. They have become absolutes in the realm of perceived values. This is true not only for individual persons but also for individual corporations as well. And it is infinitely true for mega-corporations that are so large and influential in the economic world that they are often beyond the control of governments.

At La Salette, Our Lady closes her discourse with the following command: "*...you will make this known to all my people.*" And she repeated it a second time before disappearing, "*Well, my children, make this known to all my people.*" This is a hope that her message would touch hearts and turn them to the Lord. This is a hope that Christians would become more conscious of their relationship with God and with one another to renew that sense of collaboration that is needed for our overall wellbeing. Pope Francis, in his Encyclical, *Laudato si*, put it this way:

> "Many things have to change course, but it is we human beings above all who need to change. We lack an awareness of our common origin, of our mutual belonging, and of a future to be shared with everyone. This basic awareness would enable the development of new convictions, attitudes, and forms of life. A great cultural, spiritual, and educational challenge stands before us, and it will demand that we set out on the long path of renewal" (Pope Francis, *Laudato si*, #202).

*[As I write this, we are in the midst of the Coronavirus (COVID-19) pandemic. This virus has forced us to realize that we are amid the "global-village" spoken of by Marshall McLuhan. Whether we like it or not, our actions do affect others, even to the point of impacting the entire world as this virus has so brutally shown.]*

The Pope has challenged us to enter a new lifestyle. One that considers the reality that the wellbeing of one needs to mirror the wellbeing of all. Isolation is not a Christian value, but community is. We need to educate ourselves on self-control which promotes responsible consumerism and respects the needs of all and builds on a willingness to learn from one another. Pope Francis puts it this way:

> "If we want to bring about deep change, we need to realize that certain mindsets really do influence our behavior. Our efforts at education will be inadequate and ineffectual unless we strive to promote a new way of thinking about human beings, life, society, and our relationship with nature. Otherwise the paradigm of consumerism will continue to advance, with the help of the media and the highly effective workings of the market" (Pope Francis, Laudato si, #215).

There is no doubt that this demands a true conversion of hearts as well as minds.

Our Lady at La Salette also called for a change of minds and hearts: *"If they are converted..."* Our Lady speaks of that drastic change that is echoed in Pope Francis' *Laudato si*. Without a strong spiritual backing, such a radical change becomes practically impossible. The forces of the marketplace are too enticing. Pope Francis is aware of this:

> "The rich heritage of Christian spirituality, the fruit of twenty centuries of personal and communal experience, has a precious contribution to make to the renewal of humanity. Here, I would like to offer Christians a few suggestions for an ecological spirituality grounded in the convictions of our faith, since the teachings of the Gospel have direct consequences for our way of thinking, feeling and living... I am interested in how such a spirituality can motivate us to a more passionate concern for the protection of our world" (Pope Francis, *Laudato si*, #216).

The Pope shares with us the reality of expanding deserts in the world because, as he says, "the internal deserts have become so vast" (Pope Francis, Laudato si, #217). Because of this, we need a profound interior conversion. When we speak of concern for the environment, we face ridicule and passivity; both express the unwillingness to change habits. We need to see the connection between the ecological environment and our encounter with Jesus Christ.

Our Lady at La Salette speaks the same language when she says, "*If they are converted, rocks and stones will turn into heaps of wheat, and potatoes will be self-sown in the fields.*" These are expressions that are meant to convey that conversion brings about harmony with God, nature, and the rest of humanity. It brings about blessings and general well-being. "Living our vocation to be protectors of God's handiwork is essential to a life of virtue; it is not an optional or secondary aspect of our Christian experience" (*Laudato si*, # 117).

This is a relationship which St. Francis of Assisi understood: the need for a healthy relationship with nature or as we would put it today, with the environment. A conversion calls for the recognition of the abuse we have imposed on our environment, which is God's creation, through our actions and our failure to act. We need to experience a true change of heart to achieve reconciliation with creation. This is but the beginning when speaking of ecological change. This is also a social problem.

Pope Francis clarifies the challenge:

"This task 'will make such tremendous demands of man that he could never achieve it by individual initiative or even by the united efforts of men bred in an individualistic way. The work of dominating the world calls for a union of skills and a unity of achievement that can only grow from quite a different attitude' (*The End of the Modern World* by Romano Guardini, p. 66). The ecological conversion needed to bring about lasting change is also a community conversion" (Pope Francis, Laudato si, #219).

As believers we have a keen awareness of our connectedness with God and the rest of his creation. Since we all share the same resources on this planet, we are really joined in a type of communion. We know that the Father, through his creation, finds that "all is good." Because of this connectedness, we should understand our interdependence; as Pope Francis says, "We do not understand our superiority as a reason for personal glory or irresponsible dominion, but rather as a different capacity which, in its turn, entails a serious responsibility stemming from our faith" (Laudato si, #220).

This responsibility is part of a lifestyle which responds to the care for nature and appreciates all of God's creation. Since we are all part of God's creation, we are in harmony when we recognize that God is our common Father – not only for humans but for all of created reality. Pope Francis challenges our sense of independence:

"We must regain the conviction that we need one another that we have a shared responsibility for others and the world, and that being good and decent are worth it. We have had enough of immorality and the mockery of ethics, goodness, faith, and honesty.

"It is time to acknowledge that light-hearted superficiality has done us no good. When the foundations of social life are corroded, what ensues are battles over conflicting interests, new forms of violence and brutality, and obstacles to the growth of a genuine culture of care for the environment" (Pope Francis, *Laudato si*, #229).

With the development of a sense of solidarity, the weakest and most in need receive from the abundance provided by the Father of us all.

The grandeur of nature, when contemplated, helps us realize what has been entrusted to us and how precious a patrimony it is.

This patrimony reflects on our spiritual life especially in the Sacraments where the natural elements of water, oil, fire show their symbolic power when they are incorporated in our acts of praise. Water is used in the cleansing action of Baptism while oil is used in the administration of Baptism, Confirmation, Holy Orders and the Anointing of the Sick as a tangible sign of our union with God through the redemptive action of his Son.

> "For Christians, all the creatures of the material universe find their true meaning in the incarnate Word, for the Son of God has incorporated in his person part of the material world, planting in it a seed of definitive transformation" (Laudato si, #235).

> "It is in the Eucharist that all, that has been created, finds its greatest exaltation. Grace, which tends to manifest itself tangibly, found unsurpassable expression when God himself became man and gave himself as food for his creatures" (*Laudato si*, #236).

Of all the human elements at our disposal, certainly bread and wine, common food in many countries, expresses our deepest desire for union with Christ, our Savior and his deepest desire for union with us.

At La Salette, Our Lady complains about the carelessness of Sunday worship:

> *"I gave you six days to work; I kept the seventh for myself, and no one will give it to me. This is what makes the arm of my Son so heavy…In the summer only a few elderly women go to Mass. The rest work on Sundays all summer long. In the winter, when they do not know what to do, they go to Mass just to make fun of religion."*

These words certainly apply to us today with the exception that people do not participate in the Eucharist any more often during the winter than they do during the summer. Yet, as Pope Francis points out, our Sunday participation in the Eucharist has special importance. It is that day on which the Savior rose from the dead and that day on which the Holy Spirit descended upon the apostles, initiating the age of the Church. Our Sunday worship is at the very foundation of who we are as Catholics and as Christians.

As Justin Martyr (165AD) attests, "But Sunday is the day on which we all hold our common assembly, because it is the first day on which God having wrought a change in the darkness and matter, made the world; and Jesus Christ our Savior on the same day rose from the dead" (St. Justin, Martyr, *First Apology*). Sunday, the day of the Resurrection, is the first day of the new creation.

As Our Lady at La Salette tried to tell us, if we lose our sense of Sunday worship, we lose the core of our Catholic identity, our union with God through the Gospel of his Son and the reception of his Son's Body and Blood in the Eucharist. We weaken our understanding of union with God and the universe on which we depend. That sense of interdependence is lost. The precious gift of creation needs to be lived in mutual interdependence for our wellbeing as well as the wellbeing of the earth on which we depend.

I would like to close this reflection on La Salette and Ecology with a quote from the beautiful Encyclical Letter on *The Care for Our Common Home* (*Laudato si*) of His Holiness Pope Francis:

"At the end, we will find ourselves face to face with the infinite beauty of God (1 Corinthians 13:12), and be able to read with admiration and happiness the mystery of the universe, which with us will share in unending plenitude. Even now we are journeying towards the Sabbath of eternity, the New Jerusalem, toward our common home in heaven. Jesus says: 'I make all things new' (Revelation 21: 5).

"Eternal life will be a shared experience of awe, in which each creature, resplendently transfigured, will take its rightful place and have something to give those poor men and women who will have been liberated once for all" (*Laudato si*, #243).

### Reflection Questions:

•At Creation, God made us in his image and likeness and gave his First Commandment: "...Be fertile and multiply; fill the earth and subdue it. Have dominion over the fish of the sea, the birds of the air, and all the living things that crawl on the earth" (Genesis 1:28b). How do fulfill your commission practically?

•What's "new" that Mary at La Salette and Pope Francis in *Laudato si* are calling us to develop in our lives?

•How is the Eucharist, especially Sunday Eucharist, helping us to build the world together?

The grandeur of nature surrounds the site of
the La Salette Apparition in France

# Chapter 12 —
# La Salette: A Study of Scripture Parallels
## By Fr. Isidro Perin, M.S.

**Editor:** *This article was originally presented by Fr. Isidro Perin, M.S. at the First International Encounter of La Salette Laity held on the Holy Mountain of La Salette from Sept. 1-10, 2011. It was translated from Portuguese to English by Fr. Norman Butler, M.S. The two other articles were given on other occasions.*

...The two questions Mary poses in her apparition remind us of two fundamental dimensions of Christian spirituality:

a) *contemplation* of the loving presence of the Lord and

b) *transforming* human action based on justice and solidarity.

Fr. Isidro Perin, M.S., La Salette
Superior General from 1994-2006

Mary shows us that these are two intertwined realities. The modern mind tends to contrast spirit with matter. In biblical Hebrew there are two complementary expressions: *"ruah (the breath of life)"* and *"shekinah (the loving presence of the Lord)"*.

The term spirituality comes from 'spirit' and, in a common understanding, 'spirit' is opposed to matter. However, in biblical language, 'spirit' is not opposed to matter or the body. It is opposed to the 'flesh' (that is, the fragility which is destined for death); it is opposed to the law (that is, imposition, fear, and punishment). So, in this semantic context, spirit means life, construction, strength, action and freedom.

The spirit of a person is basically the best part of the person. The spirit is the deepest self, where we find root motivations, ideals, utopias, passion and the mystique with which a person lives and struggles and transmits enthusiasm to others. (1)

Biblical Parallels to the La Salette Message:

Mary's message at La Salette, following the bible usage, is built around these two pillars: spirit as divine breath in our life and in creation, and therefore in bread. Here are a few expressions from the apparition that have biblical resonance:

Mary said: "*Come closer, my children.*"
> Scripture says: "Come, and you will see" (John 1:39a).

Mary said: "*Do not be afraid.*"
> Scripture says: "It is I. Don't be afraid" (John 6:20b)

Mary said: "*I've come to tell you great news.*"
> Scripture says: "I proclaim to you good news of great joy that will be for all the people" (Luke 2:10b).

Mary said: "*If my people refuse to submit...*"
> Scripture says: "When everything is subject to him, then the Son himself will [also] be subjected to the one who subjected verything to him, so that God may be all in all" (1 Corinthians 15:28).

Mary said: "*The arm of my Son...*"
> Scripture says: "He has shone might with his arm" (Luke 1:51a).

Mary said: "*The name of my Son...*"
> Scripture says: "Mary gave birth to a Son" (Luke 2:7).

Mary said: "*I gave you six days to work; I kept the seventh for myself, and no one will give it to me.*"

> Scripture says: "On the seventh day God completed the work he had been doing, he rested on the seventh day from all the work he had undertaken" (Genesis 2:2).

Mary said: "*If they are converted...*"
> Scripture says: "By waiting and by calm you shall be saved, in quiet and in trust shall be your strength..." (Isaiah 30:15b).

Mary said: "*During Lent, they go to the butcher shops like dogs.*"
> Scripture says: "Do not give what is holy to dogs or throw our pearls to swine, lest they trample them underfoot, and turn and tear you to pieces." (Matthew 7:6).

Mary said: *"Do you say your prayers well?"*
> Scripture says: "...Jesus departed to the mountain to pray and he spent the night in prayer to God" (Luke 6:12).

Mary said: *"Here, my child, eat some bread."*
> Scripture says: "(Jesus) taking the five loaves and the two fish..." (Mark 6:41a).

Mary said: *"Well, my children, you will make this known to all my people."*
> Scripture says: "Go into the world and proclaim the gospel to every creature" (Mark 16:15).

These comparisons make it clear that spirit and body are interrelated and inseparable in the human person. The human being is a whole which is totally unique. Therefore, our spirituality and our charism must take this into account.

Mary at La Salette knows how to read the signs of the times as she did in Palestine. She knows how to speak of "God's things" in the details of the life of her people. In both she urges us to live a spirituality attentive to the signs of the times, inviting us to be immersed in the events and the daily routine of our lives so as to discern in the world "the seeds of the Word" and the whisperings of the Spirit.

This spirituality permits us to have an experience of God's fidelity, the God who continues to do wonders in spite of our human fragility. It teaches us to listen and pay attention to what happens around us, perceiving with the eyes of the heart where the spirit is trying to lead us as we journey on the path of her Son.

## La Salette – An Incarnate Marian Spirituality

### LA SALETTE AND ITS SYMBOLS:

La Salette is an event and a message full of symbols:

- The *globe of light* that surrounds Mary and the children.

- The *tears* that constantly flow from the eyes of the Beautiful Lady and vanish as they fall into the intense light radiating from the crucifix, she wears;

- The *chains* that form a border to her shawl, symbols of oppression and of rejection of the fraternity and solidarity offered by her Son

Jesus.

• There are *roses* that accompany the chains of her shawl, and surround her head and her shoes, symbols of love, of new life so that creation no longer needs to suffer birth pangs but can become a paradise of brothers and sisters.

• She is *dressed* like the country women of that area who struggle to feed their families in times of scarcity.

**La Salette Icon painted by a Russian immigrant woman**

• The *fountain of water* has never ceased to flow since that day of the apparition, reminding us of the "living spring that rises up for eternal life".

• The *mountain* is a symbol of human limitations and of God's presence.

There are *three phases* of the apparition:

In the *first phase*, Mary is found *seated on a stone* and weeping. She is the compassionate mother. Like a mother who has no more to say, she sweeps.

In a *second phase*, Mary is *standing and conversing* intimately with the two children. She continues to cry. She says that her own people are insensitive to the tragic realities of the period, "*and (they) take no account of it*". Her people are indifferent to God's loving presence in their lives, they "swear throwing in my son's name." She proposes a radical change of life: "*If they are converted, rocks and stones will turn into heaps of wheat, and potatoes will be self-sown in the fields.*" She is saying that a different world is possible.

In a *third and final phase*, Mary floats into the air and vanishes in the light, returning to heaven, that definitive place of light for reconciled and reconciling human existence.

The event and the message of La Salette, rich in symbols go beyond rational analysis and introduce us into the mystery beyond appearances. This grace-filled event helps us identify what is essential in our daily life: God is a loving presence in our midst and always at our side, taking us as we are, as the event at Coin reminds us.

## A Marian Spirituality:

Mary at La Salette invites us to develop a spirituality attentive to the signs of the times so that in those signs we can enter into the mystery of unconditional Love. This is no easy task in our post-modern culture where almost everything is taken to be relative and society discards things without thinking.

We can notice the following elements of Mary's spirituality:

a) **Value beauty** (Maximin and Melanie call her "the Beautiful Lady") and silence, contemplation and adoration.

b) **Recover** in our celebrations and preaching the value of symbols that bear within them rich spiritual significance.

c) **Challenge the trivialization** of life and death, the loss of the gospel values of justice and solidarity, fraternity and peace.

The La Salette event with its rich symbols is a bearer of a solid spirituality centered on Christ present in the life of all who travel their land of Coin or, in biblical terms, travel the road to Emmaus.

This spirituality should guide the life and mission of all La Salette religious and all La Salette Laity. This spirituality requires constant deepening and updating so as to respond to the signs of the times. From this rich spiritual itinerary born of the apparition, we can bring out the best of the old and the new.

The general context of the apparition which takes into account the attitudes of the Beautiful Lady – her message, her symbols, her call to conversion, the situation of the people of that time, and their response of Christian life, the plain and courageous presence of the first missionaries on the mountain, the devotions that were born there – lead the pilgrims to underscore an important dimension of the faith; that is, reconciliation.

The Marian La Salette Invocation, proclaimed by anonymous pilgrims in those early days, expresses the theological dimension most typical of the apparition: "Our Lady of La Salette, Reconciler of Sinners, pray without ceasing for us who have recourse to you."

## MARY, RECONCILER OF SINNERS AND OUR LA SALETTE RULE:

The expression, "Reconciler", as attributed to Mary, though restricted in its use, was known to theologians of the Middle Ages. Pope Leo XIII, in 1879, ordered that the statue of the Beautiful Lady be solemnly crowned as "Our Lady Reconciler." This is the same statue looking over the main altar in the Basilica on the Holy Mountain of La Salette. Later on, the Holy See approved the text of the La Salette Mass and the Office for "Our Lady of La Salette, Reconciler of Sinners."

The La Salette Missionaries immediately latched into the dynamic of reconciliation as flowing from the apparition and its message, contemplated and announced in light of the Gospel and an apt theological reflection of the time. The first version of the Rule of Life of the Congregation in 1852 asks the La Salette Missionaries to be:

a) *Men of prayer*, in union with the "divine advocate of sinners".

b) *Men of zeal*, charged with the mission of shaking sinners out of their lethargy.

c) *Men of expiation*, permanently asking Mary for grace and mercy for sinners.

These men will define themselves in the first Rule of Life of 1858 as "Men of prayer, of penance and zeal." These three elements of penance, prayer and zeal capture three fundamental relationships in our life:

a) *The relationship with God* through prayer, as openness to God's will in union with the example of the Beautiful Lady.

b) *The relationship with others*, cultivated in zeal, as an expression of love for our brothers and sisters.

c) *The relationship with oneself*, lived in penance as the expression of a longing to overcome the egocentric tendencies of the human heart.

This trilogy was understood and lived in the "theology of expiation" and the practices of "reparation" common to the Confraternity of Our Lady of La Salette and/or the movements of "Reparation to God for blasphemies" which were typical of the period. Simplifying this concept, penance, prayer and zeal were privileged ways of "expiating" sin, of "repairing" the evils caused to God and assuaging God's wrath.

Expressive of this same idea is Fr. Giraud's comment to his novices: "Consider me your clay, mold me as you see fit. Self-denial, sacrifice, the offering of one's life to others for the glory of God... the Host and Victim of expiation through sacrifice, prayer and love were the theological-ascetical pillars of the spirituality that guided our founders.

It did have a biblical basis: "...unless a grain of wheat falls to the ground and dies, it remains just a grain of wheat; but if it dies, it produces much fruit" (John 12:24). Undeniably this can lead to certain exaggerations and an often intimistic, individualistic and sacramentalistic view of reconciliation and the practice of adoration of the Blessed Sacrament as a way of expiation and victimhood (rescue/repayment for the sacrifice of a victim).

**MARY'S CALLS US TO CONVERSION:**

For a long time Mary's call to conversion found these expressions: "Reconciler of Sinners, prayer, penance and zeal" which later was re-read and reinterpreted in the light of the theological-pastoral evolution of thought in the Church, especially around the time of Vatican II.

Conversion is seen as metanoia, a change of our mentality, spirit, and attitudes. This change implies self-denial, passion for the kingdom of God, attention to the gift of self. Conversion and reconciliation are not two separate acts but inseparable parts of a permanent and life-giving process.

The evangelical values of penance, prayer and zeal (the gift of self) (2) which are inherent in our charism and spirituality become "the way of personal and community conversion and of our mission in the world. We live them in the spirit of compassion, mercy, communion and solidarity, especially in relation to the poor for whom we are called to be a sign of the compassionate love of God and of the maternal gentleness of the Virgin of La Salette for her people." (3)

## A Few Concluding Thoughts:

The charism of reconciliation reread in light of the La Salette event "engenders a style of fraternal life, a manner of being and a structure appropriate for a community that is reconciled and reconciling and at the service of the mission of the church." (4) We La Salette Missionaries want to share with the other Congregations born from the inspiration of the presence of Mary at La Salette, and especially, with the Sisters of Our Lady of La Salette, with our La Salette Laity, and with all persons we are called to serve.

Herein lies a great richness for the spiritual and charismatic patrimony of our Congregation, hopefully overcoming any tendencies to the intimistic, individualistic and even sacramentalistic concept of reconciliation. The horizon of the spirituality and the charism of reconciliation opens us up to the whole world.

In the face of the demands of today's world the La Salette Missionaries, the La Salette Sisters and La Salette Laity are "called to bring the La Salette charism up to date in a personal and community commitment in favor of peace, justice and the true development, respect for ecology and ecumenical and interreligious dialogue. We are passionate about the Kingdom of God so we give ourselves up to the task of freeing our brothers and sisters from every kind of oppression and from personal and social sin, helping them to be reconciled with themselves, with others and with God." (5)

"La Salette is a message of hope! (6) I hope this encounter awakens in us a new passion for the charism of reconciliation and for a Salettine spirituality and a renewed passion for God's Kingdom as John Paul II recommended to us La Salette Missionaries, saying:

> "I ardently desire that your General Chapter stimulate the members of the Institute to achieve a renewed awareness of participation in the reconciling mission of the Church which is at the heart of your missionary vocation, tirelessly helping Christians to welcome the divine pardon of which you are witnesses in all the world." (7)

## 1) How did the Bishop of Grenoble and the first missionaries view the La Salette event?

On September 19, 1851, after a precise and rigorous investigation, Philibert de Bruillard, Bishop of Grenoble pronounced his judgment in a pastoral letter of instruction. He declared that "the apparition of the Blessed Virgin to two shepherds, September 19,1846 on a mountain in the Alps, located in the parish of La Salette, ...bears within itself all the characteristics of truth and the faithful have grounds for believing it to be indubitable and certain."

a) In another pastoral letter, dated May 1, 1852, the Bishop of Grenoble announced the construction of a Shrine on the mountain of the apparition, and went on to add:

"However important the erection of a Shrine may be, there is something still more important, namely the ministers of religion destined to look after it, to receive the pious pilgrims, to preach the word of God to them, to exercise towards them the ministry of reconciliation, to administer the Holy Sacrament of the altar, and to be, to all, the faithful dispensers of the mysteries of God and the spiritual treasures of the Church. *These priests shall be called the Missionaries of Our Lady of La Salette; their institution and existence shall be, like the Shrine itself, an eternal monument, a perpetual remembrance of Mary's merciful apparition.*" (8)

Philibert de Bruillard: Bishop of the Diocese of Grenoble from 1826-1952

b) Silvain-Marie Giraud, who professed a deep love for the mother of Christ, posed this question: "In looking at La Salette, what do we often see?" In the *Book of the Spiritual Exercises of Our Lady of La Salette*, he indicates that our response is far from appropriate.

"La Salette is not what the outer eye perceives and perhaps admires.

It is not a simple Shrine where one might spend a few days in recollection and peace. It is not simply emotions surging within the soul because of the tears shed for sinners by the Queen of Heaven. La Salette is neither a few extra prayers said before the altar, nor a few pious thoughts and desires that visit the soul to mislead and beguile without making us better persons.

"Our Lady is the Mother of thankless people sent to La Salette by God to weep and to thrust upon the world, in her immense sorrow, the threat which was a sword in her own heart: *'If my people will not submit, I shall be forced to let go the arm of my Son.'* It is obvious to those whose eyes are open that a dreadful evil has overtaken our modern society, a spirit of rebellion, a disregard for authority, and a violent yearning for absolute independence and unrestrained freedom... La Salette is a courageous and energetic protest, a tireless struggle against the deplorable but clever incursions of the world's spirit, before which always all of us, priests and faithful alike, have been weak until now." (9)

c) At the first General Chapter, held in 1856, after having reflected on the contemporary evils, the delegates identified the basic elements that should characterize the missionaries: "The Missionaries of Our Lady of La Salette must consider themselves the messengers of the Queen of heaven... disseminating and making known, more so by their example than by their words, the divine warnings she herself graciously brought to earth." Further, the Chapter stated that the missionaries were to be characterized as 'men of prayer, men of zeal, men of penance.'"

Slowly, the understanding grew among the missionaries that their mission was to shine as a light of God's reconciling love. They were to be inserted within the world as ambassadors of reconciliation. In their lives they were called to safeguard the faith and to prophetically proclaim it:

  • by allowing reconciliation to take root in their lives that it might gain a foothold in the world; and•

  • by allowing the light of reconciliation in their lives to draw others to Jesus, "the Reconciler".

In this tradition, today, La Salette Missionaries in twenty-one countries have as their principal ministry the challenge to reconcile humankind with God, with one another and with the environment.

## 2) In what does our mission consist? In what does "following the Lord" consist?

The La Salette Rule says: "Christ is the rule of our life." (10) Some basic phrases give meaning to this invitation: "I chose you ... to be with me... and to be sent."

**"I Chose You ..."**

Our vocation is a gift from God, our Father, who chose us and calls us to maturity in Christ for the holiness of his body, the Church. (11) No one is a disciple unless invited. (12) The core of being a disciple is biblically expressed in the phrase "When did you come here". It is the recognition of the presence of Christ already in our lives. To be a disciple means:

- to share in a fundamental experience made and communicated by the master;
- to be caught up in the vision of the master;
- to be on fire with the fire of the master;
- to become like the master.

To be called by God ultimately means to be drawn into God's own plan, into the mission of his Son in order to be sent and become a co-worker with God for the salvation-transformation of the world into God's final design.

**To Be Called to Be with Him...**

Being taken into God's plan for creation is to be consecrated in God. Each person, chosen in God is "holy, consecrated, set apart." "As disciples of Christ, we live in communion with him." (13) A disciple is one who has made a fundamental choice for Christ, wanting to experience fully a "Christ-presence"... the unconditional, compassionate, forgiving love that is always with us.

**And to Be Sent...**

Here the invitation is to engage actively in God's mission, to be "fishers of men." (14) "By our baptism we are incorporated into the Church and share in its mission." (15) Mission is therefore the ultimate aim of a calling in this life. Being called is not for ourselves, not for taking any special place of honor or to be treated with reverence and awe. It involves being sent. A disciple is someone who starts living his daily life out of his experience of being one who participates in Jesus' own mission.

## 3) Exploring the Future:
## What do you see as the dreams and hopes of the future?

Pope John Paul II has invited each of us 'to look at the new things his predecessor addressed... to look around at the new things which surround us and in which we find ourselves caught up... to look to the future at this time of the Christian era, so filled with uncertainties, but also with promises... part of our responsibilities as pastors being to give careful consideration to current events in order to discern the new requirements of evangelization." (16) In other words, "our future holds equal measures of uncertainty and promise, of hesitation and hope." (17)

We live in a world that is rapidly changing – can we respond adequately? Indeed, our Congregation has responded to the challenges of the past century. Now, as the future unfolds, it will be our task to discern the "criteria of judgment, determining values, points of interest, lines of thought, sources of inspiration and role models," that will serve our choices. (18)

The message of La Salette can serve as a guide for us to discern today's signs of the times. We will need to "look back... look at... and look around." How? As Mary taught Maximin and Melanie to be in touch with the actualities of their world, we, too, are called to reflection and contemplation upon our world. In this, we will discover the presence of God.

Some twenty years ago, Malraux suggested that the "21st century will be the century of religion," while Karl Rahner felt that "the Christianity of the 21st century will be mystical." John Paul II, in the same context, has said: "my contact with representatives of non-Christian spiritual traditions ... has confirmed me in the view that the future of mission depends to a great extent on contemplation. Unless the missionary is a contemplative, he cannot proclaim Christ in a credible way." (19) Indeed, the Holy Father calls our time a time of "religious revival." (20)

Looking about and around us, we can see the truth in the words of André Malraux, Karl Rahner and Pope St. John Paul II. Religion has an important place in shaping the sociological and political changes that are shaping the end of this century. Some examples:

- *In Islam*, despite an undesirable proselytism, there have been evident indications of a new awareness of transcendence...

- *Hinduism*, containing a powerful sense of sacred immanence, served Gandhi as he led India to independence...

- Both *Buddhism*, with its metaphysical strains leading to inner freedom, and *Confucianism* which searches for cosmic, political and sociological harmony have promoted the Chinese revolution...

- In *Christianity*, it is important to note the influence of new varieties of prayer, commitments of solidarity to support poor immigrants in both North America and Europe, the work of basic communities in challenging African dictatorships, while becoming a major force in reestablishing human rights in Latin America and Asia, as well as the Polish Church's significant role in a new political model being established in Poland and the rest of eastern Europe.

In all of this, many of the people of God identified as Christians, have been putting aside a routine to their practice of the faith for a committed way of living the Gospel. The influence of religious conviction is therefore clear, often positive, and unfortunately more than occasionally negative as the arrogant ways of blind fundamentalism in each of the aforementioned movements has reared its ugly head.

## 4) Discerning the signs of the times... How do you read the signs of the times?

The times of the Apparition were fascinating because it was an era of change.

"Our times are both momentous and fascinating. While on the one hand people seem to be pursuing material prosperity and to be sinking ever deeper into consumerism and materialism, on the other hand we are witnessing a desperate search for meaning, the need for an inner life and a desire to learn new forms and methods of meditation and prayer. Not only in cultures with strong religious elements, but also in secularized societies, the spiritual dimension of life is being sought after as an antidote to dehumanization." (21)

All changes contain that which is good and often that which is less than good. In the face of change, there is always the danger of living in fear, of closing in upon oneself, of returning to the past... We, the Missionaries of La Salette, in light of our tradition, ought to be able to discern the signs of the times and make the necessary decisions to direct our apostolic action.

I hope that all may be open to... make this year a privileged time of personal, community and apostolic renewal... Do not be afraid to be creative in responding to the problems of the Church and the world today, and to find the necessary solutions to these challenges. Do not fear to let yourselves be guided by the Holy Spirit who wishes "to make all things new," (22) until "God may be all in all." (23) Under the protection of Mary, continue to discern the signs of the times and to respond with fidelity and courage.

**Reflection Questions:**

- Fr. Perin asks us to reflect on our personal mission. What does "Following the Lord" call forth from you?

- What are your dreams and hopes of the future: for the world, for the Church, in the La Salette Family, and in your life?

• We are called to discern "the signs of the times". How do you understand or see the signs of the times these days?

**Endnotes:**

(1) Pedro Casaldaliga and José Maria Vigil, *Political Holiness: A Spirituality of Liberation*, Orbis Books, 1994.

(2) Pope John Paul II, *Letter to the La Salette General Chapter*, May of 2000.

(3) *La Salette General Chapter*, Rome, 2000, Decision II

(4) Ibid.

(5) Ibid.

(6) Jaouen, Jean, M.S., *La Salette au regard de l'Église*, 1981, pgs. 284-287.

(7) Pope John Paul II, 1996, *Letter to the Bishop of Grenoble, in honor of the 150th anniversary of the La Salette Apparition.*

(8) Mgr. William Bernard Ullathorne, Bishop of Birmingham

(9) Fr. Donald Paradis, M.S., *The Missionaries of La Salette: From France to North America*, 1992, pp 26-28

(10) Rule of Life, n. 7

(11) Ibid., n. 29

(12) Cf. John 6:25

(13) Rule of Life, n. 24

(14) Mark 1:17

(15) Rule of Life, n. 3

(16) *Centesimus Annus*, n. 3

(17) Fr. Donald Paradis, M.S., idem, p. 122

(18) *Evangelii Nuntiandi*, 19

(19) *Redemptoris Missio*, 91

(20) *Idem.*, 38

(21) *Idem.*

(22) Cf. Revelation 21:5

(23) Cf. 1 Corinthians 15:28

# Section 3 –
# Mission and Activities

# Chapter 13 —
# Essays on Reconcilers for the World

## By Very Rev. Silvano Marisa, M.S.,
## Superior General of the Missionaries of La Salette

Our common baptism is a call to intimacy with the Lord. It is a vocation which is a lifelong call given to all. In the past, speaking about vocations used to center on priest and religious. Now we more correctly speak about a vocation or call to the church for every baptized member of the church.

At La Salette Mary gave us an invitation to "make her message known to all her people." She echoed the words of her Son: "Go, therefore, and make disciples of all nations, baptizing them in the name of the Father, and of the Son, and of the holy Spirit, teaching them to observe all that I have commanded you" (Matthew 28:19-20a).

Fr. Silvano Marisa, M.S., La Salette Superior General (from 2012 - )

## A Marian Call to Unity and Reconciliation:

But our call to La Salette is a Marian call, a gospel way of life and a response. For Mary's call, we should look at her example. She was the one who called us to serve the Lord, be available to serve our fellow humans, meet them. She asks us to put our life at the service of mercy, love and forgiveness.

Our La Salette vocation is to unity – among ourselves, with God and with the Church. All this is in view of our call to be reconcilers. This was the theme of our 2012 General Chapter: *"May all be one for the mission of reconciliation."* Reconciliation should imbue our entire life and all our ministries since it is the specific charism of our congregation.

# Our Vision of a Gifted and United Community:

Our recent distillation of our common vision comes from our 2012 General Chapter:

"We are a *Christ-centered community* committed to the ministry of reconciliation with the laity, as a living out of the event and the message of the apparition of Our Lady of La Salette. *Attentive to the voice of God*, who speaks through the signs of the times, our life and mission are lived out in the light of the option for the poor and the demands of justice and peace. *Enriched by our multicultural diversity*, through collaboration and solidarity between provinces and regions and manifested in intercultural living and work situations, we move beyond the limitations of Provinces and Regions. Our community life and shared leadership are based on dialogue, discernment, sincerity and the active participation of all."

**CHRIST-CENTERED COMMUNITY:** Our vision is centered on Christ; he is "the rule of our life," as is mentioned in our La Salette Rule (#5). In community we daily try to live in the spirit of reconciliation.

**WITH THE LAITY:** Our La Salette call and charism is not limited to religious and priests and sisters alone but is a more open call to every person of faith, young and old, men and woman. With us, we make a grand La Salette family; our charism is living, actual and for the participation and benefit of everyone. It is also a much-needed charism in our world of today.

Although the La Salette Missionaries cannot be everywhere, our La Salette laity can enter in unencumbered and without hesitation. We thank God for all the youth who are responding positively to the call of Mary, first to Maximin and Melanie, and now to even more "Maximins" and "Melanies" who wish to make her message known today by their life and service.

Attentive to the voice of God: In order to do this, we should also be attentive to God speaking through the signs of the times. It is a mission which must be accomplished with the help of the people we serve. Some of the elements of our call are traditional (our history) and some brand new (new ways of presenting the message of Mary, based on the core message of the Gospel). Also, we are to concentrate on the church's "preferential option of the poor."

Enriched by our multicultural diversity: Another aspect of our call is to try to live in a community which is international and transcultural. Those who wish to join us should realize this is part and parcel of La Salette life everywhere. There is no culture which we as La Salettes can't serve in some way at some time. All situations are part of and effected by the incarnation of Jesus. All God's people can benefit from Christ's care and service, concretely and lovingly given. This is what Jesus meant by making disciples of all nations.

## Our Future in Serving God's People:

By nature, I am an optimist and my vision is quite positive. The world of today needs our message of reconciliation and hope. The Virgin invites us to share her message and live within the support of a caring community. This is certainly the spirit of the Gospel.

We have a great mission before us, with the help of God. Our ministry is needed and truly limitless. The words of Jesus before his passion were: "I pray that... they may all be one" (John 17:20-21). This is our prayer, our mission, our call, and our life.

## Reconcilers for the World:

Every year, September is a welcome invitation for La Salette Missionaries and all those devoted to her merciful Apparition. Her feast on September 19th challenges us to reflect on our personal history and call, as well as on our religious and apostolic identity in the light of the La Salette event (*La Salette Rule*, 1).

This is a grace we share in particular with the La Salette Sisters and with the growing movement of La Salette Laity. They work by our side in proclaiming the Gospel in so many apostolic contexts throughout the world, and with numerous friends and benefactors, ever present to us, humanly and spiritually, in prayer and solidarity...

This year's celebration comes a few months after our 32nd General Chapter, which took place in Las Termas de Rio Hondo (Argentina) and traced the path that the Congregation is called to walk over the next six years...

Every Province and Region is called in the coming years to adapt its own formation program to the... one approved by the recent General Chapter. I hope this collective effort will allow the Congregation to grow as a whole chiefly as a community seeking an identity in harmony with the spirit and charism rooted in the La Salette event.

Furthermore, the Chapter insistently asks us all to "revisit" our manner of being religious and priests in today's world and Church, in order to respond ever better to the Lord's urgent call to be "salt of the earth and light of the world."

To this end I believe it necessary to raise a few questions that require of us the dearest and most committed response:

• As La Salette religious and laity, missioned to witness joyfully to a life filled with the experience of God, *are we still capable* of renewing the fervor of our hearts, of making it beat with free and total love like that of Christ?... (La Salette Rule, # 10cp)

• *Are we still capable*, by the example of our lives and the courage of our words, to renew the fervor of the hearts of the men and women whom the Lord places on our ministerial path?

• And finally, *are we truly convinced* that the exemplary nature of our life as religious and laity... is our first and primary mode of evangelization, capable of reaching everyone, everywhere?

I am fully convinced that the future of our "specialized" and charismatic presence in the Church and the world will depend on our personal and community response to these questions.

May the celebration of this lovely anniversary become, then, for all of us an opportunity for deep renewal of heart and spirit, in the light of the Beautiful Lady's message, without which our life may prove to be empty, arid and pointless. May all touched to the heart by the message and ministry of La Salette bring all her people closer to her Son Jesus.

Fr. Beatus Christian Urassa was ordained Bishop of Sumbawanga, Tanzania, on June 24, 2018 and was in Rome for the Program for

Formation for New Bishops. He knows La Salette quite well since he was a welcome guest in our Roman community for several years in the early 2000's while pursuing further studies. We wish him a fruitful ministry as Bishop among the people God has entrusted to his care.

May the Virgin Reconciler of La Salette, our Patroness, help us all to live in fidelity to her Son's Gospel, to which we are called to witness... and make known, without hesitation or fear, to every human being on God's good Earth.

## Our Religious Call to an Intercultural Way of Life:

**Editor:** *This portion of the article was addressed to La Salette Religious but applies well to our common baptismal call to all God's people that "all may be one" (John 17:21); edited for length.*

Something significant has been happening right before our eyes: many religious communities in the first world, including our own, have become or are in the process of becoming international, as more and more of their members come from various parts of their respective congregations. To keep this unfolding phenomenon from giving rise to needless crises, fears or preoccupations, we must see it with the eyes of faith. Then, what we see is a gift of the Holy Spirit.

### New Horizons for Us to Discover:

The challenge facing all these communities, as well as our own, is how to prepare to boldly welcome new horizons for our future religious life, both in community living and in ministry. We will need

Beatus-Christian-Urasa, Bishop of Sumbawanga, Tanzania, friend of La Salette

to be open to new experiences of genuine communion, unimaginable not that long ago. Our world is rapidly evolving, and at this point, it is sick of exaggerated personalism and deeply wounded by never-ending divisions.

It is a world fearful of those who seem different to the point of wanting to erect walls and barriers between people. It is in this world that we religious are called to build bridges, to foster dialogue and to show the way that leads to collaboration and working effectively at a common task together. It is in this world that we are called to lead people to value whatever is good and creative in the other person so that together we might better live our gospel mission.

## To Become Prophets of Reconciliation:

Simply put, the challenge before us is to become prophets for a different kind of world, a world in which people are able to forgive, to reconcile differences and to love. Then, no longer will cultural diversity be optional but an everyday reality of life.

Our international dimension is our starting point and it can lead to an intercultural way of living providing we are willing to commit ourselves to listening and dialoguing with others. As La Salette Missionaries, this way of living should come naturally to us. It is part and parcel of the DNA we inherited from the Marian event of September 19, 1846.

What we need to do is to make sure that, when we look at the other person, we see the differences that are there, but we recall that those very differences are gifts and sources of wealth for ourselves and for our entire community.

Inculturation has a role to play in an intercultural way of living, as the Venezuelan, Fr. Arturo Sosa, S.J., Superior General of the Society of Jesus, points out.

"There are two complimentary aspects to inculturation. First of all, we must become inculturated in our own culture and that calls for acquiring a critical appreciation of it. Without a proper inculturation in one's own culture, there can be no real personal growth nor actual participation in its social dimensions. It is an essential condition allowing for the possibility of relationships in a diverse cultural context...

"The second aspect is inculturation in some other culture. It's as if we were to move into another family. We come with who and what we are, and we enter into a whole other world of social relationships, relationships which give meaning to life, give rise to community and provide for the necessities of life. It's always a dialogue between the culture out of which we came and the one into which we are moving... To arrive at the home of someone else, wholly intent on making one's home there, is the incentive that allows us to draw from our own culture what we will need to eventually become fully part of the new culture."

## "Abram" Became "Abraham"
## When He Placed His Life in God's Hands:

What we are talking about here is an experience often found in the bible. Abram, for example, was living peacefully in his own home, quite content being with his own family and the people who made up his extended household. After hearing a call from the Lord, he leaves his country and heads for a cultural unknown, strengthened by his enduring faith in God and fully open to whatever new experience this journey might offer. He did not cling to the personal tranquility he had been enjoying nor to the reassuring stability his own culture provided...

The call of Vatican II to return to our foundational sources is a call to an ever more creative faithfulness to the very dynamic of the Incarnation that Jesus underwent, as well as to a genuine openness to meet head-on the challenges each moment of history might place on our path, as we pursue our mission as vowed religious. We are an integral part of the Church for whom evangelization is its very reason for being...

This brings us to this simple description of an intercultural way of living:

"It's a reciprocal exchange between cultures which has the potential to transform and enrich all those involved... Inculturation has led religious life to experience a multi-cultural way of living as the normal state of congregations and communities around the world. The very fact of living peacefully in a multi-cultural setting is the fruit of authentic inculturation and represents a significant step forward in the lived experience of vowed religious." (Arturo Sosa, S.J., *Interculturation, Catholicity, and Consecrated Life*, Meeting of Union of Superiors General, 2017).

## Revealing Our Intercultural Attitudes – Near and Far:

Every day, we can witness for ourselves the international dimension of our own La Salette Congregation. There are La Salette Missionaries on all the continents. And yes, sometimes, our intercultural way of living is not all that evident. It is not a given. It remains a major challenge as we look to our future.

It is the same challenge now facing our entire Church and our whole world. We can safely say however that it is being built up ever so slowly. But if we truly want it to become a concrete reality among us, each one of us will have to foster genuine openness to all those who are from another culture, so as to see them as they are and listen to them attentively. This we need to do as we plan and work together, always respecting our respective differences even as we collaborate...

On the wider congregational level, it is fair to say that there has always been some intercultural life since the day we began to spread throughout the world. Presently that is the case in Haiti and Canada (Madagascar and USA), in Tanzania (Philippines and India), in Mozambique (Brazil and Angola), and likewise at our Shrine at La Salette in France.

The latter has truly become a kind of laboratory for intercultural community life and ministry, with its distinctly new way of bringing many cultures together to live in the same community and to share the joys and concerns arising from a common ministry. Let's also call to mind the collaboration between Poland and Switzerland, as well as between Italy, France and Madagascar, and again between the Philippines, India and the United States.

Our international gatherings have certainly been prime moments when the members of the congregation have had the opportunity to see for themselves that intercultural living, far from being a mere utopia, is actually feasible and clearly has the potential to open up new horizons for the future of religious life and ministry...

## The Lay Mission of Reconciliation:

**Editor:** *The following was a homily given at the closing Mass of the First International La Salette Lay Encounter, held in La Salette, France, from September 1-10, 2011.*

Dear pilgrims, La Salette laity and other friends, all of you are welcome here at the Shrine of La Salette! We gather in this place dedicated to the Virgin Mary, to celebrate the Eucharist at the place visited by Our Lady on September 19, 1846. From all over the world we have gathered here to recognize how the message of the Virgin in tears has affected and continues to affect our personal lives, and that of our families, as well as our work and efforts. We were called to be messengers of the gospel in this world today which, as Pope Paul VI said, needs more credible witnesses than teachers.

## The Basis of La Salette Spirituality:

La Salette Laity of Europe meet with others in 2012

Reconciliation, dialogue and listening to the Word of God and each other, to forgiveness and hospitality, to the fight against social and economic injustice, is the basis of La Salette spirituality that draws its prophetic energy from the very mystery of the apparition.

Here at La Salette, Our Lady tells us that God needs us, that the Church needs us, that our world needs us. And we, by our presence, want to proclaim loudly that we are willing to place our lives at the service of the cause of the kingdom of God with all our brothers and sisters around the world.

You are not alone because the La Salette Missionaries, whose congregation was founded just a few years after the apparition, on February 2, 1852, with the first religious profession of the early Fathers of La Salette, walk with you today and share the same concerns and expectations that deal with the challenges of witness and proclamation of the Gospel in today's world.

By living the spirituality and charism that result from the apparition, you participate fully in the life and ministry of the Congregation of the Missionaries of Our Lady of La Salette. You are likewise a member of the great spiritual La Salette family which, ultimately doing its best, seeks through all of you to reveal a new face of the Church and, at the same time, also a new way of acting and living in the Church.

## The Identity of La Salette Laity:

Be proud, therefore, to be sent as Lay La Salettes, sent by the Beautiful Lady to proclaim the Gospel and bear witness in our society, which is deeply thirsting for the Infinite and Absolute, for the love of God the Father who is full of tenderness and rich in mercy.

What identifies you as La Salette Laity? We spoke a great deal during this First International Lay Encounter in which all participated with enthusiasm and profited on behalf of so many other fellow associates scattered around the entire world.

Summarily we can say that the La Salette Laity must have close ties to the La Salette Missionaries or the Sisters of La Salette, to a religious woman or man, or to a La Salette community, feeding on his or her spirituality of reconciliation stemming from the apparition.

155

Furthermore, one must strive to live out the challenges of one's baptism in the Church and in one's own community. These are essential commitments, but which could be amazingly effective in our mission every day. It is up to us to live them and put them into practice.

## A Mission of Witness and Reconciliation:

When we say Gospel, we speak of renewal, not only because the spirit gives life and life is in itself a continuous movement but also because the Word of God is yeast which heat causes the dough rise, enlivening the search for new ways of approaching the message of salvation to all people and in all places. Lay Christians are called by God to give themselves, wherever possible, to the sanctification of the world by witnessing to the beauty of being Christian and living as Christians. Living in the "secular world" means to be fully and consciously in this world of ours – this is the specific vocation of any lay Christian.

In September of 2011, in his message sent to the Asian Catholic Laity Congress convening in Seoul, South Korea, Pope Benedict XVI identified key areas of special emphasis in evangelizing today, to witness to the evangelical truth: marriage and family life, defense of life from conception until natural death, care of the poor and marginalized, the forgiveness of enemies, the practice of justice and solidarity in all the different work environments.

And he also invited every single Catholic to follow the example of St. Paul to bring to others truth, joy and beauty that give meaning and direct their whole lives, taking care, of course, not to be discouraged in confronting the problems that normally accompany their presence and mission in the world and in the Church today.

*"Do not be afraid"* – the Beautiful Lady still tells us today to be credible witnesses of the Good News of her Son and tell the world that God is a Father who loves his children with an infinite love, especially those who have fallen away from him. He is always ready to meet us, embrace us, forgive us, and then invite us to share a moment of rest, of joy at the table of his Word and of the Eucharist.

May the Virgin of La Salette protect each of you as well as your families and friends and bless all your efforts along your mission journey.

She needs all of us!

**Reflection Questions:**

• This article shares a strong hope for the future based on a new partnership of Missionary Fathers, Sisters, Brothers and Laity. What signs of hope and growth of the mission of spreading the message do you see?

• There has always been a relationship between the Congregation of Missionaries and Lay People, beginning with, of course, Melanie and Maximin spreading the message, pilgrims visiting the site of the apparition well before the religious community was formed. In every country and ministry, the partnership of priests, brother, sisters, and lay people has created a strong foundation for mission and development. What has been your experience of this partnership? What roles have you played?

• The messenger shares more than the Story. We are called to witness to the spirituality and charism to others. Share some experiences of your witness and activities that have fostered reconciliation and evangelization.

# Chapter 14 —
# What is Mission?
By Fr. Jack Nuelle, M.S.

Crucifixion, St John of the Cross Church, Middlebury, Connecticut

As Jesus was dying on the cross, he was very conscious of what was happening to him and around him. In the relative silence of his agony and crucifixion, Jesus left a final testimony to his life and mission. Few words, but a stupendous summation!

All four Gospels record Jesus speaking and dialoguing while suffering on the cross. In its own way each instance reflects the meaning of Jesus' life, Passion and awaited Resurrection. In other words, his mission. They can help us understand both the divine mission on which the Father sent him, and the human life through which he accomplished it. On the cross Jesus' life and mission of reaching out to others were bound together in an unparalleled collaboration of divinity and humanity. In his divinity he continued to forgive. He forgave his persecutors (who did not ask for it) and the repentant thief (who did). In his humanity he reached out to his sorrowing mother and to the disciple whom he loved. "(Jesus) said to his mother, 'Woman, behold your son.' Then he said to the disciple, Behold, your mother.' (1) Widowed and soon childless, Mary would have been destitute.

With filial love, he confided her to the care of one of his best friends, John, who took her into his own home. This raised her interaction

158

with all of her son's disciples to a more intimate level. Mary once again had a family. She had been involved in the mission of her son since the moment of his conception. Without hesitation her engagement took on a new form. John, and indeed the whole community of Jesus' followers, now had a mother to care for. They also gained a mother who would cherish them. With the life of her crucified Son "stored up... in her heart," (2) she would now turn to his beloved brothers and sisters to care for them, watch over them, and help them to grow.

After the Resurrection, Jesus spent time with that community of faithful followers. "He presented himself alive to them by many proofs after he had suffered, appearing to them during forty days and speaking about the kingdom of God. While meeting with them, he enjoined them not to depart from Jerusalem, but to wait for "the promise of the Father about which you have heard me speak." (3)

Following Jesus' Ascension, Mary was still among them as they awaited the coming of the Spirit. "All these devoted themselves with one accord to prayer, together with some women, and Mary the mother of Jesus, and his brothers." (4) There she witnessed the Apostles, the first whom Jesus had sent on mission, choose the one to take over the ministry and apostolate which Judas abandoned. (5) Mary had received her mission from the lips of her son on the cross – to be a mother to Jesus' disciples. It is a charge she would never abandon.

The Apparition of Mary at La Salette, almost two millennia later, would reflect that same attitude.

## Understanding Mission:

Mission, as an English word, has undergone significant changes since it first became part of every-day usage at the end of the sixteenth century. Today, it has a large variety of meanings. Every industry, school, church, or organization has its "mission statement." So often the word refers to a goal, campaign, ideal, plan, objective, or purpose. People are "on a mission" to accomplish their targeted assignment, to carry out a designated task, or to produce tangible results in a specific time-frame. Mission is used also to embody a strongly felt personal aim or ambition.

From a biblical point of view, however, those examples may underline certain aspects of Jesus' mission, but they all fall short of understanding the substance and significance of his mission.

Mission (derived from the Latin verb mittere) necessarily involves the notion of sending; it could denote a person or persons sending or being sent, as well as sending information or objects. Mission is never a static reality but a dynamic one. The reason for being "sent" can be as wide as the horizon and unlimited as the sky, short-term and long-term, fulfilled by one individual and by a like-minded cluster of people, and both secular and religious in nature.

## Scripture and Mission:

Surprisingly, the actual word "mission" is used less than 15 times in the Bible. In the Hebrew Scriptures it is often, but not always, used in reference to a divine task. We can identify some elements of mission from the episode wherein King Saul forfeited his kingship. Mission originates in God, required obedience in execution, and, when accomplished faithfully, becomes a source of blessing; but, when done half-heartedly, it results in rejection. (6)

The three times the word mission is used in the New Testament, it always refers to the apostolic task of preaching. "While they were worshiping the Lord and fasting, the Holy Spirit said, "Set apart for me Barnabas and Saul for the work to which I have called them." Then, completing their fasting and prayer, they laid hands on them and sent them off. So they, sent forth by the Holy Spirit, went down to Seleucia and from there sailed to Cyprus." (7)

This use and meaning of the word mission in the Bible are the same not only in the English language translations, but in most modern languages and recent translations. Often the reason for sending is noted as a journey, a business, an errand, or something similar.

While use of the word mission is scarce, the concept of "sending" pervades the Bible. It occurs over 2,000 times and can cover a variety of circumstances. A few examples would include sending away or dismissal: God dismisses Adam and Even from the garden; (8) sending for or calling someone: King Saul sent for David before going to fight Goliath; (9) empowering or sending a person to complete an assignment: God sent Moses to Pharaoh with the message, "Let my people go." (10) The biblical use of the concept overwhelmingly means *to send someone or to be sent with authority in order to accomplish a divine task.* The Bible could indeed be called God's book of Mission!

From the very first pages of the Bible, God, the Creator, was often the one sending: "…there was no field shrub on earth and no grass of the field had sprouted, for the LORD God had sent no rain upon the earth," (11) "…and the LORD rained down sulfur upon Sodom…" (12) When God did the sending, it was not mission. He did so with his own authority. Mission occurred when God sent another, mainly the prophets in the Hebrew Scriptures, to proclaim God's word. "Whom shall I send? Who will go for us?" 'Here I am,' I said; 'send me!'" (13) Angels were used as messengers; Gabriel was sent to announce to Mary that she was chosen to be the mother of the Savior. (14) The idea of mission is excellently exemplified when Jesus proclaims: "As the Father sent me, so I send you." (15) Later he would send the Holy Spirit to empower the disciples to be his "witnesses in Jerusalem, throughout Judea and Samaria, and to the ends of the earth." (16)

## A People Set Apart through a Covenant of Love

From their very beginnings, the Jewish people considered themselves to be a people set apart; they were descendants of Abraham to whom God had gratuitously given a mission: "Go forth from your land, your relatives, and from your father's house to a land that I will show you," (17) and an extraordinary, multi-layered promise: of a new land, (18) of numerous descendants, (19) of universal blessings (20) that would alter the path of humanity. Accepting this promise created a distinctive unilateral covenant with Abraham. It was distinct because it was a gratuitous covenant of friendship. It was unilateral because the only person needing to be faithful to the promise was God. Abraham lived up to his part of the covenant – he left his homeland. God also was faithful, and that faithfulness (21) would find fulfillment in Jesus, the Christ.

God's ways are seldom our ways. The 430-year sojourn in Egypt changed the descendants of Abraham. Tradition helped them remember their roots, but daily contact with the Egyptian lifestyle made it difficult for them to remain faithful to the ideals of the covenant. God accomplished his plan, strangely enough, by leading his covenant people, now known as Israelites, through the miseries of Egypt toward their promised land flowing with milk and honey.

## Called through Fidelity to Mission:

Mediated through Moses, another different type of covenant was inaugurated without annulling the previous one. Unlike the first covenant, this one was bilateral, with obligations and promises on both sides. It formed a singular relationship between God and his people. "I shall take you as my own people and I will be your God." (22) This

*Moses Lifts His Arms For Victory*
**by John Everett Millais**
(1829-1896)

assurance was grounded in a text from the Torah: "For you are a people holy to the LORD, your God; the LORD, your God, has chosen you from all the peoples on the face of the earth..." (23) Faithfulness was to be the touchstone. "...if you obey me completely and keep my covenant, you will be my treasured possession among all peoples, though all the earth is mine." (24) Their answer was "yes." (25) "All the people answered together, 'Everything the LORD has said, we will do.'"

God saw the Israelites as a people precious, honored and loved. But their sojourn in Egypt, especially the years of slavery, had made them an obstinate, stubborn, and stiff-necked people. To call them back, God sent his prophets over and over again to carry out a single divine mission: Moses, Joshua, Samuel, Isaiah, Jeremiah, Hosea, Joel were some of his chosen emissaries, all fundamentally repeating the same refrain: "...return to me with your whole heart." (26) God had made a promise (27) and chosen a people through whom it would be fulfilled. "Throughout the many centuries of turbulent relationship between God and people, God has always invited people to return. No offense was able to create a definitive break. No matter how many bridges humanity blew up, God always rebuilt them. The Lord is always and in many ways saying, '*Come closer.*'" (28)

Through a seemingly impossible prophesy (29). the promised Messiah would come. His name would be Emmanuel, (30) or Jesus, because he is the one who would save his people from their sins. His life would span the Old Covenant and inaugurate the New. The opening words of the Letter to the Hebrews illustrate this splendidly: "In times past, God spoke in partial and various ways to our ancestors through the prophets; in these last days, he spoke to us through a son, whom he made heir of all things and through whom he created the universe..." (31)

## The New Covenant's Great Commissioning

New Testament writings often allude to both the Abrahamic and Mosaic covenants, with the law and promises they contain. Many of the disputes between Jesus and the Pharisees were centered around blind obedience to laws. Jesus called for his disciples to be open-minded and inclusive, as shown in the Sermon on the Mount (32) and his final Great Commissioning. (33) The law on which their fidelity would be judged was that of Love. "I give you a new commandment: love one another. As I have loved you, so you also should love one another." (34)

Having chosen a specific band of followers (disciples and apostles), Jesus promised that the Holy Spirit would convey witnessing power to them. On the eve of his resurrection the Lord Jesus gave them the first glimpse of an extraordinary parting gift to them: "Receive the holy Spirit." (35) Pentecost would unleash that glorious gift into motion. From that day, His Apostles and disciples began to refer publicly to Jesus as "Messiah" and "Christ."

The manifestation of the Spirit became daily more apparent. The divine assistance of the Spirit was dynamic. Day by day they assimilated into their lives what they remembered, not only what the Master had taught them, but especially how they were destined to identify with his message. Centered on the "breaking of the bread," another miraculous gift of his love, the community experienced Jesus alive in their midst. Death had not taken him from them. Sent by the Father to become the gradual unfolding of the mystery of Salvation, Jesus revealed the Spirit dwelling also in them. From that time on, the joint mission (36) of Jesus and the Spirit began to unfurl into the lives of every baptized person, energizing them to be ambassadors. That joint mission is what formed the Church. (37)

## Power of the Holy Spirit:

The power of the Spirit, unleashed by Jesus after his resurrection, turned the world around as nothing before it. One thing, however, remained constant. As exemplified from the first pages of the Bible to our present day, God does not override our freedom to choose, nor our human weakness. The joint mission of Jesus and the Spirit continues today in the Church and in the world, giving strength and encouragement through community.

Human history repeatedly shows that God elected to call people to share in his mission. From the initial promise of Genesis 3:15 to Christ's victorious Resurrection, and onward to this day, God's economy of grace has guided the world. Although public divine revelation "culminate[d] in the person and mission of the incarnate Word, Jesus Christ" (38) the presence and action of the Spirit did not. The Spirit's transforming presence surprised us, led us beyond established boundaries, and opened for us a wealth of grace hidden in the cultures of the world.

New Testament mission was inspired by Jesus' call for transformative action (metanoia or a fundamental transformation of thinking and living). Chapters 10 and 11 of Acts illustrate that this beautiful transformation can be contagious and an essential ingredient in mission. The Apostolic Letters from Paul, Peter, John, and others exhort Christians on all sides of mission to clothe themselves with Christ (39) and put on the mind of the Lord. (40) It necessitates not just change but transformation. Modern-day Apostolic Exhortations from Popes continue that theme, as in *The Joy of the Gospel*: "Every

Christian is a missionary to the extent that he or she has encountered the love of God in Christ Jesus: we no longer say that we are "disciples" and "missionaries", but rather that we are always "missionary disciples." (41)

**Reflection Questions:**

•We have been called to mission by virtue of our Baptism and by hearing the message of La Salette. How do you feel you have been sent? What roles or ministry are you playing in the world today?

•The ability to be missionary calls for a fidelity and insightfulness of God's Covenant with us. How do you describe the love of God in your life? How does God love you and call you into relationship with Him and His Kingdom?

•The Great Commissioning and the power of the Holy Spirit combined leads us to build the Church in our midst. How have you been a minister of reconciliation and healing in your life? Share an example.

**Endnotes:**

(1) Jn 19:26-27

(2) Lk 2:51

(3) Acts 1:3-4

(4) Acts 1:14

(5) Acts 1:25

(6) 1 Samuel 15:1-24

(7) Acts 13:2-4

(8) Gen 3:23

(9) Sam 17:31-32

(10) Ex 5:1

(11) Gen 2:5

(12) Gen 19:24

(13) Is 6:8

(14) Lk 1:26

(15) Jn 20:21

(16) Acts 1:8

(17) Gen 12:1

(18) Gen 12:7

(19) Gen 22:17

(20) Gen 22:18

(21) The idea of faithfulness is central to the Bible. It implies steadfast commitment to whatever one is bound to by a pledge, duty, or obligation. It contains a universal idea of being the best possible version of yourself as you can. "Know thyself" is a Greek motto indicating that man must stand and live according his nature. William Shakespeare, in his play Hamlet Act 1, Scene III, expresses it well: "To thine own self be true"

(22) Exodus 6:7

(23) Deuteronomy 14:2

(24) Exodus 19:5

(25) Exodus 19:8

(26) Joel 2:12

(27) Genesis 3:15

(28) Normand Théroux, *The Face of the Reconciler: Sharing the La Salette Charism of Reconciliation*, Attleboro, MA: La Salette Communications Center, 2017 16-17

(29) Isaiah 7:14

(30) Matthew 1:21

(31) Hebrews 1:1-2

(32) Mathew, chapters 5-7

(33) Matthew 28: 18-20

(34) John 13:34

(35) John 20:22

(36) *Catechism of the Catholic Church (CCC)*, #689 and #690

(37) Stephen B. Bevans and Roger P. Schroeder, *Prophetic Dialogue: Reflections on Christian Mission Today*, Maryknoll, NY: Orbis Books, 2011, Chapter 1: "The Mission Has a Church: An Invitation to the Dance," 9-18.

The exposé positions that the Church's mission begins not with the church or mission, but with God whose very nature is mission. This means that the starting point for missiological reflection is not the church, but God's engagement with the world and the church through the communicating Word and empowering Spirit.

The primitive community of Jesus' followers slowly came to recognize themselves a distinct group, apart from their Jewish brethren, but not apart from the mission of Jesus. I quote from page 10: "Now, however, at least in germ, they began to see that in Jesus something new had begun, that God's mission to the world—begun in the Spirit from the first moment of creation and continued concretely in Jesus—had been handed over to them. And now they were called to continue this mission to the ends of the earth—in every nation, in every culture, in every time period. Now … what had begun to become clear is that God's mission has a church."

(38) CCC, #53

(39) Galatians 3:27

(40) Philippians 2:15

(41) http://www.vatican.va/content/francesco/en/apost_exhortations/documents/papa-francesco_esortazione-ap_20131124_evangelii-gaudium. # 120

# Chapter 15 —
# Mary Enfleshes Mission
# Through Her Apparition
## By Fr. Jack Nuelle, M.S.

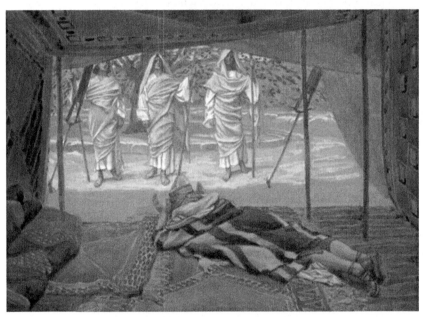

*Abraham and the Three Angels*
by Jacques Joseph Tissot (1836-1902), *The Jewish Museum*

We have quoted extensively from the Bible, which is generally understood, in Abrahamic faith traditions in which the Catholic faith participates, as "public" revelation by which God makes known his very self, his will, and his divine plan (creation and salvation) to the world of human beings. Catholics call this revelation the "deposit of faith", which came to its completion at the end of the Apostolic Age. It is more than just moral or ethical information revealed by God. "It is called 'Revelation' because in it God gradually made himself known to men, to the point of becoming man himself, in order to draw to himself the whole world and unite it with himself through his Incarnate Son, Jesus Christ." (1)

# Public and Private Revelation

God's public revelation is complete, yet it "has not been made completely explicit; it remains for Christian faith gradually to grasp its full significance over the course of the centuries." (2) "Throughout the ages, there have been so-called 'private' revelations, some of which have been recognized by the authority of the Church. They do not belong, however, to the deposit of faith." (3) They can, nevertheless, help to open our minds and hearts to a better reading of the signs of the times in the light of Gospel truths. One such "private" revelation, recognized by the authority of the Church, is the Apparition of La Salette.

I wish only to mention the essential part of the canonical judgment of approbation, signed on the fifth anniversary of the Event, September 19, 1851, to illustrate how this event complies with the ecclesial requirements for "private revelation". Bishop Philibert de Bruillard, Ordinary of the Diocese of Grenoble in which the event occurred, exercising the authority granted by the Hoy See, promulgated that Pastoral Letter by having it read in solemnly at all parish Masses on November 16, 1851:

> "We judge that the apparition of the Blessed Virgin to two cowherds on the 19th of September, 1846, on a mountain of the chain of the Alps, situated in the parish of La Salette, in the arch-presbytery of Corps, bears within itself all the characteristics of truth, and that the faithful have grounds for believing it indubitable and certain." (4)

"His judgment does not compel us to theological faith. But it does express the prudence of the Church and appeals to ours in order to enlighten it, to strengthen it...." (5) By an act of its ordinary magisterium, the Church has spoken in favor of the authenticity of the apparition. "This means, that because the fact appears as morally certain to her, she invites the faithful to commit themselves to it and receive it as a grace." (6)

# La Salette as Mission – The Beautiful Lady:

Mention is often made to the person who appeared on the slopes of Mount Planeau as "the Beautiful Lady". Both Maximin and Melanie referred to her as such on the day of the Event. (7) That evening, when both of them recited what had happened to them that afternoon, "[t]he old mother of Baptiste Pra began to cry, and with the intuition her simple faith gave her exclaimed: 'This Beautiful Lady can be none other than the Blessed Virgin.'" (8) The next day, Sunday, they retold their story to the pastor of the parish of the town of La Salette, Fr. Jacques Perrin. "As he listened, the good Curé could hardly restrain his tears. 'How fortunate you are my children', he stammered, 'you have seen the Blessed Virgin!'" (9)

Two weeks later, reporting to the Bishop, the parish priest of Corps, Fr. Mélin, attested to his own belief. "The people naturally understood that it was the Blessed Mother. ... My personal conviction, after gathering every proof I could, is the same as that of the faithful." (10) The official verdict from the Church would not be so quickly given.

For the next five years there would be investigations – by church authorities, court lawyers, politicians, and the media. The two children would be drilled on the message, promised money to detract their original statements, threatened with jail time – all to no avail. All pertinent and even non-pertinent facts concerning the Apparition would be debated, pondered, discussed. As mentioned above, in the doctrinal declaration, Bishop de Bruillard would use that same title for the Blessed Virgin, Mary, the Mother of Jesus. Consequently, when people speak of the Blessed Virgin who appeared at La Salette, she is still given the title of "the Beautiful Lady."

## Mission through Presence:

In the opening pages of this article, it was noted that biblical mission, as part of God's special relationship to humans, is understood as sending someone or being sent with authority in order to accomplish a divine task. The overall La Salette Event conforms to that meaning. In fact, certain aspects of that Event can only be fathomed in the light of biblical mission.

Taken as a whole, and therefore in conjunction with the Economy of Grace wherein all is brought together in Christ (11), the apparition of La Salette highlights distinctive aspects of mission. A divine task is not undertaken on one's own initiative. In his Pastoral Letter alluded to above, Bishop de Bruillard notes that "the wonderful consequences of the fact of La Salette are the testimony of God Himself manifesting Himself by miracles..." (12) That declaration confirms the Apparition as not just a simple presence, but presence with a divine intent. Mary's appearance on the slopes of Mount Planeau was seen as an extraordinary way of bringing God's graces into the lives of people. Her message, so easily seen as an indictment of the world in 1846, must also be interpreted as words of hope, calling to repentance. Why else would she have come?

We have testimony of this from a meeting in the Bishop's house already in 1847, wherein was highlighted the "prompt and sustained conversion" of the whole township and its environs in favor of the apparition. On Ascension Day the previous year, not one man had been present in the church; now many came prayerfully. Explaining how conversion might have waned off famine, he stated that, in the Corps township with a population of five to six thousand people, hardly one hundred had not returned to church. (13)

## Mission through Motherly Concern:

It was noted in the opening statements of this chapter that Mary, at the time of her Son's crucifixion, had received her mission from the lips of her son on the cross. She was to be a mother to Jesus' disciples. It is a charge she would never abandon. Similar to the attitude with which Isaiah, centuries before, personalized his mission – "I will go! Send me!" – Mary's intervention at La Salette was personal. She was a mother attentive to her children even in the seemingly insignificant happenings of their lives. The last section of her message – the incident at the Field of Coin – demonstrates this clearly.

The Apparition began in a startling way, reminiscent of God's attentiveness to the needs of his people. God had startled Moses through the burning bush. (14) It was an extraordinary event that showed God's constant care for his people. Similarly, the Event of La Salette shows the motherly awareness Mary has for the needs of her children. At La Salette the Event began with a dazzling light which caught the children off guard when they descended the slopes of Mount Planeau to retrieve their knapsacks. First Melanie, then Maximin were brought to an abrupt halt, struck with amazement by a small, brilliant globe of light below them, scintillating and revolving around itself with great rapidity.

Astonishment turned to fear as the globe expanded and began to open from within.

They first saw a pair of hands covering a face, and, as the globe expand more, they saw hands, arms, sleeves, and finally a person sitting on the rustic stone bench where they had eaten their noonday meal. It was a woman, and she was weeping. Fear immobilized the children where they stood. Melanie, raised her hands in fear, letting go of her shepherd staff. With the bravado of a small boy, Maximin said: "Keep your stick, now! I will hold on to mine, and if she does us any harm, I'll give her a good whack!"

La Salette Madonna seated, painted in Germany

The light surrounding the woman continued to expand as she stood to full stature. The children remained motionless on the slope. The Lady, still robed in light and her face bathed in tears, advanced a little toward them and said, *"Come closer, my children, do not be afraid; I am here to tell you great news."*

As the major protagonist of the Apparition, the Beautiful Lady showed herself to be a mother. With maternal kindness, solicitous for the welfare of her children, she sought to calm their fear. With her first words strange things began to happen. First, the children's fearful attitude changed. They felt reassured, by her voice, irresistibly drawn to the Lady as one would be to a mother. Later they would compare her voice to being like music. Second, they joyfully ran down the slope to meet her, ending up so close that another person could not have passed in between her and them. They could have touched her. Thirdly, they themselves thereby entered the globe of light which a few moments earlier had startled them. It was so englobing that no shadow was cast. Fourthly, they felt that a tender gaze had settled upon them, as if she knew them intimately.

Countless times, Melanie and Maximin would voluntarily retell their story. Interrogations, cross-examinations, insults, quizzes to trip them up, and threats were endless. One facet of their encounter with the Beautiful Lady which they inevitably spoke of on their own, was the quality of the Beautiful Lady's voice. Despite the fact that, she was continually weeping, it was described as tender, soft, sweet, melodious, comforting. In their experience, the children captured the sense of sound and words conveying more than the human ear could detect. "In their childlike simplicity, they declared that her words were rather edible than audible. 'It seemed as if we ate her words.' Truly, her voice flowed into their ears and distilled into their hearts." (15) How close this was to the biblical passage wherein Ezekiel eats the words of God as he receives his mission. (16)

In later interviews, Maximin said: "It takes time and plenty of words to describe the scene of the Apparition, but everything unrolled itself so rapidly before our eyes, that it all happened as it were in the mere twinkling of an eye." (17)

## Mission through Light:

Often mission has been associated with light and grace. Prompted by the Spirit, the elderly Simeon pronounced the notions of light and grace to be synonymous with Jesus. "Now, Master, you may let your servant go in peace, according to your word, for my eyes have seen your salvation, which you prepared in sight of all the peoples, light for revelation to the Gentiles, and glory for your people Israel." (18)

Later Matthew quotes the prophet Isaiah, "...the people who sit in darkness have seen a great light, on those dwelling in a land overshadowed by death light has arisen." (19) Jesus later would transfer that quality to his disciples: "You are light for the world." (20)

The Apparition began with a globe of light. The children heard the words of the Beautiful Lady inviting then close, into the light, as they left their fear behind. Up close, they discovered the source of that light; it was the figure of Christ on the cross which, resting on the breast of the Beautiful Lady, hung around her neck. Fr. Atico Fassini, M.S. helps us to reflect on the phenomenon of light in the message:

"If the Apparition of La Salette carries with it the signs of the Cross of the Lord, it is also very much marked by the Light of the Resurrection. The Apparition was all made of light. It was marked by an intense light, which did not leave any shadow, and this light engulfed in some way the two shepherds, Maximin and Melanie. Mary, her dress, her attitudes, and actions, as well as the two shepherds, were all taken up by this wonderful light of the Kingdom of the Resurrection of Christ, as if it were a new Transfiguration. The tears of Mary flowed down translucent from her eyes. They fell down and disappeared without touching the ground, according to the testimonies of the favored shepherds.

"Everything was Light, Mysterious Light which emanated intensely from the Cross of the Lord, placed on the Heart of the Mother of Sorrows. On this Cross, the Crucified-Risen Christ was resplendent as the Light of the World. It was a cross of suffering and of death, as a result of humanity's sin. The Cross was resplendent of the Life of God. The Cross indeed was the source of the Light of the World. On the Cross, Christ gave himself, freely and totally, for the divine pardon of humanity. By this Cross, Life rises as the Victory over sin and death. Cross and Resurrection! Pardon and Life! The Mystery of Faith!" (21)

## Prophetic Mission:

In early Hebrew Scriptures, prophecy is generally portrayed as human speech on behalf of God, either in written form or verbally. Sometimes this is portrayed as God's own self communicating personally. We see this in the portrayal of the theophany covenant on

Mount Sinai; God speaks and writes the Decalogue, using the first person "I". (22) The later prophets sometimes presented God's revelation, using these same forms. (23)

We encounter this prophetic use in the message of Mary at La Salette. Mary speaks in the first person, just as the Prophets did in the Hebrew Scriptures: "*I gave you six days to work,*" she says, "*I kept the seventh for myself, and no one will give it to me.*" Her whole message brings into focus a bilateral covenanted relationship with a loving God, with duties and promises. Once again, faithfulness would be the touchstone.

## Mission through Tears:

In the initial perception of the Beautiful Lady, the children saw her sitting, her face in her hands, weeping. As she stood, she removed her hands from her face. It was bathed in tears. She wept all the time she spoke with them. Melanie said, "I saw the tears flow from her eyes – they flowed in a steady stream." (24) This abundant flow, in the course of the apparition, is so evocative of Jesus crying over the people of Jerusalem. (25) His were tears of love and pain over a people who refused his message of redemptive love and salvation. Mary's tears reflected that same love and pain.

There was another instance when Jesus wept – as he stood before the tomb of Lazarus. Scripture simply says: "And Jesus wept." (26) Those tears expressed deeper feelings, understood by many around him. "See how he loved him!" (27) Mary's "mysterious tears" were her unvoiced message of love. They spoke eloquently for themselves. They never reached the ground but disappeared as they fell into the light. This unique feature of the weeping mother's presence hopefully still touches the hearts of those who hear her loving message through her tears.

## Mission through Conversion:

The merciful message of the Beautiful Lady was delivered amidst the pain and suffering which people were experiencing daily: ruined crops, famine, disease, poverty, premature infantile death. At first her words seemed to be blaming and condemning. Yet they were delivered in sorrow and tears to draw attention to what humans had done to themselves as they abandoned God. This brought to the forefront the loving relationship God always seeks with us – I will be their God and they will be my people!

Contextualized in the lives of the people of the district of Corps in 1846, this seeming condemnation gave way to pivotal words of hope: *"If they are converted, rocks and stones will turn into heaps of wheat, and potatoes will be self-sown in the fields."* How can one not parallel these words with the critical preaching of Jesus in the Gospel, "Repent, for the kingdom of heaven is at hand." (28) To be part of that promised kingdom, (29) requires a metanoia experience, accepting a new heart. "I will place my law within them, and write it upon their hearts; I will be their God, and they shall be my people." (30) With her words she reinforces the meaning of metanoia and faithfulness.

Conversion or reconciliation, as it is so frequently shown and said in both Testaments, remains the condition for intimacy with the Lord. The figure of speech used here by the Lady is clearly an exaggerated expression to articulate unspeakable love. Of course, there have never been self-sown potatoes or stones that have become mounds of wheat. But this is divine language using potatoes and stones to describe for people the soaring, wonderful quality of God's affection for his own.

The Lady is telling her people that there is nothing on earth that will adequately describe the joy of God at the sight of his people returning to him. It is as if the Lady were saying, "'God's love for you will be as unreal and as incredible as self-sown potatoes and rocks that become piles of wheat.' A God who performs such miracles is obviously a joyful, dancing God, eager to reward and show how overwhelming is God's presence on earth. (31)

From her first inviting words to the last dialogue with the children, Mary's message was a prophetic plea: "Return to me with your whole heart" (Joel 2:12). The last image Mary leaves us with is that of a father handing bread to his child as famine approaches. That man was Maximin's father at the fields of Coin. His return to faith is a singular one; from blatant indifference – if not out-right hostility toward God – to total surrender. Mary's cry for conversion came to him through his boy's testimony.

## *Come Closer...* **Go Forth:**

It was in this encouraging sprit of hope and joy that the Beautiful Lady ended her apparition. *"Well, my children, you will make this message known to all my people."* That mandate was first delivered directly to the children, as they stood enveloped by the light of Mary's presence. Then, as the children followed her on her final ascent up the slope of mount Planeau, she repeated it again confirming that monumental mission. Only after confiding her message to the care of two seemingly insignificant children, did she cease to cry. Then she slowly disappeared.

**Make this message known to all my people, Mary's final mandate**

The Beautiful Lady's apparition began with an invitation and culminated in mission. She gave them no hint, no instructions, no advice about how to accomplish that mission. They were to make her message known. That is all. Their task was one of fidelity. As with every divinely inspired mission, the outcome was not in their hands. Only God can change hearts.

She left with them, however, some tools and inspiration: her hope-filled message, so reminiscent of her Son's mindset, along with a treasure trove of symbols for their creative spirits. Besides her tears, which she never made allusion to, there were other intriguing icons which could be stepping stones: the hammer and pincers, the multicolored roses, the weighty chains, the simplicity of her attire, the light, the prayerful solitude of the mountains, the water bubbling from the earth where she began to weep. Though trivial and seemingly of no consequence, God uses even those smallest sands of creation to further God's mission.

In her magisterial work, *God for Us*, treating of the Trinity – a mystery which seems to be "locked up in itself and unrelated to us" (32) – Catherine Lacugna writes:

> "The 'to and fro' of divine life is the perfect communion that results from love consummately given and received. The eternal processions exist in time and history as the missions of Incarnation and deification. God goes forth from God, God creates the world, God suffuses its history and dwells within us, redeeming the world from within. God makes an eternal gift to the world as God's very self. Through the outpouring of God into our hearts as love, we become by grace what God is already by nature, namely, self-donating of love for the other." (33)

The words are theological and may seem lofty, but they clarify how God's dynamic and outpouring love is a fundamental concept of mission, and, therefore, anything but "locked up in itself and unrelated to us." Of course, the simplest expression will always be "God is love." (34)

The church deigned to assume follow-up elements contained in the mission left to the children. Metanoia often takes on a sacramental form – the Sacrament of Reconciliation. Over many years, the miracles of reconciliation have flowed as constantly as the tears of the Beautiful Lady. In another Pastoral Letter, dated May 1, 1852, Bishop de Bruillard announced the construction of a Shrine, and went on to add:

> "However important the erection of a Shrine may be, there is something more important, namely the ministers of religion destined to look after it, to receive the pious pilgrims, to preach the Word of God to them, to exercise towards them the ministry of reconciliation, to administer the Holy Sacrament of the altar, and to be, to all, the faithful dispensers of the ministries of God and the spiritual treasures of the Church. These priests shall be called the Missionaries of Our Lady of La Salette..." (35)

In celebrating the yearly anniversary of the blissful Apparition of our Blessed Mother, the Beautiful Lady at La Salette, we recognize that so many other ways of discovering the beauty of the Event and its mission remain to be uncovered. At this juncture of time, we can all ask ourselves what part of the mission we are willing to assume.

**Reflection Questions:**

• La Salette is a private revelation that is shared with the faithful because it has been deemed faithful to the Church and Scriptures and worthy of belief. How did you come to hear and believe in the Apparition? How has this belief called you to mission as a messenger by word and action?

• Mission through: Presence, Motherly Concern, Light, Tears, and Conversion are all describe in the article. Which of these are part and parcel of your mission as La Salette Laity? Which touches you the most and why?

• *Come Closer and Go Forth* are a constant duality in the life of every Christian and especially in the life and ministry of La Salette Laity. How have you been invited to a deepening relationship with God and Mary? How do you "feel sent" by this reality? What do you proclaim?

**Endnotes:**

(1) For a deeper understanding, see the *Theological Commentary* by Cardinal Joseph Ratzinger: http://www.vatican.va/roman_curia/congregations/cfaith/documents/rc_con_cfaith_doc_20000626_message-fatima_en.html

(2) CCC, #66

(3) CCC, #67

(4) James P. O'Reilly, M.S., *The Story of La Salette: Mary's Apparition, Its History and Sequels*, ed., Attleboro, MA: La Salette Communication Center Publications, 2017, 113.

(5) Jean Jaouen, *A Grace Called La Salette: a Story for the World*, trans. Normand Théroux M.S., Attleboro, MA.: La Salette Publications, 1991, 87

(6) Jaouen, Forward, xv.

(7) The "Event" of La Salette is often used in reference to the Appari-

tion of La Salette. It embraces all aspects of the Apparition, including but not limited to the light, the Beautiful Lady, the message, the symbols, the children.

(8) O'Reilly, 19.

(9) O'Reilly, 22.

(10) Jaouen, 53.

(11) Ephesians 1:10

(12) O'Reilly, 113.

(13) Jaouen, 182.

(14) Exodus 3:1-3

(15) Emile A. Ladouceur, M.S., *The Vision of La Salette: The Children Speak*, Hartford, CT: Missionaries of La Salette Corporation, 2016, 103.

(16) Ezekiel 3:1

(17) Ladouceur, 27-28.

(18) Luke 2:29-32

(19) Matthew 4:16

(20) Matthew 5:14

(21) "The Cross and La Salette" in www.lasalette:org; https://www.lasalette.org/about-la-salette/reconciliation/spirituality-and-charism/1449-the-cross-and-la-salette-spirituality.html

(22) Exodus, chapters 19 & 20

(23) Jeremiah 22:21-28

(24) Ladouceur, 36.

(25) Luke 19:41

(26) John 11:35

(27) John 11:36

(28) Matthew 3:2

(29) Jeremiah 31

(30) See Jeremiah 31:33

(31) Normand Théroux, *The Face of the Reconciler: Sharing the La Salette Charism of Reconciliation*, Attleboro, MA: La Salette Communications Center, 2017, 86.

(32) Catherine Mowry Lacugna, *God For Us: The Trinity and Christian Life*, New York, NY: HarperCollins Publishers, 1991, 2.

(33) Lacugna, 353-354

(34) 1 John 4:16

(35) Extract from the *Rule of Life of the Missionaries of La Salette*, 1987, Prologue, 21

# Chapter 16 —
# God's Tenderness and La Salette

## By Fr. Joseph Bachand, M.S.

One of the things I have had to do in the past five years that I never expected, and so never prepared for, was learn a new language – notably, Italian. Then, when I moved to France, it was clear I had to brush up on the French that I learned in elementary and high schools. "Brush up" may give the wrong impression. I knew language was organic, but it never occurred to me that what I learned fifty years ago might not apply today! A person learns a lot undertaking language studies: about communication, certainly; but also, about life and culture and lifelong assumptions. Someone sent me a Facebook page claiming that learning a second language increases one's intelligence. Given the frustration at times, I'd just as soon remain happily ignorant!

*La Salette Madonna* **from Angola**

## The Languages of Prayer:

What I want to share with you, however, is my surprise at another area challenging my assumptions: that of Scripture and prayer. In Rome, we pray the Divine Office and celebrate Eucharist in Italian; here, at La Salette, of course, our daily prayer and Mass are in French. Little by little it dawned on me that even in these areas, language is nuanced; and obviously, translators of the texts had to choose the most apt translation. (*Here in France we might say "le mot juste [the right word.])*

One of the things that surprised me was the number of times I was running into the word for "tenderness" when speaking of God. In Italian, the word is *tenerezza*; and in French, *tendresse*. (And since Romance languages all require gender [strictly grammatical] of their nouns, let me tell you – for the sake of full disclosure – that the article "la" would precede both these words.) And I began to wonder, "Have I slept through a lot of Masses and prayers during my years as a religious and priest?" This, of course, was a distinct possibility in the early years when morning seemed too early to pray.

Now that I'm older, the reverse seems to be the problem: I think I actually drifted off during rosary last week! However, the Church's public prayers depend on a repeated pattern: the texts and readings for Mass come in predictable cycles, as do the Psalms we pray during Morning and Evening Prayer. So, I began to suspect something else was at play here; and the next time I came upon *tenerezza / tendresse* in our prayers, I looked up the English translation.

It happened to be Psalm 111 (110 in some versions of the Bible). If I were to translate line 4 from the French, I would put it something like this: He leaves behind a reminder of his marvels. God is tenderness and pity. But the New American Bible puts it this way: He has won renown for his wondrous deeds; gracious and merciful is the Lord."

Solomon's prayer in the book of Wisdom (Chapter 9) begins this way in the French: *Dieu de mes pères et Seigneur de tendresse, par ta parole tu fis l'univers*; which seems easily translated into English as: God of my fathers and Lord of tenderness, by your word you made the universe. The New America Bible Revised, however, has, "God of my ancestors, Lord of mercy, you who have made all things by your word." (Wisdom 9:1).

Curiously, where the French uses *tendresse*, and the Italian uses *tenerezza*, the English most often uses "mercy" – "merciful" for the adjectival form. I say "curiously," because a perfectly good word for mercy exists in French and Italian. We used them frequently during the recent Jubilee Year of Mercy: *la miséricorde* and *la misericordia*.

The closest I have found English approaching the Romance languages when they use "tenderness" is in the Canticle of Zechariah (Luke 1:

68-79), which we (the Church) pray daily at Morning Prayer (Lauds). After a while, one memorizes these remarkably familiar prayers. So, for years I have prayed, "In the tender compassion of our God the dawn from on high shall break upon us, etc." Our French version would be more literally translated, "...thanks to the tenderness, to the love of our God, when the star from on high visits us." I imagine the English choice of "tender compassion" translates both "tenderness" and "love" found in the French. Perhaps because of the use in Scripture, the word "tendresse" is found frequently in French hymns and prayers.

## Our Language and Our Way of Looking at God:

My reflection here is not on the art of translating. After all, the French, the Italian and the English are all translating the Bible from other languages – Greek and Hebrew definitely, perhaps Latin and Aramaic. My reflection is meant to be on the way we image God, and how that is conditioned by our language. I was prompted to write this reflection, because I realized I had images attached to the words: "tenderness" and "mercy" –- and they are not the same.

I imagine we all have images attached to these concepts. Let me share with you a few of mine. When I reflect on tenderness, I see a mother holding her infant child cheek-to-cheek; I see a young couple at a coffee shop (or food court) oblivious to all around them, leaning across the table so their heads touch, holding one another's hands and speaking to one another in hushed tones – or not speaking at all; I see a father consoling his son who just struck out at the Little League game, his arm around his son's shoulders and the promise of an ice-cream cone on his lips; I see an elderly couple walking slowly down the street – as if on cue they reach and gently take one another's hand. When I image mercy, however, something like this comes to mind: the judge was merciful and imposed life in prison instead of the death penalty. That may be merciful, but it surely is not tender.

## How Do We Speak about God?

You might suggest that tenderness would not be befitting a judge anyway; and that may be truly relevant to the point I am trying to make. I wonder, would it make a difference if the primary image we had of God as we grew up was one of tenderness? Do we tend to grow more like the God we worship as we move through life? If the image of God as judge has been predominant, that could go a long way in explaining our way of speaking about and praying to God; it may even explain something about our Church, our teaching about God and our way of relating to one another; and let us not forget our (Western) society, which is purported to be "Christian" in its foundations. God as judge certainly seems to have been operative in most of these areas – or in all these areas most of the time.

So, is ruminating about God's tenderness of no import, or is it constitutive of Jesus's image of God and foundational to his mission? Is this an image of God that Jesus came to restore? I say "restore" because, obviously, if this descriptor is found in the Psalms, it is not new with Jesus. Moreover, I remember being taught that the fundamental characteristic of God deriving from the Covenant forged with Israel is that of *chesed*. I was taught to translate this term from the Hebrew as "loving kindness." To me this is a fascinating primary characteristic to ascribe to God.

Meanwhile, the term for speaking of God's compassion in Hebrew is, interestingly, connected to the same root as the word "womb"; one professor therefore suggested that the more appropriate (or revealing) translation may be "womb-love." This is a feminine concept, then, comparing the love God has for the people of Israel to the love a mother has for the children she has conceived and borne. To me such concepts are not indicative of justice and mercy, but of tenderness and love.

## God's Tenderness and Vulnerability:

Here's the thing about tenderness: as a way of acting, once in a while, it suggests a choice that we make when we find ourselves with those we care about; but as a way of being, a characteristic describing someone's (that is, God's) nature, it suggests a basic vulnerability. When we act tenderly, we expose ourselves to the response of the other. Our tenderness can be rejected, rebuffed, returned with violence or indifference. The Scriptures suggest God has suffered all these things. Who wants to be treated so?

Which brings me back to the question of imitating the God we worship. I believe we all like to be treated tenderly, but living tenderness is something else. Our vocabulary is full of references to the opposite of tender living: "hardness of heart", "thick-skinned", "he/she has a wall around them," "an aggressive personality," "a good defence is a good offense," "once bitten, twice shy," and the theme of many a pop song, "I'll never love again." God's ongoing vulnerability/tenderness assures us of being forgiven, of being given a second chance. But that second chance becomes rather pointless if it does not then inform our own relationships. "Love one another as I have loved you," Jesus said to his disciples - and, perforce, says to us. And with a vulnerability that led him to the Cross, I suggest his love has been, and always is, characterized by tenderness.

## Mary's Tears at La Salette:

And so, we arrive at La Salette. If "womb-love" is indicative of the love God has for us, then that is embodied in Our Lady of La Salette. She appeared in tears, which is a sign of both tenderness and vulnerability. She was not wracked with sobs: the children testified that her tears flowed throughout her discourse – a symbol, then, of the concern a mother has for her children gone astray.

Her vulnerability is suggested in the choice offered in her discourse: "*If my people do not submit... If they are converted...*" (I sometimes hear "if only" in such a plea.) I say this is indicative of vulnerability because she is incapable of forcing such a conversion. It is the free choice of anyone who hears her appeal and chooses to respond. But we seek her help. In her discourse, she said, "*you can never repay the trouble I have taken for you.*" So we call upon her "ceaseless intercession."

We do that literally here at the Holy Mountain in France by reciting the "*Memorare to Our Lady of La Salette*" at the end of Lauds and Vespers every day. As a result, it is without doubt the longest prayer I have memorized in French! In the prayer, we mention the certainty that Our Lady will not abandon us, her children. The French and Italian versions go on to say,

"Comforted by your tenderness, Mother, we come begging before you, in spite of our lack of trust and gratitude." That's my translation, because our English version of the prayer – citing the same fidelity on Mary's part – goes like this: "Inspired by this consoling thought, we come to you pleading, in spite of our infidelities and ingratitude."

A friend and fellow La Salette Missionary has pointed out to me that the translations have not been synchronized, and I have no idea if or when that might happen. I did, however, ask Father Roger Castel, one of our acknowledged La Salette scholars, where this prayer came from. He surprised me by admitting that he is responsible for the present French version, composed when he was director of scholastics. He said he had found the wording in the original too preoccupied with self and personal salvation.

So, counting on the tenderness of Our Lady of La Salette, the French version ends by asking her for "the grace to love Jesus above all else, and to console you by a life spent for the glory of God and the love of our brothers [and sisters]." (The French do not apologize for the lack of inclusive language!) The English, perhaps indicative of the version Father Castel was dealing with, asks for "the grace to love Jesus above all else, and to console you, too, by living a holy life, that we may share the eternal life Christ gained by his Cross."

## Mary's Vulnerability
## Offers Herself in Forgiveness and Love:

At this point, I am not asking for a new translation of the *Memorare*. However, the reference to Mary's tenderness – a mother's tenderness – is much different from a "consoling thought." It bespeaks a relationship, and counts on that relationship, considering it as orienting us on the path toward God. And the closing reference to loving our brothers and sisters suggests to me what a life of tenderness is all about: the vulnerability that offers itself in forgiveness and love.

Given that Jesus's tender vulnerability led him to the Cross, we do not embark upon such a course unawares. As Saint Paul tells us in Romans 6, however, we who share in Christ's death also share in his life. It is our faith that "in the tender compassion of our God, the dawn from on high" will indeed shine on all of us who have dwelt too long in darkness. I believe that our own efforts to mirror God's compassion and tenderness are a part of the coming of the reign of God that Jesus preached in word and in deed. They are certainly a reflection of the tenderness and compassion shown by the "Beautiful Lady" at La Salette towards "all her people." Perhaps the call to submit, was always a call to submit to *God's tender love*; and we have resisted far too long.

## Learning the Language of God:

So, do I believe the Italians and the French are more tender, loving, and compassionate than us Anglophones because they have been exposed to such an image of God? Well, it really doesn't work that way, does it? Do we even pay attention to the words we use in rote prayers? To move from praying to a tender God to believing in a tender God to forming a relationship with that God and becoming [tender] like God - well, that would be the road of conversion. And so I suggest, not that we all learn Italian or French, but that we learn the language of God, which God, I suspect, is only too eager to teach us.

**Note:** *I gratefully acknowledge the help of my La Salette brothers, Fr. Tom Leclerc, M.S. and Fr. René Butler, M.S. with technical aspects of the ancient and modern languages involved.*

## Opening Address:
## First La Salette Lay Ministry Summit
## (Smyrna, Georgia 2011)

### La Salettes and Laity:

A sincere and hearty welcome to all of you attending this historic gathering. Since we have never held a gathering such as this, expectations can be all over the place, from "Let us try to do it all" to "Whatever happens is good." The truth and success of what we do here will probably lie somewhere in the middle.

You are here, however, either because you have been invited or because your interest has been piqued by the pre-Summit advertising. Even more profoundly, you have been invited or your interest has been piqued precisely because you have a connection to La Salette: you may work closely with La Salette Missionaries or La Salette devotion/spirituality holds an attraction for you. Whatever the case, you are welcome here.

I am taken by the title of this gathering, "La Salette Lay Ministry Summit," and I see it as my task to draw out the connection between "La Salette," "laity" and "ministry." I do not know if that is your understanding of my task, but I hope our expectations converge at some point, and that point may prove both interesting and challenging to you. I undertake this task as a Missionary of Our Lady of La Salette, and so you know the perspective from which I speak.

**The Laity and La Salettes:**

For a long time, the Missionaries of La Salette would have described the connection between ministry and the laity as the latter being the recipient of the former. In other words, we missionaries ministered, and the laity were ministered to. This pretty much describes the way things were in the universal Church. We were not so different in this from other religious communities or diocesan priests. This was not all bad: at its best, it meant that clergy and religious were called to serve – an image Jesus applied to himself. However, it could also lead to a one-sided approach to understanding that service and ministry.

A major shift occurred with the Second Vatican Council, and it became clear that the laity minister by right because of their baptism and out of the workings of the Holy Spirit. As the gifts of the Spirit were discerned, we came to see that there are not two static groups in the Church: one doing ministry and one being ministered to; rather, ministry can be seen as a function of needs being met by gifts, a more fluid understanding and one more in keeping with the nature of ministry as relationship, rather than a function of state. This theology may be spoken of in more detail by other presenters. My task is to get back to La Salette. However, I would ask you to remember and reflect on that connection between ministry and relationship.

La Salette Rule in three different languages

We Missionaries have a book simply called *The Rule*, containing our Constitutions and the Norms governing our life and mission throughout the world. I was unable to find the term "laity" in the Index. Still, there are two passages I would like to share with you. The Constitutions #28 reads: "To provide more effective service we work in close collaboration with the laity, the diocesan clergy and other congregations, under the authority of the Bishop and in keeping with the pastoral guidelines of the local Church." Please note that this number sees the laity as a group with which the Missionaries are to collaborate – closely! And note that the purpose is to render more effective service.

Please keep that in mind as I read Norm #52: "The Missionaries always work in close collaboration with the laity, listening to them, sharing responsibilities with them, being available for their formation and lending them the spiritual support they may need."

I hope you are able to see how these latter two functions are in place for this gathering: it is intended as continuing formation for those of us gathered, as well as a source of spiritual support. One also hopes that we will be listening to you throughout these days (some of us being better at that than others).

Besides the Rule, the ongoing life of the Missionaries is governed by a meeting (called a Chapter in church-speak), convened every six years to choose leadership and tend to the needs of the Congregation. In Brazil in 1994, the Chapter, reflecting on the Norm I read above, recognized "that the laity who share in the mission of reconciliation are empowered in virtue of their baptism to be agents of evangelization and to create just structures in the Church and in the world." It encouraged every Province throughout the Congregation to concretize this principle.

In 2006 in the Philippines, the General Chapter urged each Province and Region to "create a program of Meetings, Encounters, and Workshops to deepen and develop La Salette spirituality for the laity. La Salette Communities will offer this program to men and women who are actively engaged in our works and mission."

Putting these two decisions together, we begin to paint a picture of how La Salette views the laity: as empowered agents of evangelization, capable of creating just structures, nourished by a shared spirituality, all under the rubric of reconciliation.

Our Province in North America recently put together a Vision Statement. In the middle of that statement there is the simple sentence, "We unite our gifts to those of the laity." I believe the placement of that sentence acts as a hinge describing our relationship in ministry.

This brief look at our Rule and official documents shows the explicit connection among the La Salette Missionaries and laity in ministry. I would like to draw your attention to another source of inspiration for us – one considered a grace for the whole church – and one that shows the implicit connection between the terms noted above. That is the story of the apparition of Our Lady at La Salette.

## The Message of Reconciliation:

If you work with La Salettes, chances are you have heard the story in whole or in part. In fact, some of you are probably able to recite the story better than my confreres. (We will not test this.) I suspect you are aware that La Salette is not opposed to the Gospel, nor does it add anything to it. Rather, La Salette provides a focus or lens through which we look at Jesus's life and ministry. It is as if this lens puts the rest of the Gospel in perspective. We are used to referring to this focus as "reconciliation." It is a word mentioned nowhere in the Apparition, but one which arose shortly after the apparition to explain the message and purpose of Mary's appearing.

The term reconciliation has an honored place in Saint Paul's writings. He portrays Jesus as reconciling us to his Father, and reconciling us to one another (for example, Jew and Greek), as well as reconciling the world to himself. Paul says that we in turn are given this ministry of reconciliation. In general, one gets the impression of subjects once alienated being brought back into relationship. But reconciliation is not a word that features often in our ordinary vocabulary. So, I would like to share with you what I have come to see at work beneath the term reconciliation.

The call of Our Lady to remember her Son and to remember what Church is all about, is the result of God's initiating love. Recognizing the central place, the Cross has at La Salette, the words of John 3:16 come easily to mind: "God so loved the world..." I couple this with a line from John's First Letter, "Love consists in this: not that we have loved God, but that God has first loved us."

If we do not understand that love is at the foundation of the apparition, we can easily misinterpret the resulting call to ministry as badgering people into attending Mass and berating them into cleaning up their language. I believe this dishonors the seriousness of the apparition. It is God's initiating love that underlies the plea of a Mother in tears, and I paraphrase her message: "Come back; don't remain alone, isolated, victimized; that's not what God had in mind for you."

What God "had in mind" for us is rather portrayed in our Lady's message as a life in abundance: rocks turned into heaps of wheat and potatoes self-sown in the fields – enough for all. And it all centers on the powerlessness of a God who graced us with free will – the ability to choose, or not. In the words of La Salette, "*If my people are converted...; if my people do not submit.*"

This freedom to choose is at the heart of the message, at the heart of any response to Jesus's preaching and person, at the heart of the possibility of a moral life and at the heart of the La Salette ministry of evangelization. I mention the latter because this is the task entrusted to us through the witnesses of La Salette: "*Make this known to all my people.*" The "this" to be made known is the possibility of a response, of things being other than they are at present. Choosing things (and one's self) to be otherwise is at the heart of a response to Our Lady's message, and we call this conversion. In the words of Twelve-Step spirituality, it is the possibility of being restored to sanity through submitting to a Power greater than oneself.

This ministry of proclaiming a message of conversion is not simply a matter of learning the right words and getting across the proper content. We are called to embody the message of reconciliation. That's what is most convincing. As May Sarton once wrote, "being something irresistible converts more surely than demanding something impossible." I think that's why the popular story of St. Francis found an immediate response in my heart.

The story concludes with the maxim, "Preach the Gospel at all times; when necessary use words." Our lives speak more loudly than our words, and perhaps it has to be so among a people who celebrate the Incarnation as a central truth of faith. This is what I think lies behind the ministry of La Salette and our understanding of reconciliation.

## Relationships are Central:

The ministry in which we engage as a people drawn together by La Salette will ultimately be seen in the relationships we form. After all, any sense of reconciliation has to include the restoring of relationships. To one who has experienced rupture or alienation in a relationship, nothing will be so convincing of the possibility of new life as healthy, positive relationships. In a society where function is emphasized and evaluations subject us to constant measuring, relationship is a bit intangible.

Yet I encourage you to reflect on this, because relationships are at the heart of Jesus's own preaching, especially the relationship that formed people into community. Relationships can only be formed over time; nothing instant about them. It is not as if someone comes to us with a problem and we hold the secret book where we look up the answer. What we offer people in need is ourselves.

Relationships are also organic – flexible, living things, which grow in mutual trust and are liable to breakdown now and again. But I believe La Salette calls us to a particular kind of relationship, and I will do my best to convince you.

# Mary's Three Commands:

It was only recently that I asked the question as to why Our Lady at La Salette suggested we pray the Our Father and the Hail Mary, when commanding the children to *"pray well."* As I reflected on this, it occurred to me that this is one of only three commands in the entire message at La Salette. The first command is the opening invitation to *"Come closer;"* the second is: *"be sure to pray well, my children; say at least an Our Father and a Hail Mary..."*, and the third is: *"Make this known to all my people."*

There are only three commands in Mary's entire message at La Salette

In her command to pray, Our Lady is inviting us to address our prayers regularly to the Father of Jesus and the Mother of Jesus. In doing so, of course, we are to recognize that Jesus's Father is Our Father; that his Mother is Our Mother. (Recall how she refers to the two witnesses as *"my children,"* – never by name.) If we share the same father and mother as Jesus, we are his brothers and sisters – and therefore brothers and sisters to one another.

The relationship that describes our ministry of reconciliation is that of adoptive siblings – a relationship of care and one attuned to justice. Make this known to all my people: all are brothers and sisters in Christ; all are called to reconciliation; all are loved by the God who created them. La Salette ministry involves the ongoing discovery of new brothers and sisters in all corners of the earth.

This ultimately displays the relationship between our spirituality and our mission. These two terms – spirituality and ministry – are not opposed; and neither is optional. The two are in a mutual relationship, where our own belonging to God is nourished and valued, and it is this connection that enables us to proclaim that truth to others. This is what I believe all of you know on some level.

To know oneself loved by God is convincing on a deep level, and all of us struggle at times to put that into words. But we act out of that deep awareness, because it is ultimately the only strength we can rely on. We work collaboratively in ministry because we recognize the strength that kind of support gives us as well as the way it speaks more clearly the very message we are trying to communicate.

## The Signs of the Times:

I return to the Chapter decision that refers to the laity as empowered to create just structures in the world. We have a time-honored phrase in La Salette that has to do with paying attention to the "signs of the times." I find this particularly appropriate in deciding how we are to listen to you. Vatican II said the laity find themselves in the heart of the world. I think this puts you in an appropriate place for being aware of the injustice that binds people. This is why we need to listen to you.

One way to be aware of this injustice and the needs of God's people is to notice your own heart: as children of the Weeping Mother at La Salette, you do well to pay attention to your own tears, whether those be internal or external. Where does the suffering of others grab your heart and hold your attention? These are the situations that need to be addressed, these are the relationships that need to be restored, these are the places God's Spirit calls us to be instruments of reconciliation.

We do that through a ministry of intercessory prayer when we do not know where else to start (very Salettine). We do that by proclaiming the hopeful possibility of restoration I spoke of above. But in the kind of "preaching that does not need words" (of which St. Francis spoke) we may find ourselves setting up programs and providing alternative structures that address real needs and enflesh God's abiding mercy and justice. These are limited only by our imagination: if we can imagine it, we can do it. The needed resources always have a way of turning up.

# An International Gathering of La Salette Laity:

In closing, I remind you that this takes place on a global stage as well. In the past, laity and La Salettes from around the world gathered at the site of the Apparition from September 1-10, 2011, to listen to one another and reflect on the internationality of the ministry we share.

This global perspective helps call us away from a narrow, self-absorbed approach to anything we do. At the same time, we recognize the locus of our attention and activity as an important embodiment of what that global perspective is all about. It is as if we were saying, "The whole world cries out for reconciliation; and here's the place I/ we can be of service in that."

The original message of La Salette was made known by two innocent, unpretentious children who found their lives forever changed by a loving encounter with the Divine. May you be blessed by such an encounter, and may you too be effective in making known the message that is thus made known to you.

**Reflection Questions:**

• The words of prayers are translated to various languages and the translation can change meanings or clarify important points. How do you understand the tender compassion of God and of Mary in your life?

• The first La Salette Lay Ministry Summit occurred in Georgia parishes in 2011. Since then the title has changed to La Salette Laity Summit, reflecting the fact that we now have a formal La Salette Laity group and presence. Have you attended a Summit? If you have been, share some experiences or learnings that have helped form you as a member of La Salette Laity?

• The International Gathering of La Salette Laity were held in 2011 and then again in 2016. They created a partnership of Laity around the La Salette World. Share what you have learned about this International Movement.

# Chapter 17 —
# Our La Salette Missions:
# Reconciliation in Action
### By Fr. Thomas Vellappallil, M.S.

## Introduction:

There are about 1,000 La Salette Missionaries in thirty countries. Each of us has a million stories to tell. We live them out in our daily lives. The greatest story of all is how God intervened in our lives when he granted us the gift of faith and called us to become Missionaries of La Salette.

When I reflect on my own faith journey I marvel at the mysteries of life, at the people who influenced and inspired me, at the love that sustained me, at the grace that protected me and the helping hands that encouraged and guided me. Through our missionary efforts we in turn reach out to others. We help them come to an awareness of God as revealed by and through Jesus. We offer them the possibility of hearing the greatest story of all – The Gospel of Jesus.

African La Salette Logo

The joy of the Gospel fills the hearts and lives of all who encounter Jesus. Pope Francis develops the theme of the proclamation of the Gospel in his Apostolic Exhortation, *Evangelii Gaudium.* " One concrete sign of such openness is that our church doors should always be open, so that if someone, moved by the Spirit, comes there looking for God, he or she will not find a closed door. There are other doors that should not be closed either. Everyone can share in some way in the life of the Church; everyone can be part of the community, nor should the doors of the sacraments be closed for simply any reason... The Eucharist... is not a prize for the perfect but a powerful medicine and nourishment for the weak." (#47)

Sharing makes all the difference in the world – to us and to everyone. Some of the stories in this article have been told before. My humble attempt is to highlight particular situations in different mission countries and how the charism of reconciliation challenges and continues to play a role in the lives of peoples in different cultures. These stories need to be told again and again. Because they are stories of people's brokenness, healing and reconciliation, a relevant message for the whole world always. These are true stories of people and their lives that I have experienced during my mission visits over the years.

## La Salette Mission in Angola:

Angola: Provincial, Fr. Celestino Muhatili (center)
with La Salette theologians

When the Swiss La Salette missionaries came to Angola in 1946, they shared with Angolans the message of reconciliation conveyed by our Lady at La Salette which is first and foremost a gospel message. This message motivated the lives and commitment of these men who came from afar. La Salette has been present in Angola, since 1946, the 100th anniversary of the apparition. On their arrival, the missionaries did not know the people of the country; they knew nothing of their culture or language. So, they had to deal with learning the local languages especially Umbundu, the language of most of the Angolan population.

Reconciliation remains a great challenge for Angola. Even though the twenty-five years of civil war are over, the country is still deeply scarred and wounded by a past that cannot be very easily forgotten. The war of arms and bombs may be over, but the war of cultural, tribal, and ethnic prejudices continue. In that context of the civil war, it was not easy to be a missionary. To make things worse, after independence, the ruling party adopted communism as the ideology of Angola.

A Missionary was not only a pastor but at times was a doctor, a nurse, a non-government representative, a teacher, etc. At times, the missionaries shed their blood for their people. One could be blamed and threatened to death as an enemy by either party (Government or rebels). There have also been cases in which a few missionaries (priests, brothers, sisters), catechists and other lay people who have been assassinated just because they were Christians. The La Salette missionaries gave a wonderful witness to their faith and they saved many lives under mysterious circumstances. Honor must be given for their bravery!

Thank God, since the civil war ended in April 2002, Angola is on the road to peace and reconciliation. The Gospel says, "You will hear of wars* and reports of wars; see that you are not alarmed, for these things must happen, but it will not yet be the end" (Matthew 24:6). The La Salette missionaries dedicate themselves, without ceasing, to reconciling the wounded and resentful hearts.

The war has left in its wake many persons who died, often in cruel ways. Some have lost father, mother, brothers and sisters, cousins, nieces, and nephews. In certain cases, they know who killed members of their own families. The tendency is to avenge the atrocities committed. The La Salette missionaries are opening paths of reconciliation by preaching, teaching, and living the message day by day.

# La Salette Mission in Argentina:

Argentina: High School students in Las Termas, Argentina

Argentina is the second largest country in South America in size and population. It has a population of forty-two million people. Many Argentineans are nominal Catholics who attend Church only on specific social occasions like weddings and baptisms. Roman Catholicism remains the official religion of the State. The society, culture and politics are deeply imbued with Roman Catholicism. The La Salettes are serving in parishes in Cordoba, La Banda, Las Termas and Santa Fe.

The city of Las Termas has a vibrant parish, divided into four sectors with 138 missions spread out far and wide. With financial assistance from St. Oliver Plunkett in Snellville, Georgia, they have built a primary school and then a high school, which grows in enrollment each year. Education for these children has brought many families closer to Church. They are now twinned with Good Shepherd in Orlando, FL as well. It is so impressive to see the joy and the smiles in the faces of these young people.

Thanks to the La Salettes for the great work they do to help shape the future of these children. There are so many unfinished projects. They need lots of help expanding the school, assisting in many *comedors* (*soup kitchens*), in completing mission chapels and places of worship.

The parish in La Banda has 10 mission centers. This is one of the most remote and poor places. You see lots of unpaved roads even the one that runs in front of the parish church and the rectory. The Sunday collection usually amounts to $20. Administering the Sacraments to the sick in far flung places is always a challenge especially when transportation is limited, and they have to drive through unpaved roads for miles. Once we entered a small shabby house, I saw a woman in her 70s lying in bed close to death. I was touched by what the missionary said. "We are going to the poorest of the barrios. It is quite a distance to travel. But to the poor I must go. They have no one to care for them."

Cordoba is the second largest city in Argentina. Next door to the Cathedral in Cordoba is a place unforgettable for Argentineans where the military, (presumably hand in hand with the Church) are believed to have killed thousands of innocent and poor people. Between 1976-1983, Argentina was wracked by a war in which successive military regimes hunted down, tortured, and took away about 30,000 citizens. It surely has played a role in the life and faith of the people in relationship to the Catholic Church.

In the suburbs where our missionaries serve, the people are very poor and simple but they are a people of great faith. No matter what the future holds for the Region due to lack of members and vocations, they are led by the conviction that "we are called to serve others with love" (Galatians 5:13).

## La Salette Mission in Bolivia:

Bolivia: (from left) Frs. John Higgins and David Cardoso
in white t-shirts with prospective candidates

Bolivia is a land-locked country in the heart of South America, which remains one of the least known of all South American countries. Bolivia is one of the 10 South American countries with a population of 10 million or greater. The Church is the most credible institution in the country. The Church is on the side of the oppressed, in general. The Church has many social services in defense of the minors. The crisis is how to live together with a socialist government, which denounces the Church as a privileged institution. Jesus said to them, "Repay to Caesar what belongs to Caesar and to God what belongs to God." (Mark 12:17). Our parish of Mary Queen in Friendswood, Texas, has recently twinned with these parishes and are developing a mutually supportive relationship.

The only La Salette parish in Bolivia is in the city of Cochabamba. Like anywhere else, vocations to religious life and priesthood are scarce and so everyone is concerned about the future of La Salette in Bolivia. The parish has two active mission chapels around the area, the Church of the Exaltation and Christ Reconciler. What is quite impressive is the beautiful practice after Mass. Every person in Church would come up front to have their heads and hands sprinkled with holy water by the priest. It is only then that they feel fully blessed and are ready to go home. In rural areas indigenous rituals are often mixed with Catholic belief.

When a Bolivian is ill, he or she is more likely to visit the local *curandero*, (*healer*), then arrange an appointment with a doctor. Bolivians are nothing if not superstitious. People would buy miniature cars and trucks and have them blessed by a priest so that the real thing can be theirs within a year. It is not just vehicles, they would buy miniature houses, suitcases, banknotes, college diplomas, which they feel might require a little divine intervention. One could only imagine the challenges a missionary could face in this situation.

## La Salette Mission in Haiti:

Haiti made the headlines around the world lately and this is not the first time. Civic uprisings, political related violence and natural disasters have been part of the life of Haiti as a nation for years. Unfortunately, the poor people suffered the most from this political instability. In addition to natural disasters off all kind, the political situation does not help them to flourish and to enjoy the many blessings this people inherited from their ancestors. Back in 2010, Haiti was hit by a major earthquake that killed 316,000 people and left millions homeless.

It is a fact that there are two distinct categories of Haitians living in Haiti. There is a group of rich people. They can afford good education, three meals a day, nice and comfortable homes. On the other hand, the majority of the population is suffering. They barely eat once a day, they have meat maybe once a week or once every two weeks. They are the ones who suffer from the results of political problems and corruptions at all levels of the government and the public administration in Haiti.

Haiti: Three Madagascar La Salette priests who went to Haiti (from left): Frs. Evariste Ralohotsy, Mamy Rakotondraibe and Maximin Rarivoarivony

Roman Catholicism is the official religion of Haiti but voodoo may be considered the country's national religion in fact. The central and key aspect of voodoo is healing people from illness. Beliefs include zombies and witchcraft. It tells the future and reads dreams. There are fundamental differences and certain similarities between Voodoo and Christianity that make them irreconcilable. Both venerate a supreme being and believe in the existence of invisible evil spirits or demons and in an afterlife. Voodoo is elusive and endangered, but it remains the soul of Haitian people. The practices of necromancy, divination, witchcraft, magic, and sorcery of the secret societies of Voodoo are incompatible with the Christian faith.

This is the cultural and religious context to which the bishop of the Diocese of Gonaives entrusted to the La Salette missionaries two newly erected parishes: St. Augustine of Petite Riviere des Bayonnais and St. Joachim and St. Ann of Haute Feuille. They also manage to run three schools with hundreds of students, provide primary health care with the numerous church based small clinics, give food for the children and the elderly through soup kitchen programs, and provide them with clean and hygienic water.

They, as part of the Catholic Church in Haiti, approach the reality with our charism of reconciliation. The goal is to preach the good news to a people devastated with an extreme poverty, to reconcile them with their past and their dignity as human beings.

Fresh are the thoughts about many people I met that live in dire poverty, some without even a home. For me it is not about just money to help them financially but participating and sharing in the life of people who are less privileged and less fortunate. The road to recovery and to rebuild this nation will take many years but the healing has begun. Jesus said, "Much will be required of the person entrusted with much, and still more will be demanded of the person entrusted with more." (Luke 12:48).

## La Salette Mission in India:

India: La Salette Shrine Church in Kayakunnu, Kerala, India

India is the seventh largest country in the world with a population of 1.3 billion people, making it the second most populous country after China. There are 17 major languages with 844 dialects. India is the birthplace for many religions such as Hinduism, Sikhism, Buddhism and Jainism. Two main religions are Hinduism (80%) and Muslim (10%) and Christianity is the 3rd largest religion with more than 30 million followers, constituting 2.6% of India's population.

For generations of Indians, the caste system has defined how people earn a living and whom they marry. Caste system is a class structure that is determined by birth. Loosely, it means that in some societies, if your parents are poor, you are going to be poor too. The same goes for being rich. Despite reform efforts, deep-rooted prejudices and entitlement hold firm among higher castes, while those on the lowest rungs still face marginalization, discrimination, and violence. The caste system affects Christians all over India because most converts to Christianity come from the lower castes, the so-called "untouchables."

The level of violence and persecution against Christians and other religious minorities in India is vast and shocking. Led by radical Hindu nationalists, who seem to operate with little interference from local, regional, or national governments, persecution against Christians in India has reached epidemic levels. Pastors and members are beaten, sometimes so badly that legs are broken, nuns are raped, and some instances killed, churches are vandalized. Hundreds of Christians are being imprisoned on false charges of converting Hindus to Christianity.

The view of the Hindu nationalists is that to be Indian is to be Hindu, so any other faith including Christianity is viewed as non-Indian. In taking steps to solve the religious conflict, different religions and denominations may meet to simply tell stories, share their religious convictions with each other and seek common religious understanding. Is reconciliation possible without compromising one's religious beliefs and convictions? Psalm 82:6 says, "God's though you be, (you are) offspring of the Most High."

This is the context in which the La Salette Missionaries have been serving in India since 1988. The majority of students in our schools are children of Hindus and some of them coming from extremely poor families. Our missionaries work in rural communities where Christians are only a minority. Though difficult, the La Salette Missionaries are committed to work towards peaceful co-existence regardless of color, creed and status. Today the Province of India (La Salette Matha) is blessed with many members and vocations.

## La Salette Mission in Madagascar:

Madagascar lies in the Indian Ocean off the southwest coast of Africa. It is the world's fourth largest island and has a population of over 22 million. Around 92% of Malagasy live on less than $2 per day.

Running water and electricity are supplied by a government service which is unable to service the entire population. Only 6.8% have access to water while 9.5% have access to electricity. Most roads in Madagascar are unpaved and impassable during the rainy season. Half the country's population is Christian and the other half practice traditional Malagasy religion.

Many Christians integrate their religious beliefs with traditional ones related to honoring their ancestors. There is an inseparable relationship between the dead and the living in the Malagasy culture. The Malagasy pay a lot of attention to their dead relatives and put much effort building ancestral tombs which are opened from time to time so the remains can be carried in procession before being rewrapped in fresh shrouds and replaced in the tomb.

Madagascar: Fr. Mémé and two other priests with a local La Salette Laity group

They call this practice as "famadihana". It is an occasion to celebrate the beloved ancestor's memory, gather with family and community and enjoy a festive time together. It is believed that by showing respect for ancestors in this way they may intervene on behalf of the living. The veneration of ancestors led to the widespread tradition of tomb building. There is no cemetery. Tombs are built near the homes.

A family may have one hundred cows and be quite rich. They will not sell one cow to take care of the sick, but they would kill as many cows as they need to celebrate their dead. Likewise, a family may own hundreds of pigs and not sell even one to send their children to school but would be willing to kill ten to celebrate their dead with a banquet with their extended family and friends. Here lies the challenge for our missionaries as to how to preach the gospel of truth without compromising it. Dt. 4:39 says, "Yahweh, He is God in heaven above and on the earth below; there is no other".

Bishop Donald Pelletier, M.S., Bishop Emeritus of Morondava, is gathering data on the history of American La Salette missionaries in Madagascar and gave me permission to quote from the introduction of the book he has begun writing.

"American La Salettes have generously served the Church of Madagascar for well over ninety years. It has been not only a long but phenomenally successful mission: one we can be proud of, one that deserves to be known and remembered as it highlights the missionary spirit of American missionaries. To this day the La Salette Missionaries are the only religious community of men to evangelize on what is known as the Red Isle. They were the first to take up residence, moving into an area that had never seen a Catholic priest.

"When the **first three priests and a brother** arrived in 1928 there was nothing and they had nothing. They lived in a rented house using crates as chairs and tables. Today there are three flourishing dioceses because the first missionaries laid solid foundations of the faith by sowing the seeds of the Word of God among whom they lived. Never could they have dreamt in 1928 how God would bless their self-sacrificing gift of life for the Good News."

## La Salette Mission in Mozambique:

La Salettes serving in Mozambique: (from left) Frs Hélio Katombela Kaheka João of Angola, Edegard Silva Junior of Brazil, João da Silva Holek of Brazil

Mozambique is a multilingual, multiethnic and multicultural country. The people of Mozambique received independence on June 25, 1975, but this was followed by a 16-year civil war which ended on

October 4, 1992. The economy is mainly agricultural for subsistence. Religions in Mozambique are approximately 23.8% Catholics, 17.8% Islamic, 17.5% Zion, 16.2% Evangelicals, and 21% without religion.

We started our mission in Mozambique, in the Diocese of Pemba, in the northeast of the Province of Cabo Delgado on December 17, 2017. In the recent past, the government of Mozambique was threatened by suspected Islamist armed groups from the Province of Cabo Delgado, which now has developed into a national crisis. The bishop has called our missionaries back to the diocesan center for their safety and security. It is unclear if and when they will be able to go back to their mission field.

Thousands were displaced as armed men who attacked the villages, burned houses and killed people. The population of the province in which we work are predominantly Muslims (55%) and Catholics (33%). The parish includes about 30 different communities and a population of about 7,000 people. Our community is in the district of Muidumbe and the Mission is called Nangololo. The La Salette community is made up of three confreres: two Brazilians and one Angolan.

## La Salette Mission in Myanmar:

Myanmar: Blessing of small La Salette Facsimile
in front of Myanmar Novitiate house

For more than a century, Myanmar remained a world apart, isolated from other nations due to foreign and military rule. Buddhism is practiced by almost 90% of Burma's population. Because the people are deeply pious, there is at least one pagoda or Buddha image in every town, city and even in villages. There are also monasteries or schools to train Buddhist monks.

Faith and superstition go hand in hand in Myanmar. Although the majority of people are Buddhists, many practice ancient animist beliefs in natural spirits. There are other religions in Myanmar, but they are not as widespread as Buddhism. Only 4% of the people are Christians and 4% Muslims and the rest are Hindus and other minor religions.

Christianity was brought to Myanmar by European missionaries in the 19th century. The La Salette Missions in Myanmar began with the arrival of five missionaries led by Bishop Thomas Newman at Akyab (now Sittwe) in November of 1937. In 1962, La Salette Apostolic School (Minor Seminary) began with 33 candidates in Akyab. However due to Government policies of taking over all the schools in the country, the La Salette Apostolic School ended its operations and sent the students back home. The government refused to renew the temporary visas for foreigners and all the young missionaries had to leave the country. The last two La Salette Missionaries left the country in November 1976 and there were no more La Salette missionaries serving in the country.

To re-establish the La Salette presence, candidates were recruited and were sent to the Philippines to be trained as La Salettes in 1992. On November 18, 2005, the La Salette in Myanmar was raised to the status of a "District." At the Council of the La Salette Congregation held in India in February of 2017, the district was raised to the level of a Region under the title of "Mary, Mother of the Missions."

The first La Salette Missionaries went through hardship and pain and even death but they have proclaimed the Word of God with courage and handed down the legacy of faith in this land of Myanmar particularly in the Diocese of Pyay (previously known as Prome, in southwestern Myanmar). They are grateful to the Lord for his guidance, for bringing the La Salette Missionaries back to Myanmar.

When they professed their first vows, they chose to surrender everything they possessed to embrace a humble lifestyle of poverty, chastity, and obedience. Through this act of consecration, they were embraced by God in return. The La Salette Missionaries are very well loved, appreciated, and respected by simple and pious Burmese people. These courageous men are living examples of Jesus' words: "No one can serve two masters" (Matthew 6:24).

## La Salette Mission in the Philippines:

Philippines: Group of teachers at La Salette School
in Santiago City, Isabella, Philippines

The Philippines is a sovereign island country in Southeast Asia situated in the western Pacific Ocean. It consists of about 7,641 islands. With a population of more than 100 million people, the Philippines is the seventh-most populated country and the most Catholic country in Asia and the tenth most populated country in the world. Protestants are estimated to be no more than 10%. Of the populace. Islam is the second largest religion with more than 11%.

Sixty-five years ago, Bishop Constance Jurgens, the Bishop of Tuguegarao, Cagayan wrote to religious superiors inviting them to help evangelize the people under his care in the Philippines. The only religious community that responded was the Missionaries of Our Lady of La Salette in the United States of America. Four young La Salette North American Missionaries left the comforts of home, family and country and arrived in the Philippines in December of 1948 to begin work in this mission area. They began their work in the Province of Isabela by establishing a school in San Mateo and beginning parish administration in Santiago. Other Americans followed and in time seven more schools and many parishes were established.

Many Filipino young men were attracted to their missionary zeal and dedicated service to the people of God to which they witnessed in the life and ministry of these early missionaries. The tiny seed of mission planted by the early La Salettes is now a large tree branching out to many other missions as Filipino La Salettes bring the message of Our Lady of La Salette in the United States, India, Australia and Myanmar.

In the Philippines, the Missionaries of Our Lady of La Salette are known as a Province by the name "Ina Ng Pag-asa" which is translated as "Mother of Hope" Province. The National Shrine of Our Lady of La Salette in the Philippines is in the South of Manila. Over two million pilgrims visit the shrine each year to celebrate the Mass, receive the Sacrament of Reconciliation and to experience retreats. The PAMANA Center of the La Salette Missionaries is the social action arm of the congregation, providing educational scholarships to children of poor families.

From Elementary through High School there are almost 5,000 students and nearly 7,000 students in College and Graduate Programs at the La Salette University in Isabela. The university and the school system have embraced education as the key to reconciliation. Rightly so, education is a powerful force for reconciliation.

As educators, they have committed to develop national and global citizens from all backgrounds who can effect change and participate in the life of the society that they live in. Programs for the Institute of Reconciliation, Lay Associates and many other ministries and apostolates will always necessitate continuous support.

There were eight parishes that were under the care of the La Salettes over the past 40 years until they were all returned to the diocese except one upon the request of the Bishop of Illagan about 13 years ago. Then they moved on to establish themselves in poorer parishes in other dioceses. In Luke's gospel, Jesus said, "To the other towns also I must proclaim the good news of the kingdom of God, because for this purpose I have been sent" (Luke 4:43). Yes, they are moving forward ... with hope.

## La Salette Mission in Tanzania:

Tanzania: Our three La Salette Missionaries (from left), Frs. Dileesh Poriamvelil, Manuel dela Cruz, and Aldrin Cenizal with a priest from Diocese of Bukoba;

Tanzania is a sovereign state in eastern Africa. It has a population that is estimated close to 56 million, composed of several ethnic, linguistic, and religious groups. Predominant religions are Christianity, Islam, Hinduism, and traditional beliefs. Approximately 68% of Tanzania's 67 million people live below the poverty line. The Tanzanian economy is heavily based on agriculture and farming. Only 20 % Tanzanians have access to electricity and less have access to clean water. There is a huge increase in unemployment, hunger, malnutrition, starvation, and various diseases.

The first La Salette mission in Tanzania was established on July 16, 2016 upon the arrival of the first three Missionaries of Our Lady of La Salette under the guidance of the General Administration. The La Salette Parish in Rutete (a parish-designate) is in the Bukoba Catholic Diocese in Kagera Region, of Tanzania. The Parish Center is situated in the village of Rutete, Bukoba. It is rural with two outer stations (Kahyoro and Rwizi). The parish is composed of less than 1,000 Catholic families or around 5,000 Catholics from 15 villages. The parish is predominantly Catholic, with other Christian denominations and Islamics composing the other members of the community.

SPENDING HOLY WEEK THERE — WHAT a beautiful experience to join the Holy Week celebrations in their parish and missions! I was invited to join at the main mission in Rutete on Good Friday, which consists of 10 villages. There were about 100 people when they started the Stations of the Cross around the Church. Never have I heard the passion readings sung by every character and a choir. By the time the veneration of the cross began there were at least 400 people in the church. Children gathered around the sanctuary for the entire service. During the veneration of the cross people lined up but genuflected three times before they kissed the cross. No doubt that the people are deeply rooted in their faith.

ON HOLY SATURDAY, after breakfast, we visited a few sick people in their homes. It took us through rough roads with rocks and mud holes and sometimes thick grass to the point of not recognizing where the road was. More than anointing of the sick, they prefer to receive communion as often as they can. Upon arrival in a home they will bring out a mat to lay on the floor in the living room where they receive you. The whole family wants you to pray together for God's healing for their sick. Our missionaries do this on a regular basis as they will drive to each village and spend the whole day visiting sometimes as many as 15 to 20 sick people.

There are times they must leave the vehicle or the motorcycle on the road and walk miles and miles to their homes due to bad road conditions. It is a great ministry these missionaries offer for the people and nothing stops them from doing it even amid challenges and difficulties. They have found a true home far away from their own personal homelands. The difference is that they do this with great joy, with no hesitation to, as Pope Francis would say, "smell like the sheep" in doing so.

EASTER SUNDAY was celebrated in a three-hour Mass at the main church in Rutete. Over 200 children sat around the altar in the sanctuary and quite actively participated in the prayers and singing. It is never boring for people as the priest engaged them throughout the homily that lasted for 25 minutes and used this moment to teach and

Fr. Thomas Vellappallil, M.S., Director of La Salette Mission Center, in front of our residence in St. Louis, Missouri

catechize them. The simple presence and personal witnessing of my brother La Salette Missionaries were a powerful way of sowing the seeds of reconciliation and love among their people who are exceptionally generous and deeply faith-filled. Acts 16:31 says, "Believe in the Lord Jesus and you and your family will be saved."

## And finally:

"Life is difficult" – these are the opening lines in *The Road Less Travelled* by Scott Peck. No doubt that life is a timeless game of problems and issues that challenge us. Our La Salette Missionaries and the people whom we serve, constantly face this reality every day. It is a great privilege and blessing for our Province, Mary, Mother of the Americas, through its Mission Office to reach out and financially support these Missionaries and the people they serve in the ten countries that I have mentioned above.

As "ambassadors for Christ" (2 Corinthians 5:20), the La Salette Missionaries around the world stand united, single-hearted in purpose, supporting one another and hoping to reconcile and liberate the world so that we can live together happily and in peace as one growing human family.

**Reflection Questions:**

• From the beginning of the formation of the Missionaries of La Salette, we have always had a sense of mission: at first in the diocese around Grenoble and in Switzerland when the Shrine was inaccessible in winter, then to Norway as the first religious community since the Lutheran Reformation, after this mission and as we left France new missions in Madagascar and Manitoba and Saskatchewan, we went to the USA, to Brazil and beyond as each Province and Region looked beyond their boundaries to reconcile new peoples and nations. Share reflections or stories you have heard or you personally experienced.

•Each of the Mission territories described but the La Salette Charism into practice based on the needs of the local people and church. How many different expressions of charism did you perceive? How would you see the Charism of La Salette better serving your location?

•How have you learned about the La Salette Missionary efforts around the world? How would you like to be further involved in this international effort?

# Chapter 18 —
# The La Salette Charism and How We Can Live It
### By Fr. Ron Gagné, M.S.

As believers, we are works in progress, always needing to learn more about God, ourselves and how we are to live with others as Christ would have us do. The following is a primer – a basic summary – of the mission of reconciliation which God gave to the Church.

The La Salette Missionaries have a special affinity for the ministry of reconciliation based on the event of the Apparition of Our Lady of La Salette on September 19, 1846. To facilitate reflection on their mission, the following are reflections from many authors about reconciliation – its origins, content and expression in the Church and the world of today.

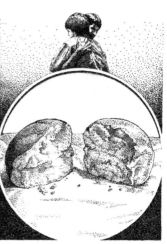

*La Salette Reconciliation* by
**Edward Tuttle**

## What is Reconciliation?

From the Merriam Webster dictionary, we read the following descriptions: to settle or resolve, to make consistent or congruous, to cause to submit to or accept something unpleasant.

In Biblical terms, "the verb 'to reconcile' ...denotes 'the action by which peace is made between personal enemies', as Moses brought together his estranged compatriots (Acts 7:26). It is the work of a mediator whose office is 'to make hostility cease, to lead to peace.'" (1)

More recently, Anglican Archbishop Desmond Tutu explained it as "...the restoration of trust in a relationship where trust has been violated, sometimes repeatedly." (2)

## From where did the Christian understanding of reconciliation come and why is it important?

"The Christian understanding of reconciliation emerges from the experience of the risen Christ... [In the words of Franciscan theologian Fr. Kenan Osborne] 'Christian life as such is a life in and through reconciliation. Were one to remove every aspect of reconciliation from the life of a Christian, there would be no Christian life at all.'" (3)

"The inseparability of the love of God and the love of neighbor in the teachings of Jesus make apparent that reconciliation with God is inseparable from reconciliation with others... Part of the mission of the Church, as alluded to in the resurrection accounts of the Gospels, is to extend the reconciling presence of Christ to the world." (4)

## What is the difference between "forgiveness" and "reconciliation"?

Since "forgiveness and reconciliation are often confused with each other," Dr. Everett L. Worthington, Jr., describes their differences. "Forgiveness is internal. I replace negative emotions or grants forgiveness as a gift. Reconciliation is interpersonal... It occurs within a relationship...."

"Reconciliation and forgiveness are related to each other but are not joined at the hip. We can forgive and not reconcile. For instance, I can forgive my father for the ways he hurt me when he was alive. Yet perhaps we cannot reconcile with him because he is dead." (5)

## What is a charism?

Each Religious Order has been given a charism (a gift) from their founder or founding event to be shared with the Church. The La Salette Missionaries have been given "reconciliation" as their charism. Concerning charisms, Fr. Marcello Azevedo, S.J., states that "Religious are not only followers but living continuations of Jesus and of their founders." (6) Therefore, their charism is embodied in their membership, in their ministries, and is shared by those who work with them.

## How did the "charism of reconciliation" first become associated with the La Salettes?

"Although 'reconciliation' did not play a major role in the expression of the La Salette community's self-understanding, it was nevertheless a major part of the devotion to Our Lady of La Salette. The invocation, 'Virgin Reconciler of sinners, pray for us,' is of unknown origin, but it is found as early as 1847...

"Perhaps the invocation came from Father Perrin, the pastor at La Salette, who founded the Confraternity of Our Lady of La Salette. For one of the conditions for membership in the Confraternity which was established on May 1, 1848, was the recitation of the invocation, 'Our Lady of La Salette, Reconciler of sinners, pray without ceasing for us who have recourse to you.'" (7)

**WHAT DOES THE NEW TEXT OF THE LA SALETTE RULE SAY ABOUT THE CONNECTION BETWEEN THE LA SALETTE MISSIONARIES AND RECONCILIATION?**

"The original spirit that dominates the new text is that of 'reconciliation':

- The first text chosen to express the charism of the La Salette Missionaries was 2 Cor. 5: 18-20. It speaks of the "ministry of reconciliation" that belongs to Christ and has been passed on to us.

- The second is John 19: 25-27, presenting the scene at the foot of the cross where Mary is being given as mother to all. A later text states that it was here that Mary 'was made Reconciler by her unique participation in the work of reconciliation accomplished by her Son.' (*Rule*, Ch. 1, par. 5, pg. 9)

- The text on God's plan for salvation puts the covenant within the reconciliation optic, viewing the mission of Christ as being sent by the Father to 'reconcile to himself all things,' (Colossians 1: 20).

- The final text deals with the Mission of the Church, 'to which has been given the ministry of reconciliation.'"

The Missionaries of Our Lady of La Salette are defined in part as "a Religious Congregation dedicated to the apostolate" and "inspired by the same Spirit who moved the Son of God to reconcile the world to the Father... (and who) strive to serve Christ and the Church devotedly for the fulfillment of the mystery of reconciliation." (8)

**WHERE IN THE SCRIPTURES IS "RECONCILIATION" MENTIONED?**

The term 'reconciliation' may not figure prominently as a theme in the scriptures, but as a theme (redemption, atonement) it runs like a red thread through all the sacred texts. From Genesis, chapters 1-11, we hear that:

• God creates a world that is good; God creates us 'in the image of God';

• There is a sin which brings alienation, injustice and death;

• "God, out of love and grace, freely chooses to overcome this alienation and redeem humanity from its bondage to sin and its consequences." (9)

Reconciliation begins, through Abraham, with the establishing of a covenant between God and God's people. Then follows the settlement of God's people in Canaan, their exile and return — another step in the story of reconciliation.

With the life, death and resurrection of Jesus, the story of our reconciliation is changed forever. The gift of reconciliation is seen as 'alive and well' in Jesus' acts of love and healing, of forgiveness and the gift of new life.

Reconciliation has to do with the way in which God relates to us as friends, by initiating reconciliation, and how we relate to God and to others. Also, reconciliation has to do with our patterning ourselves on how God relates with us, using this pattern in our relationships with others by making peace and restoring relationships. (10)

WHY IS SAINT PAUL SO IMPORTANT IN OUR CHRISTIAN UNDERSTANDING OF RECONCILIATION?

Paul is the central New Testament writer who advances and deepens the theology of reconciliation for Jew and Gentile alike. (11)

"The Greek words translated by 'reconciliation' or 'reconcile' only occur 15 times in the New Testament, and almost only in the Pauline letters. Yet they are highly significant for understanding what it is that Christians believe God has accomplished for the salvation of the world." (12)

For Paul, reconciliation is no mere theory. It "reflects (Paul's) own experiences as 'a man in Christ' who came to see life in a new way from the encounter he had with the living Lord on the way to Damascus. His 'conversion' marked the turning point and redirection of life best described by 'reconciliation'." (13)

Paul sees that "At the cross of Jesus,... the focal point of the divine 'rescue and recovery' operation... enshrines within it both past hopes and fears and a potential for turning history in a new direction...The consequences of that deed, 'once-for-all wrought out and completed, still need to be renewed in a proclamation and a contemporizing that is called by the apostle 'the ministry of reconciliation' (2 Corinthians 5:18)." (14)

St. Paul, Apostle and Martyr
(c.5-c.64/67)

"And all this is from God, who has reconciled us to himself through Christ and given us the ministry of reconciliation, namely, God was reconciling the world to himself in Christ, not counting their trespasses against them and entrusting to us the message of reconciliation. So we are ambassadors for Christ, as if God were appealing through us. We implore you on behalf of Christ, be reconciled to God" (2 Corinthians 5: 18-20).

In fact, "Paul identifies the Church's mission – its very reason for gathering – with reconciliation. Second Corinthians identifies the community of disciples as 'ambassadors' of reconciliation (see 2 Corinthians 5: 18-20)." (15) Concerning this passage, the scripture scholar, P. E. Hughes writes, "There is no sentence more profound in the whole of scripture." (16) Other passages of note on reconciliation are: Romans 5: 10-11; Ephesians 2: 12-16; Colossians 1: 22-23.

**How did Paul develop his theology of reconciliation?**

Paul did not hesitate to use pre-existing materials. "There are three texts that claim our interest — Romans 3:24-26; 2 Corinthians 5: 18-21; Colossians 1: 15-20 — where in all instances it is probable that Paul has taken and edited Jewish or Hellenistic Christian confessional, possibly liturgical, materials." (17)

Also, from his life-changing experience of conversion, we see that "reconciliation in Paul... always has to do with personal relationships. Arguably the most remarkable aspect of Paul's teaching on reconciliation is that in virtually every instance in which he uses the word or its cognates, God is the subject or agent of reconciliation... God is the one who takes the initiative in seeking an end to hostility." (18)

Another of Paul's concrete personal experiences was with the Christian community in Corinth who helped to form and deepen his theology of reconciliation. "The background to Paul's teaching is his own rejection by the Christian community in Corinth who questioned his authority and motives in writing to them. The language Paul uses is clearly intended to bring about reconciliation." (19)

From the needs of his own ministry, we can see how "Reconciliation is the way Paul formulated his gospel in communicating it to the Gentiles... For pagans, newly won over to Christ there was this pressing need: to receive assurance that the Lord who granted them pardon...was indeed the ruler of the spirit forces" from which they had been released. (20) Now they, in turn, were called to reconcile and release others.

So, again, Paul's idea of reconciliation is deeply personal. He desperately wants it to happen soon to his rambunctious community in Corinth and, by extension, to us who read his letters today. He wants all of us to become – in fact and soon –"ambassadors of reconciliation" in our daily lives.

Also, in his letter to Philemon which is only 25 verses, "Paul's recommendation to Philemon describes the Christian as one who exercises an individual reconciling role. The apostle acts as a go-between intent on bringing together the runaway slave Onesimus and his master Philemon. Each person in that three-cornered relationship was called upon to do something difficult and costly... Onesimus must return to his master and accept the consequences of his wrongdoing (vv. 12, 18). Philemon is called upon as a Christian to forgive and to welcome Onesimus back as a 'beloved brother' (v. 16) and even, it may be, to grant him his freedom (v. 21). 'And each of the three [is to do] what he is called upon to do as a Christian'. Here we see a picture of reconciliation in action on the horizontal and social plane." (21)

Simply summarized, "Paul's teaching on reconciliation bequeaths a legacy to the church, its ministers and teachers and members. It is the task of proclaiming both the bad news [we need to be reconciled with God and others, from whom we are alienated and separated] and the good news [God, through the death of Jesus for us on the cross, has forgiven and reconciled us to God, making us one family in Christ – a new creation; God is initiating our reconciliation; we must be grateful and become reconcilers in his name], so uniting man's need with God's deed." (22)

From Paul we receive the message, loud and clear, that "complete reconciliation is a future hope that shapes the way we live our lives. The Pauline trajectory of reconciliation does not come to an end with the closing of the New Testament canon... This is because reconciliation is not only a past historical event, but also the present activity of the Spirit of God in the life of the world drawing men and women into its orbit... That is why any account of the doctrine of reconciliation from a Pauline perspective is and must remain 'a relatively open enterprise.'" (23)

**WHAT ARE SOME THINGS THE BIBLE TELLS US ABOUT RECONCILIATION?**

Based on many passages from St. Paul, Fr. Robert J. Schreiter, C.PP.S., the noted scripture scholar, summarizes "major Christian insights into the process of reconciliation. It is these that form the background to the ministry of reconciliation, a ministry in which Paul exults so exuberantly in 2 Corinthians 5:20." (24)

a) It is God who initiates and brings about reconciliation:

We are invited by Christ to "cooperate in the process of reconciliation. But we must not forget whence it comes and who continues to guide it." (25) "The victim is called upon to turn to God and experience God's reconciling grace, and so, himself or herself, to become an agent of reconciliation." (26)

b) Reconciliation is more a spirituality than a strategy:

The process of reconciliation "cannot be reduced to a technical, problem-solving rationality. What undergirds a successful process of reconciliation is a spirituality, a view of the world that recognizes and responds to God's reconciling action in that world. That is why reconciliation is largely discovered rather than achieved." (27) It is more a gift that happens, a grace that is received, than a result which we directly cause.

c) Reconciliation makes of both victim and oppressor a new creation:

Reconciliation is about more than righting wrongs and repenting of evildoing. From the theology of St. Paul, we learn that reconciliation takes us to a place that we haven't been before; it makes both those involved into a "new creation." In other words, reconciliation may surprise both of us—with its transformation, results, or effects.

d) The new narrative that overcomes "the narrative of the lie" is the story of the passion, death, and resurrection of Jesus Christ:

In solidarity with suffering humanity, "God works reconciliation through the death of God's Son, Jesus Christ... The violence of our situations is met with the violence of Jesus' death; the dawning of the resurrection heralds that 'new place' in which those reconciled hope to find themselves....God reveals power where the powerful of this world least expect it. That is most evident in reconciliation itself, where those who are weak, broken, and oppressed show the way to those who had wielded power." (28)

e) Reconciliation is a multidimensional reality:

It "involves not just God's reconciling activity. It involves:

• coming to terms with the alienation that violence and oppression have created.
• lament and healing of memory.
• accepting all that is involved in the reconciliation, including those mysterious or seemingly-contradictory things we just can't understand; (29)

**WHAT IS IMPORTANT TO REMEMBER ABOUT THE MINISTRY OF RECONCILIATION?**

Cardinal Carlo Maria Martini, the Jesuit biblical scholar and pastoral leader, a friend of La Salette, shares with us his insights into living the charism of reconciliation. He outlines several qualities of the ministry of reconciliation.

1) **It is a difficult ministry:** "It is not simply an action of God meant to improve our situation, but rather a restorative act to set right a broken world, to reestablish a bond that had been torn or broken, to restore a relationship that had been undermined and weakened...The ministry of reconciliation is difficult precisely because it is a ministry that involves restoration. We are not dealing here with the spousal image of a marriage between two pure and innocent young people, approved by their respective parents, which moves ahead well and brings their union to completion. We are dealing instead with a broken marriage that needs to have a new rapport established. That is why the new covenant is hard work." (30)

Cardinal Carlo Maria Martini; photo: World Economic Forum

2) **It is very practical, a ministry of encouragement:** "...Paul says: 'We beseech you on behalf of Christ, be reconciled to God' (2 Corinthians 5: 20). I do not mean encouragement in the sense of saying that everything is fine, but that even if things are not fine, there is hope for you, there is a life of peace and harmony for you, there is a fullness of human and divine satisfaction for you. Let yourselves be reconciled to God, to the people around you, to your work, to your sicknesses, to your troubles, to your mental and emotional exhaustion—to everything you dislike in yourselves. Let yourselves be reconciled through reconciliation to God." (31)

3) **It is a ministry of peace:** "Our ministry is rooted in understand-

ing, compassion, and mercy. It is a ministry of peace...because it is a ministry that tries to understand the depths of the human heart, its sufferings, its ignorance, its resistance, and tries to approach it with sympathy, empathy, and mercy, to help people on their way, to help them take small steps. (32)

4) **It is a personal:** This ministry involves not only the life of another but of our own life, our own heart as well. "The ministry of reconciliation has to do especially with ourselves, because we cannot give peace if we do not have it. We cannot minister reconciliation if we are not ourselves reconciled. To be reconciled does not mean that we have nothing to forgive anybody; it means that we do have things to forgive and that we do forgive—ourselves and others." (33)

5) **It is a Marian ministry:** "...we should turn to Mary often for her help, for she is the mother of reconciliation... At the end of his ministry, (Jesus) entrusted Mary to John and John to Mary. This action serves as a sign of the reconciliation that has been accomplished and uses a covenant formula...The covenant is summarized in the mysterious relationship between the disciple and Mary. In the mutual entrusting of the disciple to Mary, there is a sort of foretaste, an ongoing guarantee that the mystery of the covenant resolves all the divisions and contradictions within us..." (34)

**WHY SHOULD OUR MINISTRY OF RECONCILIATION GO BEYOND PERSONAL PIETY TO CHRISTIAN ACTION?**

John W. de Gruchy, an internationally esteemed political theologian, states that "it would be a theological travesty if we tried to give an account of the Christian doctrine of reconciliation in a way that confined it to the realm of personal piety and relations, or to the sphere of the Church. If there was ever a theological theme that had to be developed in relation to the world in all its agony and hope, this is that theme." (35)

"The challenge in speaking about reconciliation from a Christian perspective is not simply that of proclaiming primary expressions of reconciliation but engaging in public life in ways that make God's gift of reconciliation and Christian hope a reality through secondary expressions." (36)

"...reconciliation is properly understood as a process in which we become engaged at the heart of the struggle for justice and peace in the world." (37) "...for Paul, theology and ethics are inseparably bound together. To be reconciled to God and to do justice are part and parcel of the same process." (38)

"The gospel of reconciliation thus leads directly to defining the mission of the Church in the world, namely to proclaim the gospel of reconciliation (2 Corinthians 5:11-20) and the eschatological (future) hope of God's restoration and renewal of the whole of creation... Reconciliation, in other words, is an open-ended process that occurs through the Spirit and anticipates the coming of God's reign of justice and peace..." (39)

**HOW CAN WE CONNECT OUR DAILY LIVES WITH THE MESSAGE AND MISSION OF LA SALETTE?**

It is important to realize the significance of St. Paul's invitation to live out our call from God to share in the mission of being a reconciler (2 Corinthians 5: 18-20). We can connect ourselves with the message and mission of La Salette by:

• reading the scripture

• praying daily

• celebrating the Eucharist regularly

• reading and reflecting on the message and mission of La Salette

• welcoming and responding to situations where reconciliation is needed

• learning more about the charism of La Salette (website: www. lasalette.org)

• supporting the ministries of the La Salette Missionaries

• not only thinking about but doing the work of reconciliation at home, at work, at church, within our local and national society

• becoming a La Salette Missionary—priest, sister, or brother

• connecting with a local La Salette Community or parish

• becoming a member of La Salette Laity

**Reflection Questions:**

• How have I been a part of a reconciliation situation between God and myself or with other people? How has that changed my life for the better?

• What does being a member of La Salette Laity call forth from me in putting the La Salette Charism into practice in my life and world?

• Jesus reconciled us to the Father through his death on the Cross and Rising to New Life how do I live out that Paschal Mystery and become one again with God and neighbor?

**Endnotes:**

(1) Ralph P. Martin, *Reconciliation: A Study of Paul's Theology*, John Knox Press, Atlanta, GA, pg. 104-105

(2) Everett L. Worthington and D.T. Drinkard, "Promoting Reconciliation Through Psychoeducational and Therapeutic Interventions," Journal of Social and Clinical Psychology (2000), as quoted in *Forgiveness and Reconciliation: Religion, Public Policy & Conflict Transformation*, Raymond G. Helmick, S.J. and Rodney L. Petersen, eds., pg. 166.

(3) Michael Weldon, *A Struggle for Holy Ground: Reconciliation and the Rite of Parish Closure*, pg. 30.

(4) *Ibidem*, pg. 31

(5) Everett L. Worthington, Jr., *Forgiving and Reconciling: Bridges to Wholeness and Hope*, pg. 170

(6) Marcello Azevedo, S.J., The Consecrated Life; Crossroads & Directions, Orbis Books, 1995, Guillermo Cook, trans., pg. 44-45

(7) Eugene Barrette, M.S., A Search into the origins and Evolution of the Charism of the Missionaries of Our Lady of La Salette, Gregorian University, Rome, for Licentiate in Spirituality, 1975, pg. 42

(8) *Ibidem*, pgs. 41-42

(9) John W. de Gruchy, Reconciliation: Restoring Justice, Fortress Press, Minneapolis, MN, 2002, pgs. 48-49

(10) *Ibidem*, pg. 51

(11) *Ibidem*.

(12) *Ibidem*.

(13) Martin, pg. 71

(14) *Ibidem*, pg. 227

(15) Weldon, pg. 33

(16) Martin, pg. 108

(17) *Ibidem*, pg. 81

(18) de Grunchy, pg. 52

(19) *Ibidem*, pg. 53

(20) Martin, pgs. 153-154

(21) *Ibidem*, pg. 231

(22) *Ibidem*, pg. 229, emphasis, brackets and italicized words were added.

(23) de Gruchy, pg. 56

(24) Robert J. Schreiter, C.PP.S., *Reconciliation: Mission and Ministry in a Changing Social Order*, Orbis Books, Maryknoll, NY, 1992, pgs. 59-62

(25) *Ibidem*,, pg. 59

(26) *Ibidem*.

(27) *Ibidem*, pg. 60

(28) *Ibidem*, pg. 61

(29) *Ibidem*, pg. 61-62

(30) Cardinal Carlo Maria Martini, *The Gospel According to St. Paul: Meditations on His Life and Letters*, translated by Marsha Daigle-Williamson, PhD, The Word among Us Press, Ijamsville, MD, 2008, pg. 118.

(31) *Ibidem*.

(32) *Ibidem*, pg. 122

(33) *Ibidem*, pg. 124

(34) *Ibidem*, pgs. 124-125

(35) de Grunchy, pg. ix

(36) *Ibidem*, pg. 19

(37) *Ibidem*, pg. 21

(38) *Ibidem*, pg. 54

(39) *Ibidem*, pgs. 55-56

# Section 4 –
# La Salette at Work Today

La Salettes and laity gather for Mass in front of the
Basilica on the Holy Mountain of La Salette in France

# Chapter 19 —
# Social Ministry —
# Reconciled with God's Plan

By Chris Austgen,
Director of La Salette Laity,
Province of Mary, Mother of the Americas

The charism of La Salette Missionaries and La Salette Laity is one of reconciliation. One way to define reconciliation is "to make compatible or consistent." Being La Salette Missionaries or Laity, we strive to be reconciled with God and should always try to be consistent with God's plan. In big and small ways, we need to always be aware of God's plan and then be consistent with that plan.

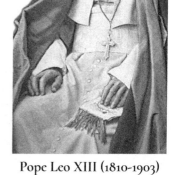

Pope Leo XIII (1810-1903)

God's plan concerning social ministry is crystal clear. You can find it everywhere in the Bible, writings of the popes, church documents, and the human heart. Official church documents on social ministry date back to 1891, Pope Leo XIII's encyclical, *Rerum Novarum* (*On the Condition of Labor*), which explained the Church's stance on the ever-growing gap between owners and laborers during the industrial revolution.

God sent his only Son, Jesus, to teach us by word and deed the importance of social ministry. In Matthew 25:31-46 Jesus tells us how to be reconciled to his Father and be consistent with God's plan:

"Come, you who are blessed by my Father. Inherit the kingdom prepared for you from the foundation of the world. For I was hungry and you gave me food, I was thirsty and you gave me drink, a stranger and you welcomed me, naked and you clothed me, ill and you cared for me, in prison and you visited me.' Then the righteous will answer him and say, 'Lord, when did we see you hungry and feed you, ... 'Amen, I say to you, whatever you did for one of these least brothers of mine, you did for me.' (Matthew 25:34b-37a, 45b).

"Then he will say to those on his left, 'Depart from me, you accursed, into the eternal fire prepared for the devil and his angels. For I was hungry, and you gave me no food, I was thirsty, and you gave me no drink, ... Then they will answer and say, 'Lord, when did we see you hungry or thirsty ... 'Amen, I say to you, what you did not do for one of these least ones, you did not do for me.' And these will go off to eternal punishment, but the righteous to eternal life" (Matthew 25: 41-43, 46).

God's ultimate plan for each of us is to have eternal life with him in the glory of his Kingdom. Living a life according to the La Salette charism of reconciliation, being consistent with God's plan, and following Matthew 25 will allow us the chance to be rewarded in Heaven.

Jesus started his public life by defining his ministry in the Gospel of Luke. He read a passage from Isaiah (61:1) proclaiming good news to the poor, liberty to captives, sight to the blind, and setting the downtrodden free. We cannot call ourselves followers of Jesus unless we take up his mission. Again, going back to the definition of reconciliation, we must live a life consistent with God's plan. We are called to:

- Bring "good news to the poor" in a society where millions lack the necessities of life.

- Bring "liberty to captives" when so many are enslaved by poverty, addiction, ignorance, discrimination, violence, or disabling conditions.

- Bring "new sight to the blind" in a culture where the excessive pursuit of power or pleasure can spiritually blind us to the dignity and rights of others. and

- "Set the downtrodden free" in communities where crime, racism, family disintegration, and economic and moral forces leave people without real hope. (Communities of Salt and Light, USCCB)

# Our Lady of La Salette is one of us:

The Apparition at La Salette begins with the words, *"Come closer, my children, do not be afraid."* This directive is at the heart of all we do each day for those who serve our local community, for instance, serving at a Food Pantry. They are called to share what we have both physically in the form of food and spiritually in the form of our love for every client who comes through their doors because they are our brothers and sisters in Christ.

Our Lady of La Salette could have been an imposing, intimidating figure, as she is the Queen of Heaven. But she is also the Mother of Mercy, Blessed among Women, Most Holy, Most Pure, and Mother of the Church. She is the mother of Jesus. At La Salette her appearance and her attitude of service and humility were on full display. She wore a long simple apron which is what the common women in France wore at that time. Her clothes were work clothes –nothing fancy or prestigious. Today she could wear a waitress uniform or a hard hat and construction vest. Her appearance and clothes made her one of her people – one of us.

Our Lady met Maximin and Melanie where they were — physically, emotionally, and spiritually. She did not wait for them to be in church before she appeared to them. She did not wait for them to graduate from school. She did not wait for them to become older and wiser. She dressed like a laborer and showed up at their workplace.

So, by Mary appearing to two uneducated, unchurched, peasant children she is showing us the value and importance of every person. Each one of us is a child of God and deserves to be treated with dignity and respect. That importance and inherent dignity of every person is the foundation of all social ministry. It is the stick by which every ministry, every parish, every person will be measured. Does what I do hurt or help the dignity of God's children? Is the way I treat people consistent with God's plan? In Genesis 4:9 when the question is asked, "Am I my brother's keeper?" the answer is a resounding yes.

*"A great famine is coming.... If they are converted, rocks and stones will turn into heaps of wheat, and potatoes will be self-sown in the fields."*

While famine typically results from a shortage of food, one can also experience a famine of compassion. When people are greedy or selfish, there is a famine of compassion and that leads to many types of famine including food. However, the opposite can also true. When people are giving and compassionate, when they are "converted," when they are reconciled, when they are consistent with God's plan, then great things can happen.

While the Gospels show us many miracles and signs of God's love for us, the Resurrection and the story of Jesus feeding the multitudes are the only two miracles recorded in all four Gospels. That makes these two miracles even more special and significant. Jesus' disciples brought him a problem and Jesus presented a solution.

Jesus didn't disperse the crowds or tell his followers where to go find food. He did not suddenly have meals appear in front of each person. His answer to his disciples was "You give them something to eat" (Matthew 14:16). So, they brought Jesus five barley loaves and two fish. Then, confused but trusting Jesus, the disciples went around feeding the hungry. An extraordinary sign that Jesus cares about our basic needs and he wants us to care about other people's basic needs.

What impact did this miracle have on the multitudes of people following him that day? Did people realize the miracle that day was also a miracle of compassion and sharing? Out of all the thousands of people who were following Jesus, maybe some of them brought food. What if the crowds who saw Jesus' disciples sharing what little they had, became aware that they should do the same thing?

When Mary said, "*If (my people) are converted, rocks and stones will turn into heaps of wheat and potatoes will be self-sown in the fields,*" she was calling us to action. Mary was calling us to become a world full of compassionate, giving people who care for each other – from helping them to clear rocks from a field to sharing what we have with others.

Every year in our local parish food pantry, we have a Thanksgiving Blessing Give Away. Families must preregister and then on the Sunday before Thanksgiving they come to the Church to receive all the groceries they need for Thanksgiving dinner including a gift card for a turkey/ham and a pumpkin pie. Funding for this large project comes solely from our parishioners' monetary donations.

This year donations were down heading into the Give Away. A few days before the Give Away, a counselor from the local High School texted asking to add several more families to our list. While I was thinking, "funding is so tight this year I don't think we can afford to take on more families", my fingers texted back, "Of course". Within a minute of sending that text, a parishioner handed me a check for $1,000 which more than covered the cost of the additional families. Striving to be consistent with God's plan and recalling the message from Jesus who fed the multitudes, I realize that we also experienced a miracle of sorts that day.

## Do you say your prayers well, my children?

*The Annunciation* (Composition Sketch)
by Dante Gabriel Rossetti (1828–1882)

During the apparition, Mary asked the children about their prayer life. Seeing that they were lacking in this aspect of their lives, she told them to say an Our Father and Hail Mary each day.

THE HAIL MARY: The first part of the Hail Mary is acknowledging her role in salvation history. Her "yes" brought Jesus to the world. Mary, under the title of Our Lady of La Salette, implores us to say "yes" to her Son.

The second half of the Hail Mary asks Mary to pray for us sinners.

Mary, again under the title of Our Lady of La Salette, brings to us the importance of identifying where in our own lives we are disconnected from God. How we are sinners in need of prayer and forgiveness. We can and should reflect on how we can better serve our brothers and sisters in Christ so that we are reconciled, consistent with God's plan.

**The Lord's Prayer:** We all know how the Our Father starts. It begins with Our Father not "My Father." That is key in social ministry. We believe that because God is *Our* Father, we are *our* brothers' and *our* sisters' keepers: the immigrant struggling with obstacles we can't imagine; the military veteran who can't quite fit back into our society; the unemployed and under-employed who just want a stable daily life. They are our brothers and sisters and are all seeking the Kingdom.

William Barclay, renowned speaker and Bible commentator, wrote, "The Kingdom of God is a society upon earth where God's will is as perfectly done as it is in heaven." As La Salette Missionaries and Laity, we are blessed with the desire to assist daily in small ways so that God's will may be done on earth as perfectly as it is done in heaven.

In this special prayer, taught to us by Jesus (Matthew 6:9-13), "Our Father" are the first two words because our Father in heaven needs to always be first. We need to acknowledge and revere God's absolute place in our lives. Sometimes in the business of helping others, we lose track of ourselves and our dependent relationship with God. For us to minister to others, we must also minister to ourselves by keeping God first. Once we have God properly placed at the front of our lives, then we can take a closer look at our needs and necessities with the next part of this Perfect Prayer.

Life on Earth is a team project and can only be truly successful when we work to build each other up. Just as there is no "I" in team there is no I, me or mine in this Perfect Prayer. The focus is on our, us and we. God has provided us with "our daily bread," yet there is hunger in the world. God has provided us with enough of everything to thrive in our daily lives, but we get in our own way and sadly we get in other people's way.

The second half of the Our Father is a prayer of sharing. Because of our commitment to social concerns, we are keenly aware of sharing and the inspiring things that happen when people share. At our parish food pantry, two men in their late twenties walked in. One was doing some contract work on a house whose owner was allowing him to sleep there. This client was sharing his good fortune with the other client by letting him sleep there too (with the owner's knowledge). This second client knew about our food pantry and brought the contractor with him to get groceries. Again, life on Earth is a team project. If we share our daily blessings from God, then his perfect Kingdom can exist on Earth.

It would please Our Lady so much if we would try to live the Our Father and not just recite it. Once we put God first, help our brothers and sisters in Christ, be God's instruments in building His Kingdom on Earth, and share our daily bread we can one day join Our Lady of La Salette and her Son in His Kingdom.

*"I gave you six days to work; I kept the seventh for myself, and no one will give it to me. This is what makes the arm of my Son so heavy... In the summer, only a few elderly women go to Mass."*

The importance of attending Mass on a weekly basis is at the heart of our Catholic faith. The Eucharist is the source and summit of the Catholic faith. However, just "attending" Mass is not enough. Just as spending time in a garage does not make you a mechanic, showing up at Mass does not make you a Catholic. Our Lady of La Salette communicates to us how troubled her Son is that we do not understand the importance of Mass. In many aspects, the importance of Mass can be seen in how we receive Jesus and then how we bring him out into our world.

The United States Conference of Catholic Bishops tell us, "We need to be a Church that helps believers recognize Jesus in the breaking of the bread and those without bread" (Communities of Salt and Light). The natural outflow of participating in the Lord's Supper is to make sure that our neighbors have supper.

In Pope Benedict XVI encyclical, *Deus Caritas Est* (*God Is Love*), he highlighted the role of social ministry. He stated that "The Church cannot neglect the service of charity any more than she can neglect the Sacraments and the Word". Service to others is not optional if you want to call yourself a Catholic. Once you fully attend Mass, incorporating the Word into your every thought and action, accepting the graces that are offered in that Sacrament, you will be drawn to serving others. Our Lady's urgent message concerning Mass attendance is so much more than just showing up on Sunday mornings.

**"May we console you by a holy life and so come to share the eternal life Christ gained by his cross" (the last line of the Memorare to Our Lady of La Salette, revised):**

May we console you by a holy life. What a beautiful thought. Each of us has the opportunity every day to live a holy life. We can decide to listen to Our Lady of La Salette's concerns and follow her guidance. We can decide to be open to be reconciled with God, either to be consistent with God's plan or ignore it. We can decide to fully participate in Mass. We can decide to follow the example of Jesus and be our brothers' and sisters' keeper. We can decide to approach the people on the margins of our society just as Mary approached Maximin and Melanie. We can decide to serve God by serving others every day.

By reminding Maximin of his conversation with his father in the field of Coin, Mary shows us that her Son is always with us and always aware of our daily struggles. In God's eyes every person and every life event are significant. God never stops listening to the hope and fears of his children. We can console Mary and be consistent with God's plan by doing our part to see everyone as a child of God and acknowledging that we are all significant in God's eyes.

**Reflection questions:**

• The Last Judgement as presented in Matthew's Gospel Chapter 25 shows us our ultimate responsibility of putting Jesus' teaching into practice. How are you personally involved in social actions for others?

• "Mary is one of us." What does the apparition teach you about her and so lead you to act in new ways towards others?

• In the Our Father we ask him to give us "our daily bread." How do we cooperate with God in providing daily bread to others? Is it more than food?

# Chapter 20 —
# La Salette: Reconciliation with the Earth
### By Fr. Paul Belhumeur, M.S.

Anyone familiar with La Salette and its spirituality knows the importance of reading the signs of the times and combating contemporary evils to live out and practice more effectively our charism of reconciliation. Issues to choose from abound in our current world. I would like to propose that we look at climate change in the light of the La Salette charism of reconciliation.

## A sign of the times:

Despite the deniers who still exist, climate change presents a huge challenge for humans. The indifference of many, in the face of the problems associated with climate change, also puts the earth, our home, at grave risk. The recent withdrawal of the U.S. from the Paris accord on climate change illustrates this. Too many in our society putting financial gain, or a strong economy, ahead of any other consideration.

"The thirst for power and possessions knows no limits. In this system, which tends to devour everything which stands in the way of increased profits, whatever is fragile, like the environment, is destroyed before the interests of a deified market, which becomes the only rule." (1)

As a consequence, species of all kinds continue to disappear from our world at an alarming rate. In that process, humans become impoverished, along with the earth.

Thomas Berry describes humans as becoming autistic in relation to the natural world:

> "We live in a world of computers, cell phones, digital photography, television, highways and automobiles, supermarkets, and trivial playthings for our children – all fostered by inescapable advertising aimed at stirring our deepest compulsions to buy and consume. Our education is focused on producing skills associated with the production, distribution, and use of such a multitude of objects with none of the exaltation of soul provided by our experience of natural phenomena." (2)

To the many reasons given as to why young people grow more absent from formal religion, we could add Berry's comment: "As the grandeur of the natural world declines, the primordial manifestation of the divine is progressively diminished." (3) This can lead to spiritual illiteracy with what some authors call the two books about God: the Book of Nature and the Book of Sacred Scripture.

In the face of all this, Berry challenges religious communities "to accept a new role, the most difficult role that any of us has been asked to fulfill, that of stopping the devastation that humans, principally those in our commercially driven societies, are inflicting on the planet." (4)

Perhaps, in all of this, La Salette Missionaries, and anyone else interested in La Salette, can find an opportunity to broaden our understanding of the charism of reconciliation. We can find much said and written about the need for reconciliation of human with human. Likewise, about the reconciliation of humans with God. Maybe the time has come to show more concern about reconciliation of humans with the earth and with all creatures of God's world.

Among other meanings, reconciliation implies making peace among warring parties—individuals, groups, nations, etc. We could say that humans seem presently at war with the earth and its creatures. Consider some of the reports in newscasts and newspapers:

> • oceans are getting more acidic because of climate warming. This negatively affects marine life and its support systems so that reefs are bleaching and in danger of dying; fish stocks are depleted, and their existence threatened.

•outbreaks of red tide and other dangerous algae become more frequent because of excessive or careless use of chemicals and fertilizers.

•forests, important for the capture of $CO_2$ from the air, are threatened in various parts of the world by overcutting or by fires.

•safe drinking water becomes scarce in many parts of the world, or is sometimes poisoned by human activity like fracking, mining or improper disposal of the byproducts of coal burning.

•We read about islands of plastic bags in the ocean. Fish, birds, and other marine life die from ingesting pieces of plastic, or plastic in the process of breaking down into invisible bits. I have read one news story that claims there is more plastic in the ocean by weight than fish.

•We read and hear about mass extinction of species. For example, "If you were alive in the year 1970, more than one in four birds in the U.S. and Canada has disappeared in your lifetime." (5)

•land is being abused through monoculture, excessive use of fertilizers, which kills natural organisms, and pesticides which kill the pollinators needed for many crops.

•rising ocean temperatures contribute to more severe storms; melting glaciers and polar ice are contributing to rising oceans.

•many places are experiencing more frequent occurrences of what used to be known as 100-year floods.

•in India and parts of Africa desertification is becoming a problem. As explained in a recent BBC News special program, this can refer to farmlands whose ability to produce abundant and nutritious food was destroyed or drastically diminished by overuse of chemical fertilizers. In other areas excessive cutting of trees resulted in the land not being able to produce because of soil erosion and inability to retain water.

•unusual heat waves: highs of 108° and 109° F in Western Europe in the summer of 2019.

•monster storms are getting more frequent and more devastating.

Judging by the huge damages caused by climate warming, we presently seem on the losing end of the war between humans and the environment and need to make drastic changes before it is too late. Again today, both the BBC News and PBS News were citing the findings of scientists who keep track of $CO_2$ stored in the atmosphere to have reached a new high (news programs on Nov. 25, 2019).

*(Note: The author assumes that anyone who has read major papers and books on global warming would accept all the above as generally known and accepted facts. See the end notes for more specific references.)*

## Where do we see the church in the face of this ecological crisis?

Thomas Berry assessed the situation in the following way. "At the present time (2009) the protest of the pillage of the earth, compassion for the earth, and commitment to the preservation of the earth are left mainly to secular environmental organizations as though the matter were too peripheral to be of concern to Christians." (6) In 2012 Fred Bahnson and Norman Wirzba treated the problem from a Christian perspective with their book, *Making Peace with the Land, God's Call to Reconcile with Creation.* Along with the facts and figures about the problem, they have many quotes from Scripture to help us consider the situation with the eyes of faith. Then in 2015 Pope Francis published the encyclical letter, *'Laudato si'*, a must reading for anyone who wants to take a serious look at the challenges we face, especially for La Salettes and our partners in ministry, because the problems desperately call for reconciliation.

We need to remember that environmental issues are justice and peace issues. Those who were the least responsible for causing the present crisis are often those who are suffering the most from its negative effects, e.g., those people who are forced to leave their homes because of the rising oceans. (7)

When a preacher attempts to

bring up environmental matters in a homily, he is apt to get serious pushback from some in the congregation who accuse him of delving into politics, and "there is no room for politics in church." For some, social justice issues are politics. This attitude is worsened by the polarization that divides people on these matters. Many conservatives see this as a strictly progressive issue pursued mainly by those, they consider radical liberals. Thus, they feel the need to dig in against them at any cost, including total denial. That helps explain why some religious people deny climate science. Their denials are "generally spurred not by theology but by an assumption that climate science is based on political beliefs—namely liberal ones." (8)

## Importance of looking at environmental issues from the perspective of faith, or the heart:

In view of the denial, and obfuscation happening around climate warming, (9) we must not put much hope on governments seriously addressing this problem. Consider the irony that on November 5, 2019, BBC News announced in the same newscast that the U.S. began the formal process of withdrawal from the Paris Accord, while announcing in the same program that 1100 scientists from 153 countries had signed a document emphasizing the reality and the dangers of climate warming and the urgent need for major action. Zak probably states it the most succinctly when he states that converting non-believers on political grounds seems next to impossible. (10)

In an article on Katharine Hayhoe, Zak develops that argument very cogently. Hayhoe, one of America's top scientists and an evangelical Christian has taken on the mission of persuading skeptics. In her talks she stresses that climate problems are "understood through science but solved only through faith." (11)

"When she put climate problems in terms of heart and soul, not just the brain and politics, her family started to see. Taking care of the planet was another way to care for people, another way to love." (12)

Mary Robinson, former president of Ireland and U.N. special envoy on climate change, decided to write her book "Climate Justice" shortly after the birth of her first grandchild. The thought of the kind of world in which her grandchild would grow up, led to her deciding to address the situation from the heart. The chapters of her book present examples of hope, action, and leadership.

Even before climate change became the issue that we hear about every day, Mary at La Salette in 1846 warned of the need for conversion when she said, "*If my people will not submit, I shall be forced to let go the arm of my Son...*" She then went on to outline some of the consequences of the sins she reminds us of. Greed was part of what made food shortages worse and caused hunger and starvation in France, Ireland and elsewhere in Europe.

In addition to the ecological crises Mary mentions, (wheat, walnuts, raisins, potatoes going bad) wheat shortages were made worse by speculators who bought up the supplies the government was trying to make available, in order to drive up the prices and increase their profits. (13) The poor could not afford to buy whatever was available and thus suffered the consequences.

Greed continues to hinder any significant progress in alleviating climate warming. The search for greater profits leads to a number of abuses to the environment: excessive cutting of forests, overuse of chemical fertilizers and pesticides, poor disposal of the byproducts of mining or energy production, fracking near dwellings or aquifers, over-reliance on fossil fuels, etc.

Many ridicule proposals to take measures to slow down climate change or keep it at survivable levels because of the costs. Some corporations are in denial because of what effect it would have on their bottom lines to take necessary measures. Politicians avoid some measures that scientists recommend but are considered political suicide—carbon taxes for example. The costs of doing nothing, however, add up to even more as storms and other climate events are more frequent and more devastating because of the warming air ( which holds more moisture and thus brings greater flooding), and warming oceans which increase the power of hurricanes and typhoons.

## Cost of Climate Warming:

When Katharine Hayhoe testified before the Budget Committee

of Congress, she stressed in her opening 5-minute introduction the massive financial consequences of ignoring climate change. When the time came for committee members to question her, they spent their allotted time trying to gain political points by ridiculing the green new deal others had floated elsewhere as a possible beginning towards a solution. They chose to ignore what she had presented and what common sense tells us: ignore a problem at the beginning and it most often ends up costing more later.

If you follow news accounts regularly, you have heard much about the cost of global warming. Keep in mind that 12% of the world's population lives along the coasts of the world's oceans. If oceans keep rising at present levels, these people will have to move. Where? At what cost? Where will the money come from?

This is not just a future event; it is already happening in low-lying countries and islands, for example, Kiribati. This is an island nation of many islands scattered across an ocean area the size of Alaska and it sits only 6½ feet above sea level. The former president of its 100,000 people arranged the purchase of 6,000 acres of forested land on Fiji's 2nd largest island for a million dollars so that they can move. Imagine the cost of moving and rebuilding!

On September 10, 2019, BBC News highlighted a report from Ban Key Moon indicating that $1.7 trillion would be needed to deal with specific problems now existing in 5 specific areas: agriculture, water, mass migration, aid to poorer areas affected, and sustainability in many areas because of heat.

Last fall hurricane Dorian devastated the Bahamas. Estimates of damages by some experts total 7 to 8 billion dollars--not counting the damages to their only industry of tourism. Having seen the damages that happened to the worst hit islands, tourists are not going to the islands that were not affected as seriously and are still open for business.

One final example. On November 14, 2019, the *Washington Post* had an article on "Venice Goes Underwater," saying historic flooding could cost hundreds of millions of dollars: highest tidewaters in 50 years, 85% of city flooded, and water peaked at over 6 feet.

"In its nine-century history, the opulent St. Mark's Basilica has flooded six times – twice in the past two years… Climate scientists predict Venice will be entirely underwater by the end of this century." (14)

## Need for Hope:

What can we do in the face of the enormity of this problem and the seeming indifference or denial of many? For starters we need to avoid giving the impression that the problem is beyond solution and that small efforts do not matter. Such an attitude can add to the problem of global warming and become a self-fulfilling prophecy of doom.

PBS News gave us an example of this in a recent book interview of David Wallace-Wells, about his book, *The Uninhabitable Earth: Life after Warming*, where the author doesn't give much hope of people attaining the 1.5° C growth in warming given at the Paris Climate Summit as a goal to avoid exceeding. He goes on to say that without drastic interventions (for example, almost total cutback from fossil fuels), we will soon reach a 3° or 4° C rise in warming, with frightening circumstances to follow. The author seems to dismiss all the small steps many are taking currently.

In this regard, Mary at La Salette uses a more balanced appeal to conversion. Yes, in her message she speaks of the dire consequences of not heeding her call to change: children will die, and adults will suffer and face famine. But she also gives reason to hope that change, conversion, will bring blessings. Speaking in prophetic language, she says: *"If they are converted, rocks and stones will turn into heaps of wheat, and potatoes will be self-sown in the fields."*

Granted, we need prophetic figures like Al Gore, Katharine Hayhoe, Greta Thunberg, Pope Francis and many others to warn us of the coming disaster if we take no action. But we also need people to keep hope alive in us and who encourage us to take whatever actions we can to help ease the problem. Mary Robinson does that well in her book, *Climate Justice*, where each chapter gives us examples of people in different parts of the world who are part of the fight for a sustainable future. Likewise, we need more articles like that of Patricia Bergen, "Hope for Christians Never Runs Dry: consciousness grew, the force of resistance grew stronger, and now children have the floor." (15)

As people who honor Our Lady of La Salette, we will want to be signs of hope. While realizing that greater measures are needed and that we need to push for them as best we can (through our voting, contacts with elected officials, activism, and the like) in the meantime let us do our bit towards a solution, rather than adding to the problem.

## What are some of the small things you can do to help be signs of hope?

This is a short list of what we can do to learn to live in solidarity with the natural world, in the hope that each of us you will draw up our own list, or at least become more aware of little things you can do.

- turning down the thermostat for sleeping at night
- caution about wasting water (*as a reminder that many do not have convenient, safe water*)
- lights off when not needed
- use of a sweater instead of turning up heat
- collecting rainwater for garden (caution re mosquitoes)
- organic gardening or purchasing of organic produce (*as a way of showing support for growers using methods that are healthier for the environment*)
- composting for reducing waste and providing good fertilizer

- worm composting for winter use
- air drying laundry
- use of tote bags for shopping
- use of cut grass for heating compost pile
- growing your own vegetables for six months of the year
- standard shift automobiles
- recycling
- encouraging others to be aware and join effort
- adaptation to one's diet, considering the problems caused by the amount of beef in human diet...

Some may look at this list and scoff – big deal! What difference does that make? I might respond by asking, what difference would it make if many of us could make millions become more aware of their carbon footprint? What if only one billion people showed more concern about the environment? At the very least there might be fewer plastic bags and things in our rivers and oceans, killing marine life and birds.

## La Salette and Climate Warming:

What does La Salette have to do with all of this? If you look at all the implications of climate warming from the perspective of La Salette, you may find many connections between the two: the place, the message, Our Lady's tears, the call to conversion, the Missionaries of Our Lady and their call to be messengers of hope and conversion (reconciliation), some of the texts used for the Mass in honor of Our Lady of La Salette — all of these can provide links to the climate warming crisis and help us to look at it from the perspective of our charism of reconciliation. In addition to calling for reconciliation of humans with God, and of humans with one another, in today's world we must call for reconciliation with the earth, which Pope Francis calls our mother and our sister in 'Laudato si'.

THE PLACE: At an altitude of 6,000 feet, the area at the site of the apparition stands way above and far from the pollution that endangers the air of some of the large cities of our world. You may remember the images of large cities in India, where citizens are urged to stay indoors if they can, because of health problems which will result from the polluted air.

**BEAUTY OF THE AREA:** In contrast to the noise and distractions of our city life, La Salette offers an opportunity to commune with nature and find refreshment. La Salette leads to prayer.

**READINGS FOR THE LA SALETTE MASS:** The Genesis reading of the flood sent by God to punish sinners of the time, could make us wonder if God has changed his mind about not flooding the earth again in that way. Is it God that has changed, or is it we humans who are causing many of the unusual flooding events that have occurred recently because of global warming? Let's not forget the rainbow of that reading that was given as a sign of hope. Today La Salette missionaries and laity can continue to provide that sign of hope by our lifestyle, our choices, and the message we give to others, directly or indirectly.

At La Salette Mary shows her concern for the things of God's creation. The Beautiful Lady speaks of grapes, wheat, potatoes and walnuts. She also shows her concern for people. She speaks of their work and their habits. She is concerned about what will happen to the people if they are not converted. She weeps as she speaks of the starvation that adults will face and, no doubt as a mother, is saddened knowing that some children will die in the arms of those holding them.

Wouldn't Mary also weep today over her people who face starvation in different areas of the world most affected by the negative effects of global warming — desertification, extremes of drought or flooding, etc., which make it virtually impossible to grow the crops they need to grow? Wouldn't Mary weep today along with those who grieve for relatives and friends killed, injured or made homeless by monster storms that have destroyed their homes and livelihood, for example, Hurricane Dorian (2019)?

Mary pointed to the only real way to bring about the changes we need to survive. Way before modern specialists studying climate warming concluded that we cannot and must not expect governments to solve the problems we face unless a change of heart and attitudes occurs in people, in 1846 Mary called for conversion. Then as now, sin caused many of the problems Mary spoke about, or made natural problems worse. Greed, for example, made food shortages worse when speculators hoarded supplies in order to have prices rise.

How many people suffer today because of drug prices and profits out of proportion to the costs of production? How many toxic cleanup sites were left behind after companies made their profits and left dangerous messes behind?

In writing to the Corinthians, St. Paul reminds us that "God ...has reconciled us to himself through Christ" (2 Corinthians 5:15b). The Gospel, often used for Masses of La Salette, showing Mary at the foot of the cross, reminds us that this was accomplished through the death of Christ on the cross.

The cross provides us with the best symbol we can find of all the elements of reconciliation that we strive for. The vertical piece reminds us we need to turn to God; the horizontal piece reminds us we have to consider others and the effects of our actions on them; finally, the cross has to be solidly grounded in the earth — and so it must happen in our efforts about global warming.

### Reflection Questions:

• The need for conversion that Mary called for at La Salette remains for today. What does that mean for us as we focus on the environment today?

• How can we personally come to a greater appreciation of our mother earth? How do we combat global warming and destructive practices in the world today as stewards of creation?

• How do we address the need to reach out in love to the poor who suffer the most from global warming and the devastation it brings? How can we become messengers of hope in a world where despair and anger prevail?

Let us do what we can even if as individuals we cannot solve the problem. At least in so doing, we do not become part of the problem. To the extent that we can, let us get involved in solutions, thus acting as messengers of hope.

**Endnotes:**

(1) Pope Francis, *Joy of the Gospel* (*Evangelii gaudium*, 56.)

(2) Thomas Berry, *The Christian and the Fate of the Earth*, p. 74.

(3) *Ibidem*, p. 80.

(4) *Ibidem*, p. 68.

(5) Gustave Axelson, "Vanishing," in *Living Bird*, Autumn, 2019, p. 45.

(6) Berry, p. 71.

(7) Mary Robinson, *Climate Justice*, especially p. 85, which summarizes chapter 7 of her book to make this point.

(8) Dan Zak, *Washington Post* article of July 15, 2019, on Katharine Haydoe.

(9) Dan Zak, *Washington Post* article of August 27, 2019, "How Should we Talk about What's Happening to our Planet?

(10) Zak, July 15, 2019 article.

(11) *Ibidem*.

(12) *Ibidem*.

(13) Maurice Tochon, M.S., *La Salette dans la France de 1846*, p. 109 and note.

(14) *Washington Post*, November 18, 2019.

(15) *National Catholic Reporter*, November 15-28, 2019, pp. 9 & 11

# Chapter 21 —
# Reconciling Racism

By Fr. Ron Foshage, M.S.

James Byrd, Jr. and his gravestone in cemetery in Jasper,
Texas; photo of gravestone: Mike Lout, reporter

On September 15, 1963, four African American girls were killed when dynamite exploded outside the Sixteenth Street Baptist Church in Birmingham, Alabama. Reacting to this tragedy, Dudley Randall wrote the poem, "The Ballad of Birmingham" which presents the perspective of the mother of one of the victims. She refuses to allow her daughter to march against racism, for fear of the police, with their dogs, clubs, and hoses. In the poem she writes:

"No, baby, no you may not go For I fear those guns will fire. But you may go to church instead And sing in the children's choir."

The irony here is chilling for you and I remember what happened next. The poem continues:

"For when she heard the explosion. Her eyes grew wet and wild. She raced through the streets of Birmingham Calling for her child."

For me, this poem testifies to the truth that it is not possible to run away from evil because it will follow us and will not go away on its own. I believe racism is a particular form of evil which must be destroyed if we are ever to live together in peace in our society. For there really can be no hiding place in the struggle against an evil such as racism. Moments of decision are forced upon us and we must decide courageously how we will act.

## James Byrd, Jr. (1949-1998):

A Hate Crime Happens in Our Own Small Town. Little did I realize in early June of 1998 that this evil of racism would so affect my life and the lives of the townspeople of Jasper, Texas. For early on Sunday morning, June 7, 1998, a hate crime took place on a deserted road just outside our town that shocked us as a community and as a nation and changed our lives forever.

I don't think I can convey to you the fear that we felt in our hearts when we saw members of the Black Panthers running down our streets with rifles in their hands – all young African-American men – telling the people in the African-American community to arm themselves and to protect their homes and their property.

Those people were our neighbors and our friends, we worship with them in our churches and serve on committees with them in our community. And now they are being told to arm themselves so they can protect themselves against "us white folks". It was a frightening thing for all of us because we never felt the need for such protection before and none of us had ever felt that kind of fear before.

## The Ku Klux Klan:

And it was equally frightening to have groups of Ku Klux Klan members with white hoods draped over their faces holding a rally on the same Courthouse Square where we had held a prayer vigil for peace just a few weeks earlier. KKK members shouting the most awful obscenities against our African American neighbors and friends. We had never ever thought those things about them. We hated hearing the KKK scream the "n-word" over their loudspeaker systems.

252

I remember tears rolling down my cheeks when I, along with everyone else in our community, stayed in our homes and listened to our local radio station broadcasting live that KKK Rally on our Courthouse lawn. I was sorry I belonged to the same race as those white-hooded hate-mongers.

We felt like our community and the town we had all come to love was under siege. And because we are a deeply Christian community, we were not about to let these groups spew forth their hatred and their prejudices. We were going to do something. We were going to stand together. We just did not know at that time what we were going to do. The Hateful Event Three young white men – Bill King, Russell Brewer and Shawn Berry – picked up James Byrd, Jr., a 49-year old African-American, around midnight on Saturday evening, June 7th. They drove him to a deserted spot off Huff Creek Road, beat him up and chained his legs to the back of Shawn Berry's old pick-up truck, dragging his body for three miles on that asphalt and dirt road.

His head was pulled from his body when it hit a drainage culvert and his left shoulder and arm were pulled from its socket as they swerved back and forth across Huff Creek Road. His elbows, back and buttocks were rubbed raw by the pavement and all but disappeared as James tried in vain to keep his head up off the road to ease the excruciating pain.

His body, when found early Sunday morning, was not recognizable at first. His head was found in front of a cemetery and his shoulder and arm in front of an African- American church. The first officer on the scene believed it might be a deer hit and drug under a car. At first our Sheriff, Billy Rowles, thought "he had a hit-and-run accident on his hands but once he understood that this man was African American and had been dragged to his death, he knew it was a hate crime of unbelievable cruelty and he knew the community of Jasper, Texas, would be forever changed.

## Finding the Culprits:

Fortunately, the three young men were arrested late Sunday evening at our only movie theatre in town where Shawn Berry was the manager. By then, the large chain used in the dragging death had been washed off and hidden in a field, the truck had also been washed and the tire that had gone flat during the dragging had been removed and hidden behind the screen in the movie theatre.

Rumors began spreading through the community by Monday, but by then, all three suspects were in custody. By Tuesday, our community was in a state of shock, disbelief and for some, denial. Events happened rapidly after that. News crews and satellite trucks from every major network and from around the world appeared at the Sheriff's office and in our downtown area around the Courthouse Square. The World Came to Speak with Us All kinds of strangers were seen throughout the city. Everyone wanted to know why and how such a horrible hate crime could take place in our little area of southeast Texas. We had no answers, but we were all asking the same questions ourselves.

At least three books, one movie, a 90-minute documentary, a town hall meeting led by Ted Koppel and thousands of editorials and magazine articles have been written. Our town has been scrutinized and studied by everyone. We have been the subject of racist jokes and universal condemnation.

We have held town-hall meetings throughout the community, prayer vigils and we have engaged in countless discussions among ourselves. We have opened our very soul and examined our community to see what needed to be changed and how we could change something so evil and so ingrained in the lives of some people.

## How We Survived This Tragedy:

Luckily, our Ministerial Alliance had been an active and strong force within the community for many years. There are fifty-four Christian churches in our small community of 8,000 people. The ministers from ten of these churches have met monthly for years. We plan four ecumenical events each year which are very well-attended.

Because of this, the ten of us have become exceptionally good friends. We genuinely enjoy being with one another and have come to respect one another. That was the glue that held us together during some extremely difficult days, weeks and months as we buried James Byrd, Jr. and lived through the trials of the three murderers and then coped with the aftermath of such a tragic event.

## My Call to Support and Strengthen:

Fr. Ron Foshage, M.S., with Stella and James Byrd, Sr. at the Byrd Family Home

Because I was the only Catholic priest in the area and because I had been highly active in the Ministerial Alliance since I arrived in Jasper in July of 1985, I think I had a unique role to play.

Bill King's Dad attended our church from time to time. I knew he was quite ill, and I later found out that none of his three children were going to attend Bill's trial with him. So, one day after church, I asked him if he needed someone to sit with him during the trial. I could tell by the look on his face that he was most pleased by my offer.

The District Attorney, Guy James Gray, is also a Catholic and he called me from time to time to ask my opinion and to seek advice since he was seeking the death penalty for all three young men. He knew well the Catholic Church's stand on capital punishment.

Sometimes I felt like I was walking a tight rope between giving advice to Guy James and giving support to Ronald King. I was with Ronald King every day of the trial of his son. We sat-in the front pew of the courtroom just across the aisle from James Byrd, Sr. and his children. Mrs. Stella Byrd chose not to attend any of the trials because of her poor health.

Partly because of my deep involvement with Ronald King, he attended the RCIA classes which I teach each Wednesday evening and he was received into the Catholic Church that next year. I visited Mr. and Mrs. Byrd on a somewhat regular basis and have come to admire and deeply appreciate this strong Christian family who helped keep the peace in our community. I was asked to preach at Mrs. Byrd's funeral a few years ago. Mr. Byrd now has Alzheimer's disease.

## We Represent our Town, Our People, Our Values:

For many years, Brother Kenneth Lyons, the Pastor of Greater New Bethel Baptist Church, the church the Byrd family attends, and I have travelled throughout the State of Texas, participating in Hate Crime Seminars and giving talks to various groups of people.

Fr. Ron Foshage, M.S., and group receive a Race Relations Award in Washington, DC with Bro. Kenneth Lyons (center), Baptist pastor of Byrd Family Parish

I have also travelled to several different States participating in week-long workshops on Hate Crimes and Racism. I have found that participating in these seminars has filled me with hope and with the conviction that I cannot remain silent and I must speak out.

In Colorado, I listened in tears as ministers spoke of their role in the days following the Columbine High School Massacre. In Idaho, learned that a group of ministers rallied together when a lone Jewish family in a small town had rocks thrown through their windows and one landed just inches away from their only son as he was sleeping in his bedroom.

The ministers decided to ask their congregations to put a Menorah in the windows of their homes to show solidarity to that lone Jewish family and to show the perpetrators of that hate crime that this would not be tolerated in their community.

In Utah, I listened as the mother of Matthew Shephard spoke of her son who was tied to a cattle fence and left to die simply because he was branded a homosexual by two men who committed this hate crime against a gay man.

In California and in Minnesota, I saw what hate crimes are doing to the fabric of our society and I am grateful that our Bishop and my La Salette Community have allowed me to travel throughout the country to be a reconciler among peoples whose lives have been destroyed, changed or ended by this ugly new evil in our midst.

## Reconciliation at Work in our World:

As a Missionary of Our Lady of La Salette, our charism is that of reconciliation. It is our unique gift to the Church. Never did I think I would be called upon to live out that charism in such a visible way. On that Saturday afternoon on September 19, 1846, in the Alps in southeastern France near the small village of La Salette, Mary asked two simple cowherds, Melanie Mathieu and Maximin Giraud to pray, make sacrifices and to speak out against the injustices in their world.

Would Mary, ask anything less of you and I today? At La Salette, Mary said: *"If my people will not submit, I shall be forced to let fall the arm of My Son. It is so strong, so heavy, I can no longer hold it back."*

Mary asked those two young people to make her message known to all her people. It was a timely message – a message for the whole church. I believe as I have traveled around the country, participating in Hate Crime Seminars and speaking to groups of people about the growing number of hate crimes and acts of racism in our country, I am very aware of our duty as committed Christians to do all in our power to educate people about these evils for it is through education that more and more people will become involved.

Mary spoke of penance, prayer, and zeal at La Salette. These three virtues are needed even more today as we face such immorality in our country.

Several years ago, Mr. and Mrs. Byrd, Brother Kenneth Lyons, our District Attorney and our Sheriff and I testified before the Texas State Legislature Committee on Hate Crimes, trying to get a Hate

Crimes bill onto the Texas House and Senate floor for a vote. We met with opposition from many legislators who were afraid to stand up for their convictions.

## Our Plea to Pass a Texas Hate Crime Bill:

I remember how nervous we were before making our testimonies, but I also remember us standing in a circle and joining hands and praying that God would give us wisdom, guidance, and strength. Each of us felt God's power, His presence, and His peace in that gathering. And when we left that House committee room, we were more determined than ever to continue to speak out.

Texas does have a Hate Crimes Law today. It is called the James Byrd, Jr. Hate Crimes Law, and it's a law with strong teeth to it.

Standing up to prejudice and racism sounds so easy when we stand here tonight in this beautiful place surrounded by fellow Christians who share our beliefs, but it can be so difficult when we stand alone, confronted by angry Black Panthers and members of the Ku Klux Klan as the people of our community were forced to do when both groups came to our city for rallies.

But Our Lord keeps his promises and when you are doing his work, he gives you the courage and the conviction to stand up to those faces of hate. He takes you by the hand and leads you through the dark valleys.

I pray that each of us will be willing to stand up to those who will not see all God's children as sisters and brothers and may we be willing to confront racism to whatever degree in whatever place we find it, so that, in the words of the late Dr. Martin Luther King, Jr., each of us can have a dream:

> "that our children will one day live in a nation where they will not be judged by the color of their skin but by the content of their character...where little black boys and black girls will be able to join hands with little white boys and white girls and walk together as sisters and brothers... when all God's children – black men and white men, Jews and Gentiles, Protestants and Catholic – will be able to join hands and sing in the words of the old Negro spiritual,

'Free at last! Free at last! Thank God Almighty, we are free at last!'"

## Only Time Will Tell:

I like to think that our community of Jasper, Texas, has come a long way in healing ourselves from the violence and hatred that was inflicted upon us after that June night back in 1998. But I am not naive to think that we have arrived at our goal. I know there are still prejudiced people in Jasper. I know there's still pockets of racism. But I have met and walked hand in hand with so many courageous people who will not be silent, who will not stay closed up in their homes, hidden away by fear, but who are determined to confront racism and prejudice wherever it rears its ugly head.

La Salette Cross overlooking the Mississippi River on our La Salette property in St. Louis, MO

Our community has paid a high price. We are a tough little town that has handled adversity about as well as anyone could expect. We have become more sensitive to potential problems. I think we have become more straightforward and honest.

We will always be known as that place where three white men dragged a black man to his death behind a pick-up truck. We cannot avoid that label. But through it all, we have stood together, and those three white men were brought to swift justice. I hope history records the events in Jasper as the beginning of a new era in race relations. Only time will tell. Only time will tell!

### Reflection Questions:

• The account of this gruesome murder and subsequent trial raise so many emotions. How did you react to the events and the people involved in this crime: The victim and his family? The culprits and their family members? The community of Jasper? The various outsiders? Recognizing our feelings and those of others is crucial to moving to reconciliation? How did the efforts of all lead to healing and justice and truth?

•Racism is a prevalent issue in our society today. It is easy to condemn murder and torture because the victim is innocent. But what about other circumstances and situation that involve less than perfect victim? Do you find ways to avoid the bottom line of a situation that a small infraction or petty crime can lead to death as in some recent cases in the USA?

•How do we heal racism, division, prejudice, opposing views in our society? Reconciliation often happens one case at a time but also needs to happen in society and in government structures and among peoples of faith. How do you think you could make a difference?

**Editor's Note:** *On Sept. 16, 2020 Catholic Extension recognized Father Ron Foshage, MS, as the recipient of the 2020-21 Lumen Christi Award. The award is Catholic Extension's most prestigious award. Father Ron has been recognized for his many years of work with the poor, with homeless veterans and with bringing reconciliation to a divided and hurting community in Texas.*

# Chapter 22 —
# What I Have Learned About
# and From La Salettes
## By Elizabeth Vasquez

### Introduction:

As a management consultant, I generally work with businesses and government agencies to help them become the best organizations they can be. I never thought I'd be asked to provide consulting support to a group of priests and brothers! However, back in 2008, Fr. Joe Bachand, M.S., who was the La Salette Provincial Superior (1) at the time, was looking for a new facilitator (2) for that year's Provincial Assembly and got in touch with me to see if I would help. I had volunteered previously at a La Salette Parish, and loved my experience there, but my education about La Salette really began that year when I started working with the Province as a whole.

Elizabeth Vasquez, facilitator for La Salette meetings

### Learning about La Salettes:

At my first La Salette Assembly in 2008, the La Salettes gathered in Orlando for the better part of a week as they do each year. That year they had two important discussions that gave me a great education about what was important to them as a community and in their ministries. In the first discussion, they agreed on how to become a stronger, more sustainable community of Religious, and in the second they decided how they wanted to focus their ministries. Here's what they said and what I learned:

## Sustaining their Community:

• Like the U.S. population overall, the La Salette priests and brothers in America are aging. This causes them to think a lot about the sustainability of their community and the ministries they provide. The 2008 Assembly addressed this question and members agreed on these priorities:

• Vocations—bringing more priests and brothers into the Province

• Religious life—deepening the experience of La Salette religious and community life

• Collaboration with laity—increasing involvement of laity in La Salette ministries

• La Salette spirituality—leaning into evangelization and the charism of reconciliation

• Geography—balancing the availability of La Salettes with needs in parishes and shrines

• Retirement—providing for medical, spiritual, and community needs of senior La Salettes

Since that Assembly, these priorities have been a major focus. For example, *vocations* has been the subject of major efforts and there are results to show for it: new vocations, along with a number of priests on long-term assignment from other countries, have strengthened the ranks considerably, though more are needed. Vocations were the theme of the 2019 Assembly, with expert speakers brought in to provide fresh ideas, and were also chosen as a focus of the Younger La Salettes (3) as well as, of course, the Vocations Director and Vocations Committee.

Another example of a continuing effort is the priority of *collaboration with the laity*, about which much has also been done. The importance of this priority was validated anew in 2017 when "What if..." discussions about the Province's needs were held in Regional meetings across the Province and engagement of laity emerged as a top finding. There are lay engagement programs at the local level in individual parishes and shrines, and there have also been four regional Laity Summits since 2011—one each in Georgia, Florida, Massachusetts, and Louisiana—attended by hundreds of La Salette parishioners. An additional important step toward increased collaboration has been the inclusion of lay people in the annual La Salette Assemblies for the past several years.

## Carrying out their Ministries:

La Salettes' charism of reconciliation focuses on helping people connect or reconnect, with their faith, their families, and their sense of belonging in their communities. At the 2008 Assembly, the community members agreed by consensus on these broad societal issues as focus areas for their ministries:

- Immigration
- Multi-culturalism
- Poverty
- Polarization
- The alienated, unchurched
- Families under stress
- Evangelization and reconciliation

The societal issues targeted as priorities in that Assembly continue to inform La Salette ministries. Just this year, the Younger La Salettes, inspired by the Province's Justice and Peace Committee, added to their charge several social justice issues identified to 2008, carrying on the effort.

I have come to understand La Salettes as a group of Religious who provide a very special kind of ministry. I see their gift as one of helping people heal and grow in their faith and in their relationships with one another. Interestingly, they do this not only for the people to whom they minister, but also for themselves as well.

## Staying the Course:

The importance of the charism of reconciliation in today's polarized environment cannot be overstated. La Salettes bring the healing balm of their charism to their parishes and shrines and in their many ministries which offer everything from faith sharing to spiritual healing to inter-culturalism to eco-awareness. The specific ministries vary widely, but the overall reconciliation charism is the thread connecting all that the La Salettes do.

I have come to appreciate the La Salettes' ability to take the long view and stay the course on important goals. They clarify their vision, chart their path, and work toward desired outcomes. Nowhere is that more evident than in their determined focus on sustaining the presence of La Salettes and their ministries in North America.

## Learning about Love from the La Salettes:

In that same first year of my work with La Salettes, I was asked to facilitate a meeting of the Consultative Body (CB) (4) in Atlanta. On the evening before the meeting was to start, the pastor of St. Ann's, a La Salette parish, hosted the CB and Provincial leaders for a dinner at the Rectory. Fr. Joe Bachand and I arrived a bit early so I could have a few minutes to catch up with the pastor, Fr. Tom Reilly, whom I knew from my work as a volunteer at St. Ann's.

A few minutes later, as Fr. Joe, Fr. Tom, and I were standing in the living room chatting, the CB members all arrived at the same time and suddenly burst into the room in a happy, noisy bunch! The effect was immediate—the already warm, comfortable atmosphere suddenly exploded with affection as the La Salettes greeted one another. It was clear this was more than just a Religious order—a formal affiliation of Catholic clergy—rather, this was a community of people who really love each other. That awareness of the strong emotional connection among La Salettes has stayed with me and I think it is an important thing to understand if we are to really understand La Salette.

## Living in Community:

La Salettes see community life as the foundation that supports the life in ministry that priests and brothers have chosen. As Fr. Jack Nuelle, M.S., said in a recent meeting, "Community life is the well-spring from which La Salettes draw energy and motivation to work in ministry;" it makes everything else possible.

Having a loving community life does not come any easier for La Salettes, however, than having a loving family life does for lay people. Living in community requires sensitivity and intentionality. Community members, like family members, need to cultivate tolerance, work through differences, and make a conscious effort to live in caring companionship. This the La Salettes regularly remind themselves to do through sharing the Eucharist, sharing the responsibilities of daily domestic life, and sharing fellowship.

Love, expressed through community and ministry, is at the heart of La Salette just as I have learned love for all humankind is at the heart of Christianity.

## Caring for One Another:

Province Retreat Gathering in La Salette Retreat Center, Attleboro, MA

The first time I prepared to facilitate a CB meeting at the Hartford House, the Provincial retirement home for La Salette priests and brothers, I was a little apprehensive. Most of the residents of the Hartford House are, of course, very elderly, and I anticipated a somber or maybe even depressed atmosphere that might affect the mood and productivity of our meeting. But that was not the case at all! It turned out that the seniors in the Hartford House are warmly appreciated and valued by the La Salettes. They are treated with love and respect, and as a result I found them to be wonderful hosts and a pleasure to be around.

The Younger La Salettes had a meeting in Hartford House recently which included a joint session with the younger priests and brothers and a number of the resident seniors. The cross-generational conversation invited the seniors to share reflections on their lives and ministries as La Salettes. Their stories were rich with missionary experience and La Salette spirituality in faraway places, like Madagascar, Burma, and the Philippines. The conversation gave me a new appreciation of how the La Salette charism looks when it's brought to people around the world.

## Learning about Leadership from La Salettes:

Because I am a management consultant, I can't help but observe the La Salettes' approach to leadership. Many organizations in the US have recently discovered two leadership ideas that I have long observed among La Salettes. The first is the idea of *inclusive leadership*, which for La Salettes means that important decisions are made by consensus of the leadership team, or of a Regional group, or even of the Province as a whole. Knotty and significant issues are often given to task forces to sort and recommend solutions which are then decided upon by Provincial leadership or by a gathering of the members at a Chapter. (5)

An example that illustrates how this works can be seen in the Task Force on the Future of the Province. As a result of proposals (*postulata*) adopted at the 2018 Chapter, a task force was established by Fr. Rene, the Provincial Superior, to work on the complex challenges of developing a shared vision of the future of the ministries, membership, community life and more. The Task Force is accomplishing that goal through a process of engagement and consensus building, in keeping with the inclusive leadership value. This approach both reflects and reinforces the inclusive leadership value among La Salettes.

The second idea popular among American business and government organizations is *servant leadership*. This notion is based on the belief that leaders exist to serve a people, not to control them. Service leadership involves creating a clear vision of the way forward, developing mechanisms for the people being led to have a voice in how things go, and ensuring that obstacles to forward movement get resolved in a way that is supported by the people led.

The Task Force on the Future of the Province, to continue the example, has a three-year plan to help the Province develop a shared vision of the future. This year, Task Force members conducted interviews of about 90 percent of the North American La Salettes to get their thoughts and feelings about the future, asking everyone about their hopes, dreams, fears, expectations. A member of the Task Force presented a report of the interviews at the 2019 Assembly and held round table discussions to give the priests, brothers, and lay people present a chance to reflect on the interview results and provide their feedback on the way forward. Furthermore, this year there will be Days of Recollection across the Province and retreats for members as well, all moving toward an envisioned future for the Province. At the 2020 Assembly, more opportunities for dialogue on the futuring process will be on the agenda. In 2021, more engagement opportunities will be provided, with the decisions about the Future of the Province being made at the 2021 Chapter in October. Those decisions will come only after three years of consultation, reflection, and consensus-building—inclusive leadership at its best!

These two leadership notions, inclusive leadership, and servant leadership, are related—both require humility and generosity of spirit on the part of leaders, both are La Salette leadership values, and both are important to maintaining an engaged, and vibrant La Salette community. I have learned a lot from La Salettes about putting these leadership principles into practice and I know that my experience with La Salette has made me a better consultant.

### Lessons Learned in Summary:

I have learned a lot from my work with La Salettes over the last decade-plus. I've gained new appreciation for the importance of community life to us all; La Salettes show us the way through their imperfect (they are still human, after all) but enduring commitment to live in communities of peace, love, and shared faith. I have also

267

learned about a way of leading that strengthens both community and ministry.

But most importantly, La Salettes have given me a deeper awareness of the values at the heart of Christianity, which I now understand to be love, compassion, and care for others. The La Salette charism is exactly what the world needs now—reconciliation—within ourselves, with one another, within our diverse communities, and in our faith. The La Salette values of acceptance, tolerance, caring, and faith offer all of us a better way to be in the world.

**Reflection Questions:**

• Is there anything in Elizabeth's impressions of La Salette that especially resonates with you? Have you seen any of the values and priorities—for example, building community, staying the course on hard-to-reach goals, caring for others who need your support, leading with inclusion—among La Salettes you have experience with?

• What kinds of words and actions (that you don't have to be a priest to say or do) might have reconciling effects—that is, would tend to unite people and make them feel like they are a valued part of a community? What can individuals do as reconcilers in their regular lives?

• Can you think of any examples of when you have been a reconciler? Think about the various communities you are a part of, for example your church community, your circle of friends, your co-workers, a sports team—any group in which to know some or all of the members, spend time with them, and have something in common with them.

**Endnotes:**

(1) The La Salette Province of the USA includes North America and Bolivia and Argentina in South America and is named: Mary Mother of the Americas.

(2) A facilitator helps people at a meeting focus on, and work through the agenda, stay on topic, finish on time, and have a good record of the meeting's decisions in the form of minutes. Importantly, a facilitator does not participate in the actual give and take, but

rather ensures that everyone else has a chance to be heard and their ideas considered.

(3) The Younger La Salettes are a group of 18 priests and brothers who meet regularly and provide input from a younger perspective to the Provincial Superior and his Council. They contribute in other ways as well, for example, attending events throughout the year where they meet prospective vocations and introduce them to La Salette.

(4) The Consultative Body is comprised of one representative from each La Salette Region and their job is, as the name suggests, to provide advice to the Provincial Superior and his Council.

(5) A Chapter is a gathering that takes place every three years, in which binding decisions are made by the La Salettes who are in attendance. A number of formal rules and conventions guide the work of the Chapter and its results are taken seriously and acted upon. It is also called to elect the Provincial Superior and his Council.

# Chapter 23 —
## *John Twigg:*
## A Case Study of La Salette Laity
### By Fr. Terry Niziolek, M.S.

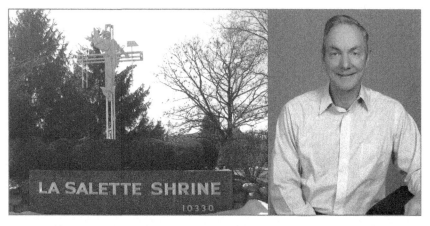

(from left) Entrance to the La Salette Shrine in Twin Lakes, Wisconsin; John Twigg, a longtime friend of La Salette

As a young man, John Twigg, was hired to do property maintenance in 1983 at the La Salette Shrine in Twin Lakes, Wisconsin. He began shortly after graduating from High School. He has always stayed close to home and looked after his mother before she passed away last year. His home is in Kenosha, Wisconsin twenty-five miles from the Shrine. He has a brother and a sister that he has stayed especially close to after his mother's passing.

He belongs to St. Peter Parish and is a minister of hospitality. John looked after his mother, saw to all her needs when she was ill. As one parishioner of St. Peter Parish noted, John would arrive early on Sunday mornings for Mass with his mother on his arm, get her seated and then begin welcoming parishioners.

# John is a member of the La Salette Family:

Even with so rich and close family ties, all the La Salettes who have served at the Shrine think of John as a member of the La Salette family. He has not professed vows, is not a La Salette associate or Laity, nor made any promises as an oblate brother. He is definitely, a member of the Shrine community, an employee, a layperson, a brother in service of La Salette, nevertheless.

During the past thirty-seven years John has become more than a La Salette employee. He has always done more than five days' work a week, nine to five. He works with us, prays with us, shares meals with us, celebrates with us, mourns our losses with us. He also looks after us when we are ill or getting on in years. He is at the Shrine often enough on weekends to serve our guests and pilgrims.

## He has a La Salette Heart:

He stays over to plow the snow in the early hours of winter mornings or drives through the snow to clear the property of snow before the faithful begin to arrive for Mass. He works on the property, in the office, in the kitchen, the garage, the chapel wherever anyone needs help, or anything needs to be fixed or found. All that would be more than enough to know his gifts but it's all done with a dedication and devotion and grace that binds him to our Mother of La Salette. All of us, who have served here, have an appreciation of what it means to have a La Salette heart.

## La Salette Laity have La Salette in their heart:

We cannot but be filled with gratitude for all the community, the employees, the volunteers, the pilgrim and event organizers of the Shrine, the Christmas decorators and Feast Day workers who give themselves to the message in so many ways. We are blessed by the dedication and closeness to the Shrine of so many laity, where the very air we breathe says, make the message known to all my people, by all my people.

Making the message known can be done in many ways. It can be done behind a snowplow, serving tables, preparing a mailing, or mending a fence or decorating a Christmas tree. Making the message known to all people needs more than our professed members could possibly accomplish. It is made known in more ways than preaching, teaching, writing, forgiving, staffing of shrines and parishes, and telling and praying and celebrating.

What does all this say about all the folks who have heard the message and pray and tell and live the message of La Salette? Fr. Edward Hayes, in his book, *Feathers on the Wind*, retells a wonderfully telling parable.

"Once upon a time there was a woman who longed to find out what heaven is like. She prayed constantly, 'O God, grant me in this life a vision of paradise.' She prayed this way for years until one night she had a dream. In her dream an angel came and led her to heaven. They walked down a street in paradise until they came to an ordinary looking house. The angel, pointing toward the house said, 'Go and look inside.' So, the woman walked into the house and found a person preparing supper, another reading the newspaper and children playing with their toys. Naturally, she was disappointed and returned to the angel on the street. 'Is this all there is to heaven?' The angel replied. "Those people you saw in that house are not in paradise, paradise is in them.""

Beyond a breathtaking mountain, a Shrine, Retreat House, Parish, La Salette Assembly, La Salette Fathers, Brothers, and Sisters, there are folks who like John carry La Salette beyond the Shrine in their hearts. As Edna St. Vincent Millay so pointedly says in the conclusion to her poem, *Renascence*:

*The world stands out on either side*
*No wider than the heart is wide;*
*Above the world is stretched the sky,*
*No higher than the soul is high.*
*The heart can push the sea and land*
*Farther away on either hand;*
*The soul can split the sky in two,*

*And let the face of God shine through.*

## Listen to Mary's heart at La Salette:

When Mother Mary says to Melanie and Maximin, *"Come closer, my children,"* she was inviting them to listen to her heart as well as to her words. Our lives begin with our hearts beating alongside the heart of our mothers where we learn that home is in the heart, just as heaven is in the heart, where we find the God whom we love with all our hearts.

Fr. Ron Rolheiser writes: "A mother's love teaches us even before we come to awareness that we were caressed by hands far gentler than any we've met in this life and where we were once kissed by a truth and a beauty so perfect that they are now the unconscious standard by which we measure everything." (*Column: Home Is a Place from Which to Understand, August 13, 2006*)

The message of La Salette is that heart-to-heart talk of a mother to her wayward children, the plea of a heartbroken mother to turn away from their sin and turn back to God. From her heart to the hearts of two children, to the hearts of all Gods' children, to the hearts of all my people.

Mother Theresa was once asked how she intended to care for all the suffering people of the world. There are so many. She said, "One at a time." She added that it begins in one's own family. "Learn to love in your own family... I have come more and more to realize that it is being unwanted that is the worst disease that any human being can ever experience."

## Our home is where reconciliation begins:

From our hearts to our families we bring our need for connection, for community or suffer devastating loneliness. There is a give and take in hearts, where we hold the message of reconciling love. The sharing happens to those who share life with us most intimately, our families. Melanie runs to her family and they go to the Church. Maximin's father's life is turned around with his conversion at his hearing of

Mother Mary's mentioning him in her discourse. It takes less than a village to make the message known in the most ordinary of places, our homes.

The telling of the message, the prayerful lifting up the message, and the compassionate living of the message happens when hearers become tellers and exemplars. It happens when one mother, one father, sister or brother, cousin grandparent, uncle, or aunt teaches the power of forgiveness, asks for forgiveness, knows it's give and take, is blessed with its power to unite in prayer, and experiences its gift of reconciling love.

## Little things mean a lot:

We once sang songs like "Little Things Mean A Lot," because most of life is about little things even though so much seems complicated. Spiritual teachers have said that all the small moments add up and become great even though in the long run they do not seem like much. Little things like "I'm sorry, or I forgive you." Blessed are the families that work to open their hearts to true and deep intimacy in communion with one another.

Like charity, the hearing and telling of mercy, compassion, healing, prayer, and reconciliation begins in the home as do vocations. And like charity, the home is only a beginning. It needs a telling beyond the sweetness of home, like a church without walls.

Two churches close to one another, one Presbyterian, the other Catholic pose an interesting difference in their names. One is the Church of The Holy Apostles. The other is the Church of Holy Apostles. The Holy Apostles are Peter, Andrew James, John, Thomas and so on. The Church simply of Holy Apostles describes itself as the Church of Harry and Jean, Maria and Jose and a long list of the faithful — all apostles. With or without walls, the church is the people.

The church needs twenty-first century apostles. Before we would invite anyone unchurched to attend Church with us, we invite them into our lives. The wisdom of the Rite of Christian Initiation of Adults (RCIA) is that sponsors walk a journey of faith with their candidates who are introduced to the Body of Christ in them. St.

Augustine in Sermon 272 on the Sacrament of the Eucharist said that before we receive the Eucharist, we need to understand ourselves as the body of Christ. He says, "Be what you can see and receive what you are. So now, if you want to understand the body of Christ, listen to the Apostle Paul speaking to the faithful: 'You, though, are the body of Christ, member for member' (1 Corinthians 12:27). When you hear (the words) 'The body of Christ,' you (should) reply 'Amen.'"

## Mary speaks about the Lord's Day:

We read the words of the discourse and hear the pain in Mother Mary's voice because her unfaithful children will not give themselves over to the Lord's Day which makes the arm of her Son so heavy. There is a price to pay for turning away from God. "God punishes but God is not silent," as Father Normand Theroux, M.S. says in, *The Face of the Reconciler*. What are we, who do give the Lord his day, to learn?

Mother Mary's call is not only a call to Sunday worship, to come to church. It is a call to be Church. Today, we face diminishing numbers in our pews, a dearth of vocations, and Communion Services in the absence of a priest. This growing awareness of our needs as a Church asks of lay people an awareness of their unique role in the Church today. Our parishes ask parishioners for their gifts of Time, Talent and Treasure. It would be well for us to know how much of a blessing we all are to one another and the wider community.

We have not just been thrown together randomly; we are given to one another to become sensitive to the presence of God among us. Together we work at what it means to be Eucharist to one another revealing the Reign of God, "Thy Kingdom come on earth." We find God's goodness, compassion, and power in our midst. We share a relationship far more basic than pastor and parishioner, or minister and parishioner. The starting point of any relationship is our humanity, not our roles, as we see in Jesus who came to serve and not be served.

God's reign needs to be seen and heard, in our ministries of reconciliation, healing, and liberation. Wherever we find Christ, we find healing. That is the message we are given in our prayer, most authentically in the Church celebrating the Eucharist. Pope St. John Paul II in his letter introducing the Year of the Eucharist in 2005 (Mane Nobiscum, Domine (*Stay With Us, Lord*) proclaimed that the authenticity of our celebration of the Eucharist is found in how we treat one another, especially the poor.

Grayson Warren Brown echoes the Pope when he says in his Mission talk.

"Jesus begins his ministry not by talking about saving souls, but saying he is about saving people. He does not begin by talking about a relationship with a God who is there only to serve us, but by laying out a mission that from the very beginning is about service to God, by serving his people. And not just people of means, but people who are poor and powerless, and who need both the mercy and the power of God. This was the only true mark of authenticity as far as the prophets were concerned."

We come to faith as we have noted in the uniqueness of our hearts, amid the faith of our families, and as members of the Body of Christ. But the message asks for the broadest of proclamations. "Make this message known to all my people." The forward of the book< *"All My People"* by Fr. Marcel Schlewer, M.S., says:

"In the same way the virgin of La Salette comes to speak to us about God and humanity without ever separating them from each other, she invites us , in the midst of all of our problems, political and social, to live in loving submission in union with Christ, to live in loving submission to God's plan for the human race. Mary thus seeks to avenge both God and humanity."

We grow up in a world of natural differences such as race and location and culture. The absence of oneness, unity, and connectedness of all humankind with one another throughout all of history is our great sin. We are born not only into divisions but into animosities that set us against one another and that define us. We do so in the face of Jesus' life testament of oneness with his Father and with us, found in all his preaching, teaching, healing, forgiving, dying and rising. It is the essence of the message of the Kingdom of God revealed in the many, the different, the diverse he embraced.

"Do you say your prayers well, my children?"

Do you say your prayers well, my children?,
window from Mary Keane Chapel in Enfield, NH

## Praying the Lord's Prayer:

We are called to a brotherhood and sisterhood in the prayer he teaches, the Lord's Prayer which begins with the very inclusive "Our." He teaches that our human dignity and worth are found in the love his Father has for us is the same love that his Father has for him. As different as we are, as diverse as we are in race, creed, culture, language, our humanity unites us with the God who became flesh, where Jew and Greek, slave and free, male and female are one in Christ, where, as St Paul says, we are *"one body and one Spirit... (with) one Lord, one faith, one baptism, (and) one God and Father of all, who is over all and in all..."* (Ephesians 4: 4-6). Reconciliation demands that we find this oneness in all of humanity's truth, goodness, and beauty.

In the letter of our La Salette Superior General from February 2, 2018, Fr. Silvano Marisa, M.S. spoke of witnessing the beauty of our diversity.

"We experience diversity in every context, at every level. We experience it in our small community, as well, as in the wider world. Living in diversity, experiencing and witnessing its beauty, means living in depth the experience of the grace of reconciliation that comes exclusively from God who made himself present to us in Jesus Christ. We suffer from a dramatic polarization in our society as well as in the church. Christianity has always embraced difference... The church should testify to the beauty of diversity, the beauty of reconciliation."

## We must do more than just tell Mary's message:

The appeal for a depth-level appreciation of one another is one we may profess but not practice or proclaim. The challenge of the gospel, in the inclusive grace of God's kingdom, needs a reconciliation that would give us hearts that beat together to the same rhythm in relationship to all of life. Is the final instruction of the message of La Salette to just tell the message to all people? There must be more to the message than its telling. And there must be more to tell the message than the only the La Salette Missionaries.

Crucial to our appreciation of La Salette is our understanding of Good News. The final words of Jesus at the end of the Gospel of St. Matthew entrust his disciples with the proclamation of the Good News. "Go, therefore, and make disciples of all nations, baptizing them in the name of the Father, and of the Son, and of the Holy Spirit, teaching them everything I have commanded you. And behold, I am with you always, until the end of the age" (Matthew 28:19-20).

Mother Mary's role has always been to bring Jesus to all her children. Marian devotion is more than our devotion and prayers. The devotion of Mother Mary was, is and always will be her devotion to her Son. Being the first of his disciples she is entrusted with the gifts of God's Spirit that she received at Pentecost. She continues to ask us to make the message of reconciliation known for we are all her children.

## Are we today's Melanies or Maximins?

We are Melanies and Maximins who have a story to tell that our time desperately needs to hear. The faith of Melanie and Maximin, their truth, their courage is inspiring. Young, unschooled cowherds that they were, they found the strength to face a skeptical world. Perhaps they found their grace in the beauty, in the love, the truth of the Beautiful Lady. It takes a great deal of faith to see into one's own life until whatever is there is loved. What they saw perhaps for the first time was an acceptance and a trust and a love they had never known.

When reading the discourse of the La Salette apparition, be a Melanie or a Maximin. Hear the message that everyone needs to hear, that you are asked to share. But also hear the love with which it is given to you personally. It will reveal your grace, your strength, and your understanding. It will reveal the love and likeness with which you were created and redeemed. It will say that you can count on this love more than talent, or success or virtue. The love of our Sorrowful Mother simply asks us to hear her message, to take it to heart, reveal it to our family, give and receive it in the community of faith and bring it to our broken world. Like Mary, we invite others to *"Come closer."*

### Reflection Questions:

• Fr. Terry describes a friend, a partner, an unofficial member of the La Salette Family. Do you have experiences of people like John who have attached their souls to the message and mission of the Missionaries? How do you expect to live out your role as La Salette Laity?

• Proclaiming the message is more than telling of the account or sharing pictures and videos of the beautiful site at La Salette. How do you share the message? How do you invite others to *Come closer*? To not be afraid? To hear the Great News?

• Fr. Terry uses the powerful expression of "Mother Mary" to describe the Blessed Virgin but so much more. We are in a relationship with our dearest heavenly Mother and she with us. When have we experienced this oneness of being her children — in fact and not just in name?

# Chapter 24 —
# La Salette and Youth
### By Fr. Ted Brown, M.S.

**Editor:** *Father Ted Brown, M.S., is the director of Post-Novitiate Formation for the Missionaries of La Salette. Prior to this position he was Director of the National Shine of Our Lady of La Salette in Attleboro, MA. Prior to that ministry, for nearly thirty years he served as University Chaplain at Long Island University: Post Campus in Brookville, NY.*

## Introduction:

Newman Club college students sing Christmas carols around the campus

There is much hand-wringing around church communities today about the rapid loss of young people. The Pew Foundation, in a recent study, found that young Catholics begin to 'dis-associate' from the church about the age of thirteen.

They may continue to attend Mass, youth group, or be involved in other ways. Yet, emotionally and intellectually, they begin to leave as early teenagers. This certainly poses a threat to the life of the Church. It also means a generation will be without one set of tools to help them negotiate through life and find meaningful ways to be human.

As Catholic Christians, we believe Christ is The Way, The Truth, and the Life. Christ brings us to the fullest expression of who God wants us to be. Christ not only points the way but is The Way. A disassociated generation will lose out on what we believe is the ultimate way of life, which we call salvation.

Every generation of young people faces its own unique challenges. The world and societal events happening at any given moment shape each cohort of young people. Even today, there are still people who faced The Great Depression, World War II, and the nuclear threat. Many faced the Vietnam War, Civil Rights changes, the AIDS crisis, the September 11th attacks, or the ups and downs of our economy as teens. As much as we wish to romanticize our youth, each generation faces a crisis of their time with the same naivete that we did.

The church's inability to connect with many young people on a meaningful level means the current cohort of young people will be less well-equipped to face life. The focus the Church often puts on –'who will occupy the pews in the future' – is the wrong focus. We should focus on the gifts do we have that will help them have a sense that God loves them, strengthens them, and dreams with them.

Rather than asking the question "how do we get them into the pews," we should show young people how a life of faith, in particular a Catholic faith-life, can help them have a happy and wholesome life. Can we help young people see that faith gives them a fuller picture of what it means to be human and how to live a meaningful life? Faith takes nothing away from life, but only adds to it.

What insight does the Apparition of Our Lady La Salette in France (1846) offer us as we search for ways to give our young people the richness of the Church's resources? How can aspects of the message at La Salette help youth grow more fully into God's image, which we believe will lead to a meaningful life?

Considering that Our Lady at La Salette spoke to young people, there may be some clues.

What drew these two uncatechized children into the circle of faith? What was in Mary's message that captured their minds and hearts? What might her message tell us today about mentoring young people into a life of faith?

# The challenge of the times:

As much as we live in a vastly different society than those who lived in that little village of La Salette, in southeastern France, there are many similarities. The world the children faced is similar to the one that young people face today.

The children were growing up in a time of political upheaval. The French Revolution had ended fifty years earlier. After centuries of a monarchical rule, the political world was fragile. Twenty years before the Apparition, the Napoleonic era had ended. France was still searching for a period of political stability. Similarly our young people face our involvement in armed conflicts around the world.

Here in the early twenty-first century, we live in a time of significant political instability. Our country's inner workings have not convulsed as France did. Still, a young person born after 1990 has watched our nation become more and more polarized. They have witnessed Americans turn on one another in unprecedented ways. Our society does not seem any more stable than the one Melanie and Maximin faced. For the children of 1846 and our young people today, the future appears unpredictable.

The technological change afoot in France was significant. The industrial revolution was rapidly transforming the world. The world went from a very craft-oriented, agricultural-based society to a factory based, mechanized world. Young people were leaving farms and moving to the cities to work in the industrial world.

Young people today live in a world influenced by the technological revolution dominated by computers and smartphones. A teen today, who has a smartphone, carries in her or his pocket more computing power than the astronauts had on the first trip to the moon. Young people today flock to the cities for jobs at Google, Facebook, and other media companies, much like the young people of the mid-nineteenth century flocked to the cities for factory jobs.

Melanie and Maximin grew up in a very secular France. The French Revolution had its focus on humanism and the secularism of the Enlightenment had saturated the culture. France, once the center of

European Christianity, became a very secular country. Today, we have moved from a society that revolved around its religious centers to a world more focused on other activities. Many young people say their religious affiliation is 'none.' Melanie and Maximin were not church-goers and barely knew their faith. Any knowledge of the faith came from their grandparents, a situation like the one in which we live.

The world of 1846 tells us that the young visionaries had much in common with the young people of the early twenty-first century.

The event of La Salette in 1846 changed the faith in France. It brought many back to the faith. The effects of La Salette even touched the United States early on. One will find a statue of Our Lady of La Salette at the museum of Notre Dame University (founded in 1842). Fr. Edward Sorin, SCS, one of Notre Dame's founders, developed a devotion to La Salette and possessed that statue.

Fr. Edward Sorin, SCS (1814-1893), founder of Notre Dame University, in his later years

Could the Apparition and the words of Our Lady help us with our outreach to young people today? I believe so.

## Come closer: A warm invitation amid disorientation:

The children of La Salette lived in a disorienting, secularized world being transformed by a technological revolution. The blinding light of the Apparition certainly mirrors the blinding light of a world changed by new technologies. They were fearful as they witnessed the light. Melanie asks: "Do you think it will hurt us?" From the middle of this disorienting light, they hear comforting words: "*Come closer, my children... I am here to tell you great news."*

Whether it is a sports team, theater group, scout troop, almost all youth become involved in an activity because someone invites them to try it out. The invitation must always be warm and exciting at the same time. *"Come closer... I am here to tell you great news"* is both consoling and holds out a promise.

Young people almost always respond to a safe, warm invitation to something that will help make sense of the confusing world they are entering. This response raises essential questions for those who wish to work with young people. What is the benefit a young person will get if he or she responds to the invitation? Do we understand their world enough to show the benefit of having a relationship with Christ? Can our invitation to follow Christ affirm their deep inner value? Today many voices tell them there is little value to their lives. The alarming rate of teen suicide (and adult) tells us that young people question their value, meaning and purpose.

The invitation young people need to hear today is one that holds out the promise that they can discover value, meaning and purpose. Young people live in a world where bullying is common. This bullying tells them they do not matter. They compare their lives to what they see on social media and feel their lives come up wanting. In a culture where they wonder if they matter at all, they just might hear an invitation to a life that matters.

## Sharing encouragement and hope:

Years ago, while working as a Campus Minister, I got a call that one of our students might be attempting suicide. It was the end of the semester. The school protocol would remove the student for hospitalization for two weeks; it was exam time and the student was upset he could not finish in time. Through the hard work of many caring adults, the student was able to take exams and finish the semester. The student had signed up to participate in our Mission Trip later that summer.

I met with the counselors at the hospital and school, who assured me that the student was healthy enough to go. During that Mission Trip, the student was able to connect with his value. He saw his life made a difference. Years later, I got a note from him, telling me how much it meant that I still saw him as someone who had something to offer the world. That young person now works as a teacher in a tough school district in New York City and is still involved in the Church.

Can our invitations be phrased in ways that will contain the good news that the Church is a place that will help them navigate the rough waters of adolescence and beyond? They yearn to know that life can and does have meaning. Can our invitations be full of hope and say that the Church says they truly matter? Our invitations have to say, "in Christ you will find a purpose and a way to be alive."

Our Lady invited the children to draw closer and the children approached her because they believed she had something important to say.

## Do Not Be Afraid:

Our Lady looks lovingly at the children and says: "Don't be afraid."

Immediately, after greeting Melanie and Maximin, Our Lady tells them not to be afraid. She must have exuded care, concern, and safety because the children calmed down quickly and entered a conversation with her.

While I was a full-time college chaplain, I asked one of the counselors what was the predominant mental health issue she was observing on campus. Her answer was one word: anxiety, and it was at the highest level she had ever witnessed.

## St. Paul urges us, "Do not be anxious":

Anxiety is the constant state of fear, worry, or dread. The fear's cause is often unnamed and unfocused. Studies show that twenty-five percent of all young people suffer from anxiety. Young people will come to a place where safety is assured.

Creating a safe place for young people should be at the top of the church's priority list. Of course, we are all aware of making our youth programs safe regarding sexual abuse. We know that young people are already confused and disoriented regarding their sexuality as they move through adolescence. The need to provide an environment where a young person doesn't have to worry about her or his safety sexually, must be paramount.

Yet they carry other fears. One fear that almost all young people carry is: what if I am not accepted? Creating a culture in a Church (and a youth group specifically) where 'all are welcome' and signaled quickly is essential. The Newman Club (the Catholic Organization) I oversaw had a 'ten-second rule.' Students were greeted immediately at the door. If anyone noticed someone was standing alone, especially a newcomer for more than ten seconds, that person had to be engaged in conversation and brought to meet other people. The group had to communicate quickly; the newcomer was welcome.

One of the most significant signs of welcome the Church can give young people is a listening ear. My personal experience as a Campus Minister has taught me that young people desire a safe, caring, and non-judgmental adult mentor in their life. They long for someone to help them explore all that is happening within them. Young people are exploding with 'newness.' The sunset they witnessed was the most beautiful one ever; no one has ever seen one like it. They want to share that!

Newman Club college students remind others that love is central

## Creating a safe place:

Falling in and out of love is part of being a young person, and so is the excitement and pain that goes with it. Who will listen, but not judge them? Who will rejoice with them? Who will cry with them at the heartbreak? Who will allow a young person to explore these feelings and learn these will not crush them? Creating a safe place for a young person to explore self is the greatest gift we can give them.

The safety that takes their fear away is also a safety that allows young people to go to the edges of their capabilities and test themselves. Providing settings for young people to try new things, explore the world, and enjoy new-found skills builds confidence. They will take up the challenge if they know they are safe.

Each year I bring young people to Mexico to build houses. One year a young woman from Brooklyn wanted to go. We accepted this fun-loving, bright Freshman into the program. Little did I know she had never flown before and was afraid of flying. The flight had terrible turbulence. I could see her white knuckles from my seat about four rows back. We landed safely, and I asked if she was ok. She nodded her head 'yes' slightly, still not quite sure. She worked hard all week and returned to the project year after year, even though she had to fly, which she still hated.

After graduating, she became a 'buyer' for a high-end fashion brand and had to travel the world. She has become quite successful. At a Homecoming/Alumni event, she told me, "If I hadn't gone on that trip with you, I would not have applied for that job because it involved flying. Thank you. I knew you wouldn't lead us into anything unsafe."

## Difficult discussions:

During the Corona Virus pandemic, a teen was talking to me. I could tell something was off, and I asked him what the matter was. He told me that his mother (a single mom) found out she had been exposed to the virus at work. She had to be tested, quarantined, and isolated until the results came back. He looked at me with tears in his eyes. "What happens to me (and my brother) if she dies?" After gentle listening, I asked, "Have you talked to her about this?" His answer was "no, I don't want to upset her, and I don't want to cry." I told him "This is worth tears." I said to him, "She is most likely thinking about the same thing and she might have a plan."

A few days later, I saw him with a big smile. He reported, his mom tested negative, would work from home, and that if anything happened, his favorite aunt and uncle would take them in. He thanked me for pushing him to talk to her. I asked: "Did you cry?" He laughed... "Yah, but it was ok."

One of the most La Salette things we can do for young people is to create a safe space for them both physically and emotionally. They need to know the Church is a place where they will not be judged. They should see the Church as a place where we will push them beyond self-imposed limits to discover themselves and learn to face fears.

## I see you don't understand, let me try it a different way:

If you are familiar with the La Salette story, you know Our Lady begins her message in perfect Parisian French. The children did not speak French but spoke a local dialect. Our Lady notices quickly and says: "I see you don't understand, let me try it a different way." She does not tell the children to go home, learn French, and she would talk with them. She switches gears and begins her whole message again in their dialect.

La Salette calls us to learn to switch from our own needs and plans and respond to the real needs of young people. Tucked away in all our programming, we must be ready to switch up our plans and meet their needs. Youth culture changes fast and knowing that reality must be foundational for working with young people.

## The times, they are a-changin':

I remember explaining to a colleague one time: "I feel like I come out to greet them, and I notice they are playing baseball. I go back and get my glove and when I come back, they are playing hockey. I get my hockey stick and now they are playing basketball." Their culture is always changing. What's cool today is out of style tomorrow. To care for youth today means to be ready for an ever-changing landscape.

As noted earlier, they are growing up in a world that is fast-paced and ever new. The technological changes have a dark side to it. This dark side is far beyond the well-known dangers of exploitation on the internet. Every young person knows that whatever he or she is learning to do, might be done by a computer or machine in a few years. All their plans could go up in smoke. Their future is marked by instability, and they know that. Our ability to deal with an ever-changing world gives youth confidence.

The message at La Salette calls for creativity when dealing with the young. First, do we recognize that often the Church talks a quite different language from our own culture, especially our youth? A religious educator once put it this way to me, "Think of language as colors. The Church often talks in the color green, while our young people are talking in orange."

We often speak in a language they do not understand. We are like Mary speaking French to the children at La Salette. Mary notices she isn't getting through and says, "Let ME try it a different way." Mary adjusts.

This often happens around controversial issues. Many Church leaders are befuddled around the issue of sexual orientation. The Church keeps talking the language of "sexual morality," but young people see the issue in terms of justice – the rights to housing, a job, loving the person they want. Young people see other moral issues at play. We are talking green; they are talking orange. We talk past one another. We need to notice their starting spot, not ours. Once we do that, a meaningful conversation can happen.

One time in campus ministry, we were holding a dance for people with Cerebral Palsy. Hundreds of students helped, and about 100 people with Cerebral Palsy attended. It was often called the best dance on campus. During one of the dances, a student walked up to me and said, "Father, this is really dope." I was not sure if it was a compliment or an insult. I had to ask another student what he meant. The student laughed and said, "Father, he means this is great." We must recognize in many ways we speak different languages. Being with young people today means a willingness to learn about their culture and their language continually. We can never fully enter it but be aware of it and appreciate it.

One final note on this topic. Young people are quickly discouraged when people put down their culture. When we do that, we tell them all they know, all they have experienced and how they have lived is worthless. It signals we have not taken time to get to know them. I have found this current crop of young people is very generous. They are very justice-oriented and care deeply about the Earth. They also see the potential of technology. It is vital that we "find a different way" and affirm what is good about their culture. It will be a different voice they often hear from their elders.

## "But if my people are converted" — the possibility of change:

One of the prophetic statements of Our Lady is the effects of conversion. *"If (my people) are converted, the stones and rocks will change into mounds of wheat, and the potatoes will be self-sown in the land."*

Teens and young adults carry a heavy burden. From a human development perspective, they face the fact that they have flaws, are imperfect, and are capable of hurting people. This uncharted and new territory for them. Any priest will tell you, hearing the confessions of young people can be full of tears. As they face themselves, their shortcomings overwhelm them.

Newman Club students gather for a selfie with
(a cardboard picture of) Pope Francis

They go through the halls of their schools, participate in sports and clubs with false confidence. As they meander through life, a voice keeps reminding them of all their failures. Often they have no outlet to face the fact; they are far from perfect. It is a new experience for them.

The message of Mary at La Salette is a perfect message for young people. Her message reminds us all, "You aren't stuck. Change is possible. A hugely different future is there for you other than the one you imagine." Mary's message says: "Goodness and fulfillment are God's plan for you. You can change if you want. You can make a different plan." Our youth need to hear that the rotting potatoes and wheat of their lives are not God's final words. Actually God's final words to them in La Salette terms are "wheat will be piled like rocks and potatoes will be self-sown." Your life can have abundance. La Salette says: You are not stuck; change is possible.

One time I was dealing with a student from another country. The student had been thrown out of several colleges, (which is very hard to do today), and landed on our doorstep. He was an "itch" for sure, but there was also something very likable about him. Sadly, he had a severe drug addiction and nearly died from an overdose. He was immediately brought into the psychiatric ward of a hospital after a trip to the Emergency Room.

I visited him every day. After that stint in rehab and months of out-patient counseling, he kicked the habit. (Now twenty years later he is still clean and has a Ph.D.)

One day while we were talking, he said to me, "You know, every other college saw me as a problem they didn't want to deal with and threw me out, but this school saw me as someone with a problem who needed help. This school believed in my potential, and they saw that I could *be* someone."

Every young person needs to learn they aren't 'stuck' in all their failures and sins. They have to hear again and again that they can change and become new. Isn't that the promise of Baptism? Isn't that the promise of our faith? Isn't that the promise of La Salette? It is all summed up in Mary's simple words, "*if they convert.*"

La Salette invites us to walk with young people towards who they can become and beyond who they were.

### "Make this known":

Mary's parting words are simple. "*Make this known to all my people.*"

Mary charges the children with a mission. She has faith in them and believes they can and will carry it out. It bids us ask: how much faith do we have in our young people? Young people are capable of much more than we think. Young people like a good challenge.

How often do we limit their 'service' to unfolding tables and chairs at the church festival? In my experience, if that is all we expect of them, they become frustrated and leave. They want to have their gifts and talents recognized. They also want to test their abilities.

Mary gives the children a 'mission' – a crucial one. To the surprise of everyone, they handle it and handle it well. You are reading this book because an 11 and a 14 year-old fulfilled the charge Mary gave them.

One day I was hearing confession while the students were at adoration. I cannot remember what was going on before, but I remember they were rambunctious coming in. I was annoyed at their lack of decorum. As I sat waiting for a penitent, God's word bubble up in me. "Ted, suffer their enthusiasm. Learn to enjoy their energy, their excitement and zeal." When you give young people a challenge in line with their development capabilities, they will do it far better than you ever expected. Yes, it will be done with lots of noise, laughter and usually at the last minute, but it will be done and done well.

The Catholic Student group with whom I worked took on a great love for the poor and the homeless. We worked at a soup kitchen in NYC that fed about 1500 people on Sundays. We had talked often about the dignity of the dinner guests and how they were Christ in the flesh. One day one of the women students told me "I made a friend at the soup kitchen; I gave him my phone number and email address." I went into panic mode. I told her," be careful."

Next time we were at the soup kitchen she introduced me to "Billy." I was still wary but warmed up to him a bit. When we were hosting "Homelessness Awareness Week" on campus, she asked, "Could Billy come and talk about what it's like to be homeless?" I said "OK" but still was not sure.

We made all the arrangements, and he was wonderful. As the years past, he became a great friend of our Newman Club, but life on the streets took its toll on Billy. He ended up in the hospital, and Pilar visited him often at Belleview Hospital in Manhattan. She was there holding the hand of "her friend" as he died.

Pilar accepted the challenge of our faith much more than I did. She was far more loving and accepting than I could ever be. Now, years later, she still goes to that soup kitchen, and continually makes friends. She has a mission to make the lives of the homeless a little less cruel.

Mary at La Salette gave a mission to the children that most of us adults would shy from, but the children accepted it and did it well. If we were to give young people opportunities that made their spirits soar, that showed them how much they were capable of, perhaps the affection for the Church would grow.

## A final word:

When it comes to Apparitions, one often wonders why Our Lady appears usually to children. In my years of youth work I have learned that young people are naturally spiritual. They are open, in touch with their own brokenness, and believe they can do great things with God's grace. Our Church offers a tradition that naturally affirms these movements within them.

The La Salette message is one of great challenge to the organized Church. The La Salette event calls us back to who we are as followers of Jesus Christ. Do we dare share such a challenge and offer it to our young people in meaningful ways?

During a Mexico Service Project to build houses for the poor, a Newman Club teen makes friends with a curious child

The La Salette 'event and message' still offers life. When offered to young people, as it did many years ago, it can re-invigorate the faith.

**Reflection Questions:**

•Could the Apparition and the words of Our Lady help us with our outreach to young people today? What can you do to help support and welcome youth into our community or Church?

•How can we challenge the Youth of today with a new sense of mission? How do we make them partners and messengers of Our Lady in their own way and not our ways?

•One of the great fears in the life of us all comes from anxiety. We worry, we doubt ourselves or our God. We become afraid. How do we calm our fears? Lower our anxiety levels? How has God helped us as we let go and put our trust in him?

# Section 5 -
# La Salette Prayers

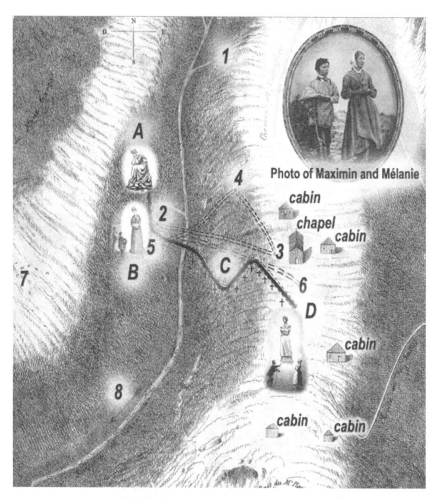

Explanation of Site of the La Salette Apparition, Sept. 19, 1846:

**Mary:** **A:** the miraculous fountain where Our Lady was seated, weeping; **B:** place of their conversation; **C:** path marked by crosses where Our Lady walked (130 feet); **D:** the place where Our Lady disappeared.

**Children:** **1:** the Men's Spring where the children ate; **2:** area where they fell asleep; **3:** the place where the children looked for their cows; **4:** place from where the children saw the globe of light; **5:** place of conversation and path the children took to top of knoll **(5-6); 6:** where children saw Our Lady disappear; **7:** the area where the cows were grazing; **8:** animals' fountain.

**Chapel:** the provisional chapel; cabin: the five cabins built after the Apparition;

**Note:** solid line indicates Our Lady's path; dotted lines indicate the children's path.

# La Salette Novena

La Salette Novena for the 175th Anniversary
of the La Salette Apparition (1846-2021)
Province of Mary, Mother of the Americas

## First Day: The Holy Mountain

**Scripture says:** "[Jesus] made the disciples get into the boat and go on ahead to the other side while he sent the crowds away. After sending the crowds away he went up into the hills by himself to pray. When evening came, he was there alone" (Matthew 14:22-23).

**Reflection:** Behind the slope of this Holy Mountain, isolated from the outside world below, the site of the Apparition reminds us of the special encounter between the Beautiful Lady and the two unsuspecting children, Maximin and Melanie.

### The Dialogue:

In our imagination, as we sit on the rock overlooking this ravine, we ask the Beautiful Lady why she has chosen this place – so isolated from the world below.

**And Mary says:** "The world has become accustomed to our busy cities and noisy streets, to a certain spirit of restlessness. The working day has become all-important and everything else seems to fade from view. In my visit so long ago in this very place, I wanted to speak to my people, expressing the desire and hope of my Son for these some-times-lost souls. I have chosen this timeless mountain vantage-point to remind my people that they are called by their baptism to love God more than anything else in this passing world. I spoke of the importance of prayer and the Eucharist and the advantage of the habits of faith to nourish and strengthen their life.

"As we sit together on this mountaintop, my hope is that you receive a renewed perspective on your daily life. I pray unceasingly that, through the grace and example of my Son, you may appreciate your ongoing need to 'come to the mountain and pray'. And hopefully you can return to your daily life renewed by a clearer vision and a stronger determination to follow the ways and message of my loving Son."

## Our Response:

**Our Anniversary prayer:**

> **Mary, Mother of Reconciliation,** in this time of celebration we rejoice that: *The Father* asked you to carry out his plan of salvation; *The Son* chose you to be his Mother and his First Disciple; *The Holy Spirit* fashioned you into his living temple, our sister in faith.
>
> **At La Salette,** with abundant tears of mercy, you spoke to the two poor children in their own language and urged us to share your message of peace and hope with needy people of every culture and nation. Pray for us to your loving Son that we may draw all your people closer to him. Amen.

[Mention intention]

**Pray:** *the Lord's Prayer and the Hail Mary.*

**Invocation:** Our Lady of La Salette, Reconciler of sinners,
pray without ceasing for us who have recourse to you.

**Reflection Questions for today:**

- What is a peak-experience in your life where you were touched by the grace of God?
- What is very important in your daily life and what has eventually

become less important?

## Second Day: The Unsuspecting Shepherds

**Scripture:** "I am the good shepherd: the good shepherd lays down his life for his sheep... And there are other sheep I have that are not of this fold, and I must lead these too. They too will listen to my voice, and there will be only one flock, one shepherd" (John 10:11,16).

**Reflection:** Melanie had been tending the cows for more than six months on the mountainside near La Salette. On Monday, the 14th of September 1846, Pierre Selme, the farmer, went down to Corps. He wanted to ask Mr. Giraud if Maximin could take the place of his hired man who was sick.

## The Dialogue:

In our imagination, we ask the Beautiful Lady: "Why do you often speak to shepherds when you visit your people?"

**And Mary says:** "Those who watch over herds of animals learn to become attentive, to have patience and to become skilled in the ways of the creatures that they guard. Everyone needs time to reflect in silence. Without some quiet time, there is a danger of losing yourself in a multitude of projects, interests and wants. I would like everyone to take the time to reflect and find peace in solitude.

"Time and time again, people who come here soon discover that they are lost, like the sheep mentioned in the gospels. My Son follows them into the wilderness of their lives, into the thorns and thistles of their difficulties and challenges. He finds them, frees them and then holds them close to himself. As reconcilers, you are to be my Son's hands and feet in search of the lost and forsaken. But first, you yourself must be reconciled."

## Our Response:

**Our Anniversary prayer:**

**Mary, Mother of Reconciliation,** in this time of celebration we rejoice that: The Father asked you to carry out his plan of salvation; The Son chose you to be his Mother and his First Disciple; The Holy Spirit fashioned you into his living temple, our sister in faith.

**At La Salette,** with abundant tears of mercy, you spoke to the two poor children in their own language and urged us to share your message of peace and hope with needy people of every culture and nation. Pray for us to your loving Son that we may draw all your people closer to him. Amen.

[Mention intention]

**Pray:** *the Lord's Prayer and the Hail Mary.*

**Invocation:** Our Lady of La Salette, Reconciler of sinners,
pray without ceasing for us who have recourse to you.

**Reflection Questions for today:**

• When have you found yourself lost and someone else lifted you up?

• When have you "shepherded" other people, helping them in their need?

## Third Day: The Fire of God's Love

**Scripture:** "Moses was looking after the flock of his father-in-law Jethro... [and...] he came to Horeb, the mountain of God... The angel of [the LORD] appeared to him in a flame blazing from the middle of a bush. Moses looked; there was the bush blazing, but the bush was not being burnt up. Moses said, 'I must go across and see this strange sight, and why the bush is not being burnt up.' ...[The LORD] then said, 'I have indeed seen the misery of my people in Egypt. I have heard them crying for help... And I have come down to rescue them...'" (Exodus 3:1-3,7-8a).

**Reflection:** The children's first impression at the time of the apparition was that a ball of fire that had fallen into the ravine. They were afraid until, out of this brilliant sphere, a figure appeared and spoke to them.

# The Dialogue:

In our imagination, we ask the Beautiful Lady: "Why did you come, seated within this globe of fire that frightened the two children so much?"

**And Mary says:** "Fire has tremendous power. Scripture often speaks of it – from the burning bush to the tongues of fire at Pentecost. It is a symbol of passion but does not necessarily destroy anything, just as the fire did not consume the bush on Mount Horeb.

"Just before I went back to heaven, the two children noticed that the grass was gently swaying in the breeze, moving under my feet, unharmed. The world is imbued with the presence of God and lives in harmony with it. The fine Fire of God's love wishes to animate and give everyone a deep enthusiastic love for God. Allow yourself to be seized by the fire of God's love, so evident during my visit at La Salette. Share it unhesitatingly – in everything you do."

# Our Response:

**Our Anniversary prayer:**

> **Mary, Mother of Reconciliation,** in this time of celebration we rejoice that: The Father asked you to carry out his plan of salvation; The Son chose you to be his Mother and his First Disciple; The Holy Spirit fashioned you into his living temple, our sister in faith.

> **At La Salette,** with abundant tears of mercy, you spoke to the two poor children in their own language and urged us to share your message of peace and hope with needy people of every culture and nation. Pray for us to your loving Son that we may draw all your people closer to him. Amen.

[Mention intention]

**Pray:** *the Lord's Prayer and the Hail Mary.*

**Invocation:** Our Lady of La Salette, Reconciler of sinners,
              pray without ceasing for us who have recourse to you.

**Reflection Questions for today:**

- In what event in your life have you felt the intense fire of God's love?

- Who is a person whom you could describe as afire with God's love?

## Fourth Day: The Two Young Children

**Scripture:** "People even brought babies to him, for him to touch them; but when the disciples saw this they scolded them. But Jesus called the children to him and said, 'Let the little children come to me, and do not stop them; for it is to such as these that the kingdom of God belongs. In truth I tell you, anyone who does not welcome the kingdom of God like a little child will never enter it'" (Luke 18:15-17).

**Reflection:** The Beautiful Lady at La Salette speaks to the children. These children, neglected by their families, are important to her. She addressed her words to us through these two children.

## The Dialogue:

In our imagination, we ask the Beautiful Lady about the place of children in our life of faith.

And Mary says: "It is always the children who suffer in the conflicts of the world. They are most often killed or maimed in war, victims when their parents separate or argue. Have you forgotten what it means to be a child? My Son, Jesus, said that we are to 'accept the kingdom of God like a child.'

"It is important to recover the childlikeness of your earlier years. Just as my Son guided Maximin and Melanie in their trials as they were subjected to intense questioning and yet remained faithful to my message at La Salette, you also can be strengthened with the purity and simplicity of a child to face the demands and responsibilities of your adult faith-life to build my Son's kingdom on this earth. You will also be able to hear more easily what they are saying. In this way, you allow them to enter into our world and the world will change."

## Our Response:

**Our Anniversary prayer:**

Mary, Mother of Reconciliation, in this time of celebration we rejoice that: The Father asked you to carry out his plan of salvation; The Son chose you to be his Mother and his First Disciple; The Holy Spirit fashioned you into his living temple, our sister in faith.

At La Salette, with abundant tears of mercy, you spoke to the two poor children in their own language and urged us to share your message of peace and hope with needy people of every culture and nation. Pray for us to your loving Son that we may draw all your people closer to him. **Amen.**

[Mention intention]

**Pray:** *the Lord's Prayer* and the *Hail Mary.*

**Invocation:** Our Lady of La Salette, Reconciler of sinners,

   pray without ceasing for us who have recourse to you.

**Reflection Questions for today:**

   • When have you been touched by the words or actions of a child?

   • What habits strengthen your life of faith – a special way of praying, certain practices of a Liturgical season, certain ministry groups in your parish or shrine, etc.?

## Fifth Day: Our Blessed Mother

**Scripture:** "Can a woman forget her baby at the breast, feel no pity for the child she has borne? Even if these were to forget, I shall not forget you" (Isaiah 49:15).

**Reflection:** At first, the two children at La Salette thought they had met a mother who ran away from her abusive children in order to cry alone in the solitude of the mountain.

## The Dialogue:

In our imagination, we ask the Beautiful Lady: "What does it mean for us to have a mother and to be a mother?"

**And Mary says:** "Your own mother may have answered this question already. Children mean more to a mother than anything else in the world. A mother is the center of the family. She is the 'knot' that holds the threads of a fabric together. No matter where or who her children may be, she carries them in her heart.

"Mothers begin by giving life and then instinctively protecting the life to which they gave birth. At La Salette, I came in tears to remind you that I am often in anguish for your sometimes-poor response to the words and invitations of my Son. His loving examples of prayer, forgiving, healing and other good works are events to be appreciated and done by you in his Name.

"You lift your hearts in prayer to me as 'Reconciler of Sinners' and that is who I am. My Son's call to a lifelong ministry of reconciliation should be the center of your life as his disciple. Hopefully my compassionate words and actions at La Salette will also encourage you to do 'motherly' acts of kindness and generosity, mercy and love without counting the cost, just as I have done for you unceasingly."

## Our Response:

**Our Anniversary prayer:**

Mary, Mother of Reconciliation, in this time of celebration we rejoice that: The Father asked you to carry out his plan of salvation; The Son chose you to be his Mother and his First Disciple; The Holy Spirit fashioned you into his living temple, our sister in faith.

At La Salette, with abundant tears of mercy, you spoke to the two poor children in their own language and urged us to share your message of peace and hope with needy people of every culture and nation. Pray for us to your loving Son that we may draw all your people closer to him. **Amen.**

[Mention intention]

**Pray:** *the Lord's Prayer* and the *Hail Mary.*

**Invocation:** Our Lady of La Salette, Reconciler of sinners, pray without ceasing for us who have recourse to you.

**Reflection Questions for today:**

- What are the qualities in a mother (yours or another's) which attract you?

- When have you been called to take on "motherly duties" (as a life-giver, consoler, protector or forgiver)?

## Sixth Day: The Power of Listening

**Scripture:** "Then [the LORD said], 'Go out and stand on the mountain before [the LORD].' For at that moment [the LORD] was going by. A mighty hurricane split the mountains and shattered the rocks before [the LORD]. But [the LORD] was not in the hurricane. And after the hurricane, an earthquake. But [the LORD] was not in the earthquake. And after the earthquake, fire. But [the LORD] was not in the fire. And after the fire, a light murmuring sound. And when Elijah heard this, he covered his face with his cloak and went out and stood at the entrance of the cave" (1 Kings 19:11-13a).

**Reflection:** When the children spoke about their meeting with the Beautiful Lady, they said: "We didn't think about anything, we simply were there, ... we were listening and absorbing her words as if it were music."

## The Dialogue:

In our imagination, we asked the Beautiful Lady: "Did the two children respond well to your presence and listen attentively to your message?"

**And Mary says:** "Did you notice how the two children were 'simply there', drinking in my words? They were in tune with the prophetic words I was drawn to share. Some were severe words of warning, yet they were honest and direct. As your mother, I was speaking my message directly to the heart of the two children and to your heart as well.

"It was also important to me to respond to each child personally. When I realized that the two children were having difficulty understanding my initial words, I changed into the local patois for their sake. Also my questioning of Maximin concerning the event at the field of Coin was a gentle reminder of his father's deep fear of not being able to feed his family. This was a troubling expression from his anxious father and I ensured that Maximin appreciated his father's concern."

## Our Response:

**Our Anniversary prayer:**

Mary, Mother of Reconciliation, in this time of celebration we rejoice that: The Father asked you to carry out his plan of salvation; The Son chose you to be his Mother and his First Disciple; The Holy Spirit fashioned you into his living temple, our sister in faith.

At La Salette, with abundant tears of mercy, you spoke to the two poor children in their own language and urged us to share your message of peace and hope with needy people of every culture and nation. Pray for us to your loving Son that we may draw all your people closer to him. **Amen.**

[Mention intention]

**Pray:** *the Lord's Prayer* and the *Hail Mary.*

**Invocation:** Our Lady of La Salette, Reconciler of sinners,
        pray without ceasing for us who have recourse to you.

**Reflection Questions for today:**

• Who has listened well to you in your lifetime?

• Which people have gotten your full and rapt attention when they spoke to you?

## Seventh Day: Her Heartfelt Words

**Scripture:** "After hearing Jesus' words about the bread from heaven, many of his followers said, 'This is intolerable language. How could anyone accept it?' Jesus was aware that his followers were complaining about it and said, 'Does this disturb you? What if you should see the Son of man ascend to where he was before? It is the spirit that gives life, the flesh has nothing to offer. The words I have spoken to you are spirit and they are life" (John 6:60-63).

**Reflection:** The children were so intent on the Beautiful Lady's words that they had the distinct impression that she spoke to them for a very long time.

## The Dialogue:

In our imagination, we asked the Beautiful Lady: "What brought you to share your words in this remote place to these untutored children?"

**And Mary says:** "As I urged the two children to come closer, they did so without hesitation. They were a very attentive audience – open and receptive to me. They seemed to drink in my every word. In their presence, I could speak from the heart. I chose to begin with austere and foreboding predictions. The words came spontaneously.

"Words have a way of finding their own path when the heart is filled with pain and concern, with the need to admonish as well as to counsel. These may be words that sometimes disturb but they are also words that are full of promise and blessings. My message was one which could catch the attention of even the hardest heart. I do believe that they also heard my merciful and tender concern for all the parts of their lives, including the possible ruin of food staples such as potatoes, grapes and walnuts. These words of mine demanded a response – not only of the mind but also of the heart."

## Our Response:

**Our Anniversary prayer:**

Mary, Mother of Reconciliation, in this time of celebration we rejoice that: The Father asked you to carry out his plan of salvation; The Son chose you to be his Mother and his First Disciple; The Holy Spirit fashioned you into his living temple, our sister in faith.

At La Salette, with abundant tears of mercy, you spoke to the two poor children in their own language and urged us to share your message of peace and hope with needy people of every culture and nation. Pray for us to your loving Son that we may draw all your people closer to him. **Amen.**

[Mention intention]

**Pray:** *the Lord's Prayer* and the *Hail Mary.*

**Invocation:** Our Lady of La Salette, Reconciler of sinners, pray without ceasing for us who have recourse to you.

**Reflection Questions for today:**

• What topic of Mary's message at La Salette gets your attention?

• How does Mary express her direct concern for the children?

## Eighth Day: Her Abundant Tears

**Scripture:** "As [Jesus] drew near and came in sight of the city [of Jerusalem] he shed tears over it and said, 'If you too had only recognized on this day the way to peace! But in fact it is hidden from your eyes!'" (Luke 19:41-42).

**Reflection:** "The Beautiful Lady cried all during the time she was speaking to us. I saw the tears running down her cheeks. They fell down... they fell down..." What was so remarkable about the tears is that they fell to the level of her feet and there, became pearls of light and just melted away.

## The Dialogue:

In our imagination, we asked the Beautiful Lady: "Why did you allow yourself to shed these constant tears?"

**And Mary says:** "We as human beings need to weep in order to express our deep-seated feelings. It just may be that we are brought to tears when we are finally overcome by a powerful overflowing of our painful emotions. Just as my own Son wept over Jerusalem, so too I wept unceasingly for my wayward children on the Mountain of La Salette.

"Of course, sorrow and its tears can soften the hardest of hearts. When I allow others to feel my concerns as my tears flow, I allow others to suffer with me. Maximin and Melanie instantly sensed my sincerity and were touched not only by my words but also by my abundant tears.

"In another sense, I brought two messages for the world: one in my words and another in my tears. In your daily life, be aware of others who are hurting and often brought to tears. They are sharing a precious part of themselves and you must respond promptly and lovingly."

## Our Response:

**Our Anniversary prayer:**

Mary, Mother of Reconciliation, in this time of celebration we rejoice that: The Father asked you to carry out his plan of salvation; The Son chose you to be his Mother and his First Disciple; The Holy Spirit fashioned you into his living temple, our sister in faith.

At La Salette, with abundant tears of mercy, you spoke to the two poor children in their own language and urged us to share your message of peace and hope with needy people of every culture and nation. Pray for us to your loving Son that we may draw all your people closer to him. **Amen.**

[Mention intention]

**Pray:** *the Lord's Prayer* and the *Hail Mary*.

**Invocation:** Our Lady of La Salette, Reconciler of sinners,

pray without ceasing for us who have recourse to you.

**Reflection Questions for today:**

• When have the tears of another affected you deeply?

• When was there a time when you expressed yourself through tears?

## Ninth Day: Our Spring of Life

**Scripture:** "...no one who drinks the water that I shall give will ever be thirsty again: the water that I shall give will become a spring of water within, welling up for eternal life" (John 4:14).

**Reflection:** On the morning of Monday, September 21, 1846, Melanie discovered a spring of water at the spot where the Virgin appeared to them. Once there was another spring located there, named "Little Spring", but it had stopped flowing a long time ago.

## The Dialogue:

In our imagination, we asked the Beautiful Lady the meaning of the abundant spring of water arising at her feet on the Holy Mountain of La Salette.

**And Mary says:** "Water can teach us much. Where water flows, it brings life. It gives itself to all who need it. Water is often good and generous. It knows how to moisten and give life to the ground. It is courageous – it flows around rocks that wish to block its flowing current. It is good-natured – its gentle force is at work, day and night, to eliminate all obstacles. It is persevering – all these qualities we should emulate.

"During my visit at La Salette, I used many symbols to remind my children about the basics of faith: light to emphasize the crucifix on my breast, the instrument of our salvation; chains to express the challenge of living a life of faith; roses to express the beauty and joy of following my Son; and finally the hammer and pincers on the crucifix, expressing the two choices we have in life – maintaining unforgiven sinful habits (nailing the nails in my Son's hands and feet) or maintaining a Christ-like life (mercifully removing the nails from my Son's hands and feet). All this we learn from the flowing spring and the other symbols of my visit to La Salette."

## Our Response:

**Our Anniversary prayer:**

Mary, Mother of Reconciliation, in this time of celebration we rejoice that: The Father asked you to carry out his plan of salvation; The Son chose you to be his Mother and his First Disciple; The Holy Spirit fashioned you into his living temple, our sister in faith.

At La Salette, with abundant tears of mercy, you spoke to the two poor children in their own language and urged us to share your message of peace and hope with needy people of every culture and nation. Pray for us to your loving Son that we may draw all your people closer to him. **Amen.**

[Mention intention]

**Pray:** *the Lord's Prayer* and the *Hail Mary.*

**Invocation:** Our Lady of La Salette, Reconciler of sinners, pray without ceasing for us who have recourse to you.

**Reflection Questions for today:**

- In your life, what is a "spring" that has given you the strength to move on?

- What place that you have visited has given you a sense of beauty or peace?

**Acknowledgements:** The Swiss Province of the La Salette Missionaries originally wrote this Novena for the 150th Anniversary of the La Salette Apparition. This was recently edited and expanded for the 175th anniversary by Fr. Ron Gagne, M.S. Sources of these La Salette materials are available on: www.lasalette.org … La Salette Library… La Salette Masses.

# La Salette Laity Prayer

## by Chris Austgen

**Loving and merciful God,**
be with us as we continue on our path of learning
and sharing the message of Our Lady of La Salette
and inspire us to apply this message to our daily lives.
Help us see our relationships
through the eyes of Our Weeping Mother at La Salette.
Help us live out our ministries of service
in the reconciling love of her Son, Jesus Crucified.
And help us pray well
as instructed by the Beautiful Lady at La Salette.
We ask all this through Christ, our Lord. Amen.

# La Salette Prayers

## Memorare to Our Lady of La Salette

**Remember, Our Lady of La Salette,** true Mother of Sorrows, the tears you shed for us on Calvary. Remember also the care you have taken to keep us faithful to Christ, your Son. Having done so much for your children, you will not now abandon us. Comforted by this consoling thought, we come to you pleading, despite our infidelities and ingratitude.

**Virgin of Reconciliation,** do not reject our prayers, but intercede for us, obtain for us the grace to love Jesus above all else. May we console you by a holy life and so come to share the eternal life Christ gained by his cross. Amen.

# Dedication to Our Lady of La Salette

**Most holy Mother, Our Lady of La Salette,** who for love of me shed such bitter tears in your merciful apparition, look down with kindness upon me, as I consecrate myself to you without reserve. From this day, my glory shall be to know that I am your child. May I so live as to dry your tears and console your afflicted heart.

**Beloved Mother**, to you and to your blessed charge and sacred keeping and into the bosom of your mercy, for this day and for every day, and for the hour of my death I commend myself, body and soul, every hope and every joy, every trouble and every sorrow, my life and my life's end.

**O dearest Mother**, enlighten my understanding, direct my steps, console me by your maternal protection, so that exempt from all error, sheltered from every danger of sin, I may, with ardor and invincible courage, walk in the paths traced out for me by you and your Son. Amen.

## La Salette Invocation

**Our Lady of La Salette**, reconciler of sinners,
pray without ceasing for us who have recourse to you.

Made in the USA
Middletown, DE
10 April 2021